A place for all people

British Library
Cataloguing-in-
Publication Data: A
catalogue record for
this book is available
on request from the
British Library.

ISBN 978 1 78211 693 6

Designed by Graphic
Thought Facility

Printed and bound
in Bosnia-Herzegovina
by GPS

Other books by the
same author:

*A Case for Modern
Architecture: The
Smallpeice Lecture
1989*

*Architecture:
A Modern View*

A New London
with Mark Fisher

*Cities for a Small
Planet* with Philip
Gumuchdjian

*Cites for a Small
Country* with
Anne Power

A place for all people
life, architecture
and the fair society

Richard Rogers

with Richard Brown

Published in Great
Britain in 2017 by
Canongate Books
Limited, 14 High Street,
Edinburgh EH1 1TE

canongate.co.uk

For Ruthie, the love of my life.

'I can't understand why people are frightened of new ideas.
I'm frightened of the old ones.'

John Cage

Introduction

'Are you sitting down, old man?' Renzo Piano asked, when I picked up the phone (he is four years younger than me). I reassured him that I was. 'We have won the Beaubourg competition,' he explained. 'The announcement is in Paris this evening. We have to be there but I can't get away from Genoa; could the rest of you fly over from London?'

We hardly had time to digest the news, let alone prepare for the dramatic change in our working lives that it heralded. My mother, who was gardening at her Wimbledon house, cried with joy when I told her of the news. John Young, Ruthie and I dashed around London collecting partners and passports – we had so little work on that people weren't coming into the office – and made it over to Paris just in time to join the celebration dinner on a *bateau-mouche* on the Seine. Dressed variously in jeans, T-shirts, sneakers and miniskirts, and hardly speaking any French, we were catapulted into the cream of the French establishment where the women wore tiaras and evening dresses, and the men white ties, medals and sashes.

It was July 1971; we were in our twenties and thirties. Over the past seven years, we had designed houses, pavilions and small factories, but this was a project on an entirely different scale – a major public building in the heart of Paris. We had built so little, but with the confidence that naivety allows, we believed we could change the world.

The competition had been to design a cultural centre in a run-down inner city area, which would accommodate a library, an art gallery, and a centre for experimental music. We had responded with a design for a loose-fit, flexible structure, but at its heart was the public piazza, which would occupy half the site, and continue underneath the building and up its façade, on escalators and walkways. This would not be a temple to high culture; rather, it would be what our submission called 'a place for all people, the young and the old, the poor and the rich, all creeds and nationalities, a cross between the vitality of Times Square and the cultural richness of the British Museum', a place for two-way participation not passive consumption, a piece of urban infrastructure rather than a building, a project driven by social and political responsibility.

These were strong political statements, but architecture is inescapably social and political. I have always believed that there is more to architecture than architecture. The first line of my practice's constitution states: 'Architecture is inseparable from the social and economic values of the individuals who practise it and the society which sustains it.'

Our best buildings do not just arise from the requirements of the client, but seek to answer broader social questions. The Pompidou Centre brought culture into the public domain. The Lloyd's Building was designed as a flexible machine for a financial marketplace, but also as a carefully considered expression of those activities, designed both for the user and for the enjoyment of the passer-by. The Bordeaux Law Courts that we built in the 1990s rethought the purpose of judicial architecture; they were designed to draw the public in and explain the role of justice in society, as a school of law, not a citadel of crime and punishment. The Welsh Assembly Building, completed a few years later, does more than accommodate a legislature. The ground floor is essentially an indoor piazza for public use, with cafes, meeting spaces and a gallery that enables citizens to view the assembly chamber, where their representatives make decisions. The Leadenhall Building is a 50-storey-high skyscraper, the highest in the City of London when it was completed in 2014. The first seven storeys are given over to an open piazza with no walls, from which escalators carry you up to the reception.

Architecture creates shelter and transforms the ordinary. Architects are both scientists and artists, solving problems in three dimensions, using structure and materials to create scale and humanise space, capture the play of light and shadows, and make an aesthetic impact. From the primitive hut to the Athenian Agora, from medieval palace to city hall, from the street bench to the great piazza, architecture shapes our lives. Good architecture civilises and humanises, bad architecture brutalises.

But architecture also structures cities with buildings and public spaces, all the defining inventions of civilisation. Cities are where human beings first came together, where we evolved from social to political animals – from pack to polis. The first cities were refuges, offering safety in numbers in a hostile world, but they soon grew into something more complex and creative. City dwellers came together to exchange ideas and goods, for the meeting of friends and strangers, for discussion, argument, trade and collaboration. In 6,000 years (only 100 lifetimes), cities have transformed human history, providing the foundation for an astonishing burst of creativity and discovery.

Nearly four billion people live in cities today – half the world's population and more people than lived on the entire planet in 1970 – and the speed of urbanisation is accelerating. By 2050, cities are expected to house two-thirds of the world's population; in 1900 they housed just 13 per cent.[1] Meanwhile, the gulf between the rich and the poor is widening, threatening civilised values. Well-designed, compact and socially just, cities are fundamental to tackling inequality and climate change – the two most serious challenges our planet faces.

Architecture is social in another sense too. Apart from its impact, it is an inherently sociable activity, an exercise in collaboration. As an architect, I am not an abstract artist in front of a blank canvas, seeking the blinding flash of inspiration and creativity. Quite the opposite, my drawings are notoriously bad. We develop designs in a team, by questioning briefs, analysing context and constraint, considering social, physical and cultural impacts, defining problems and testing solutions.

I have always been happiest working in a group; from the first gang of friends that I gathered as a teenager, to the brilliant architects who I have worked with since. The dyslexia that made me so hopeless at school also spurred me on to find different ways of making things happen, depending on and supporting others, reflecting our human nature.

Architecture is enriched by the interplay between different disciplines, from sociology and philosophy, to engineering and horticulture, and most of all by the collaborations between an enlightened client, the community and a design team. These last few make ethical principles real, and their dynamism creates the most exciting moments and unexpected results.

This book is not an autobiography, though it draws on my life. I have always been more interested in ideas and dialogue than in narrative, in the visual rather than the written, in the present and the future rather than the past.

But, working on the exhibition *Richard Rogers – Inside Out* at the Royal Academy in the summer of 2013, I started to think about how my ideas, beliefs and values had been formed and influenced, by my colleagues, my family and my friends, and by the times I have lived through. I looked back at how they have found expression in my work, in completed projects and sketches, in public speeches and private conversations, in the way my architectural language has evolved, and the ways in which my architectural practice has grown.

This book goes deeper in exploring my ideas and talking about the people who have inspired my work and informed my beliefs – in people

'A place for all people, the young and the old, the poor and the rich, all creeds and nationalities, a cross between the vitality of Times Square and the cultural richness of the British Museum.'

and fairness; in places and streets that are designed for people, for democracy and openness; in buildings that create beauty through the aesthetic fulfilment of needs; in cities that are compact, adaptable, sustainable and humane.

It gathers together relationships, projects, collaborations and arguments, interweaving stories with case studies, drawings and photographs. It can be read in a number of ways. It is a mosaic, open-ended, more like jazz improvisation than an elegant and polished symphony.

I hope this will give you something richer than a straightforward narrative; something that may inspire you to find your own ways of challenging and enhancing how we live on what remains a very small – and shrinking – planet.

Left: Our vision for the Pompidou Centre, as expressed in our competition submission.

Right: *Inside Out,* the 2013 Royal Academy exhibition of my life and work, which was the inspiration for this book.

'A PLACE FOR ALL PEOPLE, THE YOUNG AND THE OLD, THE POOR AND THE RICH, ALL CREEDS AND NATIONALITIES. A CROSS BETWEEN NEW YORK'S TIMES SQUARE AND LONDON'S BRITISH MUSEUM.'

1   Early Influences

Nothing comes from nothing. Our characters emerge from the accretion of experience (good and bad, of winning and losing) and the assimilation of influence. I don't believe in the myth of the self-made man; we are influenced from the moment we're born, by our parents and grandparents, by our friends, by education, geography and politics, by everything we see. It's not a question of whether or not you are influenced, but of understanding the influences that your mind absorbs from the world around you as you grow, and of deciding how you will adopt and adapt them as the foundation stones of your thought and work.

Influences are not destiny. But I was fortunate to first open my eyes in an elegant Florence apartment, flooded with light, filled with beautiful modernist furniture designed by my cousin Ernesto Rogers, and looking out towards the magnificent Duomo, an early fifteenth-century masterpiece by Brunelleschi, who was not just the first Renaissance architect, but also an engineer, a planner, a sculptor and a thinker. The unornamented expressive Duomo is, to me, the pinnacle of Renaissance architecture, better even than the masterworks of Michelangelo. I have always preferred the simpler expression and stripped-down energy of early Renaissance, early Gothic, early modern architecture, to the richer more decorative forms that appear as movements mature.

And I always say that I chose my parents well. My father was a doctor with a rigorously enquiring scientific mind, while my mother was an art lover (and in later life a skilled potter), with a love of colour and form. These powerful influences blended with many others over the years.

Above left: The view from the Florence apartment where I was born. It looked out over Filippo Brunelleschi's Duomo, a high point of early Renaissance architecture and engineering.

Left: With my mother.

13

Florence

Florence is the city I know best. It is the birthplace and pinnacle of the European Renaissance, a city-state that created some of the great masterpieces of art and architecture, against a backdrop of turbulent and sometimes bloody power struggles, the home of Brunelleschi, Alberti, Donatello, Massaccio, Dante and Michelangelo. I left the city when I was five, so my early memories – of hills, domes, towers, rooftops, churches and streets – may not be entirely reliable. But Florence entered into my bloodstream, and has stayed with me as a template, an ideal, for what a city can be; the River Arno and the Ponte Vecchio, its beautiful inhabited bridge; the dialogue between medieval and Renaissance buildings in the Piazza della Signoria. I am constantly revisiting and deepening my relationship with the city of my birth, and with the friends and relatives who still live there. I still love showing Florence to visitors, as my father did in his time.

My father, Nino, had been living in Florence since 1926, where he studied to become a doctor. Nino's grandfather was English, but had trained as a dentist in Paris before settling in Venice – we still have a tin of his patented 'fragrant tooth powder'. Dada, my mother, was the daughter of an architect and engineer, from a notable Trieste family. Nino and Dada had been friends since they were children and married in 1932. I was born a year later.

My parents were products of the early twentieth century, of the great flowering of civic and cultural life that followed the unification of Italy. My father was a rationalist to the core, with a strong belief in the strength of the human spirit, and a determination to succeed; echoing Nietzsche, he wrote 'My will is my god' on the flyleaves of books. Nino was deeply interested in politics too, in democracy and in Florence's history as a city-state – as a new Athens. I remember him talking me through an essay he had written on the guild system and how this had formed part of Florence's early Renaissance period of citizen government.

Reflecting his deep interest in his adopted city, Nino was perhaps more Florentine than Italian, just as I would still say that I come from Florence rather than from Italy. As Mussolini's fascists tightened their grip in the late 1920s and early 1930s, there was good reason to question the value of allegiance to the Italian state. Nino had always been drawn to England, visiting the year before I was born to investigate working there as a doctor. The rise of the fascists forced my parents' hand.

Nino loved England as only a foreigner can. He prized classic English brands – Burberry raincoats, Dents gloves and Lotus shoes – and dressed as the epitome of the saying, 'To be truly English, you have to be

My parents, Dada (top left) and Nino (below left). Our Florence apartment was furnished with elegant modern pieces designed by my cousin Ernesto Rogers.

15

a foreigner.' For him, it seemed an oasis of democracy and liberal values in an unstable world. English newspapers, Dickens and G.K. Chesterton's Father Brown stories were his favoured reading, and my name was emphatically the English 'Richard', not the Italian 'Riccardo'.

Dada was more sceptical about the prospect of moving, more attached to Trieste, the town of her birth; although Trieste had only been part of Italy since the First World War, her family was comfortably established there. It had always been a cosmopolitan place, set on the edge of the Austro-Hungarian Empire, for which it provided the only port, at that time, and looking more to Vienna than to Rome. Like many port cities, Trieste had its roots in commerce, not religion or military strength, so had a marginal and transitional character, filled with a minestrone of mysterious businessmen, writers and artists – including James Joyce, who taught my mother English.

Though she was more modern in outlook, Dada's family was more traditional than Nino's, and more passionately Italian. Her parents lived in the neo-medieval castle Villa Geiringer built by her architect grandfather Eugenio together with a funicular railway that stopped at the Villa on its way uphill. Dada was passionate about art, with a brilliant eye for beauty. I remember her delight in taking me to see the Festival of Britain in 1951, and throughout her life she retained her enthusiasm for modern art, design, writing.

I only discovered years later that both sides of the family were Jewish though Dada's grandfather had converted to Christianity, and both she and Nino were atheists. When I asked my mother whether this was true, she replied, 'Of course your roots are Jewish, but I've spent all my life getting away from religion.' I accepted the answer at the time, but looking back there was clearly an element of reticence, and a reluctance to acknowledge that being Jewish is as much about culture as it is about religion.

Choosing London

By 1938, it had become clear that war was coming, and that my father would finally have to choose between his Italian home and the risk of internment or worse and his English passport (a legacy of his English grandfather). My parents chose England, and my privileged existence as a moderately spoilt firstborn Italian child in a comfortably bourgeois family came to an abrupt end. My father came over in late 1938, and my mother and I landed in England in October 1939, accompanied by my father's brother Giorgio, a concert pianist, and a man as romantic as my father was rational. I remember him rehearsing Schubert and Chopin on a concert grand piano during the Blitz while I sat underneath hugging the legs.

We swapped the elegantly furnished flat with a view over Florentine rooftops for a single room in a boarding house in Bayswater, with a coin meter for the heating and a bath in a cupboard that we used to fill with hot water to take the edge off the flat's chill. Nino had only been able to smuggle a few hundred pounds out of Italy and though we weren't living in poverty, life was a lot tougher than it had been in Florence. The first Christmas was dark and cold, and my only present was a grey lead toy submarine. I felt my parents had let me down.

Life had switched from colour to black-and-white. London was occasionally enveloped by smog from thousands of coal fires, which in later years filled the city so thickly that all sense of direction was lost within a few steps of your front door, like being submerged in thick black oil. My mother had to learn to cook more or less from scratch, and missed Florence's rolling cityscape so much that in her first few months she took to walking the streets of London looking for hills to climb, to get a better view of her new city.

Nino urgently needed to find work. Fortunately, his previous visit in 1932 had enabled him to register as a doctor, and we moved to Godalming early the next year, where he initially took up a job in a tuberculosis clinic. Dada joined him working there, making beds and caring for patients, but despite taking all the precautions that he urged on her, she quickly contracted TB herself. She was sent to the Alps to recuperate, and I was sent to Kingswood House, a boarding school in Epsom.

Schooling During Wartime

Like so many immigrants, my parents wanted the best for their children, so spent what money they had on a private education for me. But Kingswood was a brutal and unfair place, full of arbitrary punishment and cruelty. The cornerstones of the headmaster's beliefs appeared to be that beating small children was a good thing – I was beaten regularly from my first day there – and that the Boer War was the pinnacle of British achievement. It would have been a grim experience for any child, but was particularly horrific for a homesick six-year-old Italian. I spoke a little English by then, but was certainly not fluent, and was hampered by dyslexia – as yet undiagnosed. I was bullied by other children too, but being unusually tall and later on a good boxer, I managed to defend myself.

I was miserable at Kingswood, crying myself to sleep every night – years of unhappiness that culminated in me sitting on a high window ledge at the age of nine or ten, trying to steel myself to jump. My parents were naturally very worried, and offered to move me, but I insisted on staying put; I had lost all my confidence and was too frightened of how much worse another school might be.

Eventually, following a series of disastrous school reports, I was taken away from Kingswood and sent to a crammer called Downs Lodge (I used to annoy my parents by referring to it as a 'school for backward children'),  where classes of four or five pupils were intensively coached to prepare for Common Entrance, the entrance exam for English public schools. Here, I discovered I had some sporting ability, and this combined with more focussed tuition helped me to build my confidence and improve my mental state. The atmosphere was relaxed and friendly. I remember my tutor used to tell me to 'hit the ball and forget about style', a maxim that applied as well off the cricket pitch as on it. I felt liberated, and my marks began to improve. I was accepted at St John's School in Leatherhead (a former seminary for Anglican priests), to which I could cycle every day from home. My

Me as a teenager at St John's, Leatherhead.

parents helped hugely, providing any extra tutoring that was necessary for me to scrape through exams, though my academic aspirations remained modest – to be second from bottom rather than bottom in the class.

Around this time, I also started to make friends. A gang of us began to coalesce around a small muddy pond in Epsom, where we would catch newts and tadpoles, or practise falling through trees, using the branches to moderate and slow our descent. I met Michael Branch, who remains one of my closest friends, and Pat Lillies, my first girlfriend – a beautiful tomboy three years older than me (my uncle Giorgio eventually had to convince me that we should separate and not settle down in our teens). I grew in confidence and strength. Now I had my own people close around me.

Childhood in wartime was an extraordinary experience. I vividly remember the feeling of isolation and determination that we had when we crowded round the radio to hear the six o'clock news during the Battle of Britain, listening to Churchill's speeches, the sound of the planes – Spitfires and Hurricanes – that seemed to be all that stood between us and invasion, and the strange sight of the elephantine barrage balloons flying above Hyde Park.

But the later period of the Second World War, and the Blitz in particular, was an amazing time for children. I really don't think we considered the dangers. Air raids disrupted lessons and meant time off school, or crouching in the Morrison shelter (an indoor shelter with a heavy steel top, which we used as a table during the day, and I slept under at night). We would rush off on our bikes to hunt for shrapnel on bombsites. Beneath the county hospital in Epsom, where my father worked before being called up and sent to a hospital in Poona, was an undercroft, which 'the gang' occupied, furnishing it with animal heads and what we called 'jewels' (pieces of chandelier) pilfered from a nearby historic house where Canadian servicemen had been billeted.

As a teenager I also discovered books. I had only begun to read when I was eleven, so was rushing to catch up, and my parents weren't keen on me reading rubbish, any more than they were keen on me eating, drinking or wearing rubbish. (My parents, though strict in some ways, were surprisingly liberal in others. Even as a teenager they let me have my girlfriends to stay the night, but I had to be at the table for breakfast, with or without my partner.) I would go to the library, prop myself against the wall, and spend hours racing through everything from patriotic stodge like *Our Island Story* that I was fed at school to Jules Verne's thrilling visions of the future. As I got older, I progressed to Steinbeck and Hemingway, Dickens and Graham Greene, to Joyce, Orwell and Russell, to Sartre, Gide and Camus, to Pirandello, and dos Passos.

It was my problem with learning by heart that made my school days miserable. From the age of six to 18, I had to recite the Lord's Prayer every morning, but I couldn't remember it however hard I tried. Now we have a name – dyslexia – for this learning difficulty, but then it was simply seen as stupidity. We still know very little about the workings of the human brain, and dyslexia is a term for a set of symptoms and characteristics that we barely understand. I revisited Kingswood House in 2014: ironically, the school that failed me so badly as a child had opened a new centre specialising in teaching dyslexic children, which is a sign of progress.

People who are dyslexic think differently. We may not be comfortable with traditional teaching, but some dyslexic people have enhanced visual skills, and the ability to think in three dimensions. In my case, it made me realise at an early age that there was more strength in a group, in creative collaboration, than there was in the solo high achiever.

People have asked me whether dyslexia makes you a better architect. I'm not sure whether that's true, but it does rule out some other careers, so focuses you on what you can do. It defines an area of possibility, as well as impossibility. I was lucky to find a profession where I could work with others to achieve results. But a lot of children did not have my luck; they found that their prospects were destroyed by a narrow education system and by having nobody to support them. Today there is a change. One of my pleasures in the House of Lords is meeting dyslexic children and their parents, and seeing the huge differences that good teaching and supportive local authorities can make.

1945 – A Brave New World

In the 1945 general election, the British people made an amazing decision: they turned their backs on Churchill, the great war leader, and voted Labour – for the party that promised to bring a new world into being, despite the country being almost bankrupt by the war. The gap between rich and poor began to narrow, probably for the first time in modern history, and a progressive post-war consensus was established that survived till the late 1970s.

My parents were excited by the possibilities of this new beginning, and the politics and policies of the day were discussed, sometimes loudly, at every family meal. Unlike many doctors, my father was an enthusiast for the Beveridge Report and the establishment of the National Health Service. The politicians of that era – Bevan, Attlee, Bevin and Morrison – still stand out for me as heroes of modern society.

James Chuter-Ede, who was Home Secretary in that government, was a patient of my father's. Chuter-Ede and his wife had no children of their own, and he took me under his wing, taking me out in his little boat *The Brown Duck* on the Thames near Hampton Court. I still have some of the bird-spotting books he gave me. He was the most charming, low-key and unpretentious politician I have ever met and I remember how unhappy he was to be moved from Education to the Home Office in 1945 (where he had to oversee capital punishment, against his every principle). Together with my parents he sparked in me a lifelong commitment to progressive politics. At my school elections I stood for the Labour Party – always an unpopular position in an English private school – winning about two votes.

If politics was progressive at the time, England was still reserved about culture; people bridled at the word. It was seen as something alien, faintly suspicious. Modernity in the visual arts was seen as particularly suspect. In a continental doctor's surgery, you would see a reproduction of a Picasso or Braque in the waiting room. In an English surgery, you would be lucky to see a sentimental watercolour of a landscape. The country seemed starved of visual stimulus. We didn't lack the artists – Henry Moore, Francis Bacon, Patrick Heron, Tony Caro, Barbara Hepworth, Ben Nicholson – but they had limited recognition. It would take twenty or thirty years before Nick Serota at the Tate, Michael Craig-Martin at Goldsmiths and Charles Saatchi would open up contemporary British art to the British people, and to the world.

My parents didn't share these reservations – they were excited by the modern movement and inspired by what the great Australian art critic Robert Hughes would later call 'the shock of the new'. But I remember

The Skylon, designed by Powell & Moya with Felix Samuely, at the 1951 Festival of Britain. To the very left is the edge of the Dome of Discovery. These modernist icons contrast with the ornate high Victorian style of Whitehall Court in the background.

the public outcry that greeted the Picasso exhibition at the Victoria and Albert Museum in 1945; the newspaper critics declaring that donkeys could paint better with their tails, and rolling out all the usual criticisms levelled by those who can't – or won't – understand modern art. Modern design was also seen as something foreign, as were grand city plans and there was some truth in this. British architecture had benefited from an influx of brilliant foreigners – exiles from the Bauhaus, architects like Gropius, Lubetkin, Mendelsohn and Chermayeff – in the 1930s and after the war. But there was no modern furniture or even clothing. It was as if everything had to be rooted in the distant past.

Still, the spirit of utility and austerity was starting to stimulate British modernism, and bring its architecture into the mainstream, unlocking creativity in the design of everything from dresses, to furniture, to health centres. Everything had to be constructed with minimal materials, which forced designers to eliminate the showy ornamentation of Gothic revival, Rococo and Baroque architecture. And there was a new sense of the possibility of creating a better society, and a small but growing appetite for the cleaner lines of a contemporary world. So, while England was still grey, the seeds of modernism were being sown, mingling with a more conservative and romantic tradition. It found an early expression at the Festival of Britain in 1951, where my mother and I marvelled at the way that art and science came together in the Dome of Discovery and the Skylon.

The growing influence of modernism was underpinned by an optimistic belief, amid all the scarcity, that communal action could create a fairer world – winning the peace as it had the war, building homes, hospitals and schools. The war had changed society (rationing had actually improved public health), unifying the British socially and politically in a way that would have seemed unthinkable in the 1930s. The modernist style was an expression of a deeper social purpose, letting light and air into a dark and dusty world, creating healthier places for a new generation.

Rediscovering Italy

As soon as the war ended, my parents and I began to travel to Italy every summer to visit our family in Venice, Florence and Trieste. We were hungry for the culture that seemed still to be rationed in England, rediscovering cities that I could barely remember from my childhood. At first we travelled in buses, as the war had devastated much of the continent's rail infrastructure, then we took trains.

The first place I visited with my parents was Venice, on the way to see my grandparents in Trieste, and I remember very well thinking, as we trailed round church after church and gallery after gallery, 'I suppose one day all this will make sense.' Even then I knew that, however boring the paintings seemed to me as a teenager, here was something to file away, rather than to ignore completely. I rediscovered my Italian family, staying with my aunt in Florence, my uncle in Rome, my grandparents in Trieste and my cousin Ernesto in Milan. In Florence, my father was a wonderful guide with a deep knowledge of the buildings and their history, and he would walk the streets pointing out highlights to us, as I do now with my children and grandchildren. My grandfather did the same in Trieste.

At the age of 17, I began to travel independently, hitch-hiking and jumping trains. In Italy, my aunts and uncles would give me enough money to carry on to other relatives' houses. I was adventurous; I ran with the bulls in Pamplona, and dodged ticket collectors by hanging on the outside of trains; I spent a night in the cells in San Sebastián after being arrested by the Franco-ist Guardia Civil for swimming naked in the sea.

One adventure nearly tipped over into disaster. After I had left school, I went back to Venice with a friend who had the self-explanatory name 'Big John'. We had checked into a hostel and were travelling to the old city on a vaporetto. Suddenly the captain started shouting at Big John to get off the boat, then I was being jostled by the crowd and one man in particular who seemed to be trying to push me into the water. I fended him off without much difficulty, and when the police met the boat I assumed they would be taking him away for his unprovoked attack.

On the quayside, my attacker really went for me, and I landed a punch on his jaw (my schoolboy prowess at boxing showing itself). He went down on the ground, and we were escorted to the police station. After a while, they took my passport, asked me to sign a statement and said we could go.

When I went back to collect my passport the next day, however, I was thrown into jail. I was accused of groping my attacker's wife on the boat at the same time as fighting with her husband, who now claimed he had lost teeth as a result (this, the magistrate explained, was a permanent injury, making the accusation more serious). So I passed the night in a cell with two prostitutes, an 80-year-old man who had spent most of his life inside, and two cigarette smugglers.

The following morning, I was taken to see a magistrate, and sent off in manacles across Piazza San Marco in a long line of prisoners, then to a squalid prison on one of the outlying islands. I was there for two weeks in solitary confinement, only able to see a crack of light from a high window, without even a belt to hold up my trousers.

When I was brought back in front of the magistrate, it turned out that his father worked for my grandfather. He told me that I was in serious

trouble, and could be locked up for years for the alleged sexual and violent assaults. He granted me bail, and quietly indicated that I abscond as quickly as possible. My grandfather put up the money and I got out. After spending a weekend being shown the alternative sights of Venice by one of the prostitutes I had met in jail (to my grandfather's utter fury), I made it to Trieste, which was then outside Italian jurisdiction and subsequently received a pardon after an exchange of letter between lawyers and the Vatican, which enabled me to return to Italy.

In prison, I lost all sense of time and perspective on the outside world. I was pretty fit, but that period of isolation really took its toll. It made me wonder how prisoners coped, though it had also shown me that the people behind bars were often better and kinder than the people locking them up. I began to question my assumptions about law and order, about who the good guys and the bad guys really were. It also made me realise how privileged and lucky I was. If it hadn't been for my grandfather's influence, I could have been stuck in jail, on spurious charges, for years.

Military Service in Trieste; Architecture in Milan

Leaving school in 1951, I had no idea what I wanted to do. It was made clear that I was expected to enter one of the professions. My grandfather felt that I should become a dentist, like him, but my lack of A levels fortunately ruled that out. Indeed my academic record had led one careers adviser to suggest a job with the South African police force, perhaps feeling that my boxing skills would be useful, but ignoring the fact that my political beliefs made this just about the least likely career path I would ever take.

So, to buy myself two more years I joined the army to do my National Service in late 1951, rather than postponing it till after further education. Like everyone else at St John's, I had been a member of the Cadet force, but had got into trouble for refusing to obey another boy's order to carry a Bren gun (a bulky machine gun) while on exercises. This trivial insubordination led to threats of a court martial from one of the teachers, until my housemaster, who outranked him, told him that the idea of court-martialling a schoolboy was ridiculous. Unsurprisingly, with this record at school, it quickly became clear that I was not going to be made an officer, and I was posted to the Royal Army Service Corps. Fortuitously, I had measles when my unit was being sent out to Germany. Left behind, I persuaded the sergeant that I could speak Italian and

25

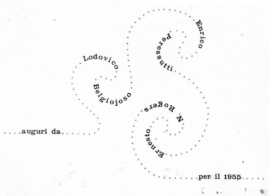

...auguri da... Lodovico Belgiojoso Enrico Peressutti Ernesto N. Rogers

.....per il 1955.....

was posted to Trieste, which was then under British and US military rule, owing to territorial disputes between Italy and Yugoslavia.

There was probably nowhere better for me to see out my brief and undistinguished military career. My grandfather Riccardo, who was a director of the insurance giant Assicurazioni Generali, gave me a season ticket to the Trieste Opera – beginning a life-long passion for opera and classical music – and I was able to visit the family's Villa Geiringer, designed and built by my great-grandfather Eugenio Geiringer, at weekends, travelling up on the mountain railway, playing chess and meeting their friends. Back at base, I worked on clerical duties from early mornings until lunchtime. This left time free for swimming in the afternoon, for drinking beer out of boot-shaped litre glasses, and for seeing Marta, my Yugoslavian girlfriend (who was also our secretary at the base).

Being in Trieste also meant I saw more of my cousin, Ernesto Rogers. He was one of the intellectual leaders of post-war European architecture, and his Milan-based BBPR was one of the best-known modern Italian practices.

Ernesto had joined CIAM (Congrès Internationaux d'Architecture Moderne – the foremost alliance of modernist architects) in the early 1950s, but he diverged from the absolutist position of the first generation of modernists, who saw their architectural – and social – task as one of creating the world afresh, starting with a blank slate. Ernesto challenged that concept when he took over as editor of *Casabella,* one of Italy's leading architectural journals, in 1953, renaming it as *Casabella Continuità,* and reinstilling a sense of historical perspective. This made him unpopular with some modernists like Reyner Banham, later a good friend of mine, who Ernesto mocked for his chilly, hard-edged modernism, calling him an 'advocate of refrigerators'.

Ermesto's blending of modernism with continuity is visible in the design of BBPR's most famous building, Torre Velasca, a mixed-use tower in Milan near the Cathedral and the Galleria Vittorio Emanuele II, with offices on the lower floors and flats above them. At 106m tall, Torre Velasca looms over Milan's Gothic and baroque galleries, squares and churches; it is modern and imposing, but also responsive to context, echoing medieval Lombard castles in its top-heavy design, forming links between past, present and future. I must admit, when I first saw the plans, they looked retrograde and heavy; I immediately preferred a steel-framed alternative, which was rejected.

Top left: An invitation card from my cousin Ernesto showing BBPR's designs for the children's labyrinth at the 1954 Milan Triennale. BBPR worked on the designs with cartoonist Saul Steinberg and sculptor Alexander Calder.

Left: BBPR's Olivetti showroom on 5th Avenue, New York, which opened in 1954. Its futuristic displays of typewriters and adding machines were lit by striped glass lamps made in Murano.

Above right: *Domus,* the architectural magazine that Ernesto edited from 1946 to 1947.

Below right: Ernesto edited *Casabella* from 1953 to 1964, adding the word 'Continuità' to its title.

Ernesto was a great humanist, and a fantastic writer and teacher, who opened my eyes to the fabric of the city that he loved. His lyrical letter of welcome, written to me as a newborn baby, told me, 'Life is beautiful. Life is curious. Break through the door, listen to the world.' He had incredible cultural breadth, and was always elegantly dressed – a *bella figura*. He talked of a design approach that could encompass everything *dal cucchiaio alla città*, from the spoon to the city. As well as making architecture, and the Bauhausian furniture that filled my parents' Florentine apartment, Ernesto was one of the pioneers of modern urban design, thinking about urban districts as complete places, formed of continuity and change, rather than as collections of buildings in space – a concept that owes as much to Renaissance masters like Brunelleschi and Alberti as it does to modernism itself. I worked in Ernesto's office during periods of leave, and immediately after I left the army, generally on pretty menial tasks. I did try my hand at drawing, with limited success; my drawings were hurriedly tidied away when clients visited, something that continues to this day!

I enjoyed my time at the BBPR office (a converted convent), the buzz of working with a group of committed young people creating exciting new designs in the heart of a beautiful city, and exploring the social possibilities that architecture created. I asked Ernesto whether I would be able to get into the Architectural Association, without A levels, and he told me not to worry: 'If you are going to do architecture, it doesn't matter where you go, just do architecture.' But I approached the AA, and managed to persuade them that, even though I had failed my exams, my breadth of education and travelling made me sufficiently unusual to admit to their diploma course.

Left: Torre Velasca, one of BBPR's best-known buildings, was being designed when I worked in their Milan office.

Right: (From left) Luigi Figini, Le Corbusier, and BBPR partners Gian Luigi Banfi and Ernesto Rogers, photographed in 1935. Banfi, who was Jewish, died in a Nazi concentration camp in 1945.

2 The Shock of the New

Modernism exploded into the twentieth century, embracing medicine, science, manufacture, travel, music, visual arts, literature and architecture. Shaped and driven by industrial manufacture, mainstream modernism challenged tradition in every field of human creativity, stripping back orna-mentation, dissolving form and embedding constant renewal. Like previous waves of change, it represented a belief in progress, and in the potential of innovation to transform society. Karl Marx's famous passage from *The Communist Manifesto* anticipates the giddy excitement of change:

> Constant revolutionising of production, uninterrupted disturbance of all social conditions, everlasting uncertainty and agitation, distin-guish the bourgeois epoch from all earlier ones. All fixed, fast-frozen relations, with their train of ancient and venerable prejudices and opinions, are swept away; all new-formed ones become antiquated before they can ossify. All that is solid melts into air, all that is holy is profaned, and man is at last compelled to face with sober senses his real conditions of life and his relations with his kind.

All good architecture is an expression of its age, materials and tech-nology - from the classical columns of antiquity to the flying buttresses of the gothic cathedral. Modernism was spare, stripped down and spartan, with a clear geometric order. Its lineage can be traced back through the Bauhaus, to Adolf Loos (who in 1910 famously asserted that ornament was crime), Louis Sullivan, Gustave Eiffel, Isambard Kingdom Brunel, Joseph Paxton and other nineteenth-century innovators. But you can go back further, to the classical Japanese architecture that inspired Frank Lloyd Wright. In the Katsura Imperial Villa in Kyoto, which dates back more than 500 years, the beauty of the building lies in the expressive use of scale and

Top left: Buckminster 'Bucky' Fuller in front of the lightweight steel and acrylic geodesic dome he designed as the US Pavilion for Expo 67 in Montreal.

Left: Joseph Paxton's cast-iron and glass Crystal Palace, built for the 1851 Great Exhibition in Hyde Park, and subsequently rebuilt in South London (shown here).

31

natural materials – the simple tapered wooden structure, the paper walls, and tatami mats inside; the sand, stones and water outside – rather than in decorations applied to them. Though it is a product of tradition rather than a rejection of it, it also embodies the modern principles of restraint preached by Buckminster Fuller, Jean Prouvé and Frei Otto – to do the most with the least.

By the mid-twentieth century, Frank Lloyd Wright, Walter Gropius, Le Corbusier and Ludwig Mies van der Rohe were presiding over a rebirth of architecture, and a rediscovery of the unadorned and rational simplicity of Japanese building, reinvented for the age of machines. Their styles were different; Wright's naturalism contrasted with the more classical approaches pioneered by Mies and Corb. Inspired by modern manufacturing techniques, they saw houses in minimalist, functional terms, as 'machines for living'; form should follow function; distracting ornamentation and historical cherry-picking should be outlawed; materials should be true to themselves; natural light, air and health should be celebrated.

Whole cities could be remodelled to replace urban squalor with rational blocks and street layouts. Le Corbusier's 1925 Plan Voisin proposed demolishing central Paris north of the Seine, replacing it with a grid of cruciform skyscrapers, connected by raised walkways separating pedestrians from cars, and topped with roof gardens. The idea was to bring the same rigour and scientific thinking to architecture that Lister and Pasteur had brought to medicine.

The tone of early modernism is uncompromising, but if you are a pioneer, you have to be uncompromising. Architects such as Walter Gropius at the Bauhaus wanted to rethink not just the shape of buildings, but the way we would live in the machine age. The Bauhaus took a total view of modern life, bringing together architects, artists, interior designers and craft workers. They felt the need to wipe the slate clean, to enable a fresh start after an orgy of decorative excess at the turn of the twentieth century. Since most critics at the time felt that what the modernist pioneers were doing was trash, should be outlawed and replaced by neoclassical and neo-Gothic pastiche, there was no space for compromise. You sometimes have to lean into the wind to make progress.

There were other currents of the modern movement too. Alongside Frank Lloyd Wright, other Chicago architects were using the steel frame, the telephone and the elevator to enable building at previously unheard of heights. In northern Europe, a Nordic modernism was developed by Alvar Aalto – more contextual, more humane, not immune to acknowledging history and the vernacular.

Left and above left: Katsura Imperial Villa in Kyoto, which dates from the sixteenth century, feels thoroughly contemporary in its simplicity of manufacturing, transparency and expression, and has influenced many modernist architects.

A dialogue between Mediterranean and Nordic modernism can be seen in the London County Council-designed Alton Estate, in Roehampton in southwest London. One of the triumphs of post-war housing, the concrete Corbusian towers of Alton East contrast with the brick-built Alton West.

Aalto's cool northern-European contextualism was tinged with elements of the Arts and Crafts movement; Le Corbusier offered harsher lines, cubist forms and brighter Mediterranean colours. As an Italian, albeit one transplanted to England at an early age, I knew where my instinctive sympathies lay – with buildings like Corb's Villa Savoye, Pierre Chareau's Maison de Verre and Mies van der Rohe's Barcelona Pavilion. Hitch-hiking to Italy every summer, I would usually sleep under the stars. On one trip, I took a detour to see Corb's socially and architecturally radical Unité d'Habitation in Marseille. Night fell, and I gave up my search and instead found a field to sleep in. I woke up to see the building itself looming over me, with its residents peering curiously down at me from their windows and balconies. A few years later, I met Charlotte Perriand, the designer who worked closely with Corb on many of his interiors, at Jean Prouvé's studio; when I expressed interest in their work together, she insisted on taking me in her car to visit the nearby Priory of Sainte Marie de la Tourette.

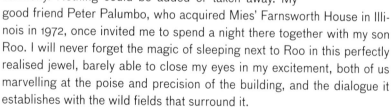

Mies van der Rohe's buildings were tightly controlled, complete works of art, which expressed their structure, but also took incredible care over scale and harmony. Nothing could be added or taken away. My good friend Peter Palumbo, who acquired Mies' Farnsworth House in Illinois in 1972, once invited me to spend a night there together with my son Roo. I will never forget the magic of sleeping next to Roo in this perfectly realised jewel, barely able to close my eyes in my excitement, both of us marvelling at the poise and precision of the building, and the dialogue it establishes with the wild fields that surround it.

These mid-century modernists carved toeholds in the ice and showed a path, but did not complete the journey – Le Corbusier acknowledges as much in the title of his best-known work, *Vers Une Architecture* (75 years later, this title must have influenced the title of the Urban Task Force's report, *Towards an Urban Renaissance,* produced under my chairmanship). My generation of architects, and the generation who taught me at the AA and elsewhere, used these toeholds to explore new pathways. We wanted a new architectural language that could flourish and add impetus to modernism, without being stifled or drowned out by this forceful collection of architectural and intellectual revolutionaries.

Left: Le Corbusier's Unité d'Habitation, built in Marseille, 1947–1952. The flat roof is a public space, with a running track and a paddling pool for children. The building still expresses early modernism's confidence in the value of daylight and fresh air. The building is constructed from raw concrete – the béton brut that gives brutalism its name – but has brightly coloured balconies, with well-proportioned rooms, and shops, clinics and restaurants on site.

Right: Jean Prouvé with Charlotte Perriand, who designed interiors and furniture with Pierre Jeanneret and Le Corbusier (and once gave me a guided tour of Corb's Priory of Sainte-Marie de La Tourette near Lyon).

Following page: Ludwig Mies van der Rohe's exquisite Farnsworth House, built in Plano, Illinois, in 1951. The house is unequalled in its lightness, transparency and simplicity, seeming to float above the ground. The night I spent there is one of my most magical architectural experiences.

By the mid-1950s, the modernist edifice was starting to crack. A new generation was stepping away from a rigidly utopian attitude, sensing that modernism was itself becoming a codified style (the much-criticised 'international style'). Reyner Banham, who later became a great friend, began to unpick the idea of a modernist style, divorced from function and from the zeitgeist. In Italy, my cousin Ernesto Rogers was imbuing his modernist towers with a sense of context and historical continuity, and in England Alison and Peter Smithson were mounting their own challenge to the clean-lined utopianism of Le Corbusier's Ville Radieuse.

The Smithsons' two best-known London schemes could hardly be more different. The 1964 Economist Building in St James's is one of London's greatest modern buildings, standing in an elegant piazza, a delicate insertion into a historically rich context. Robin Hood Gardens, their housing scheme in Poplar completed in 1972, was in an uncompromising location alongside the urban motorway that leads to the Blackwall Tunnel. There, in the heart of east London, they introduced the radical concept of 'streets in the air' – designed to replicate the street life of east London, rather than the dark, dingy internal corridors then common in blocks of flats (their earlier unbuilt scheme for Golden Lane, a social housing scheme on the edge of the City of London, adopted the same language).

Hunstanton School in Norfolk, which the Smithsons completed in 1954, was a huge breakthrough. It was a rough building, owing plan and section to Mies van der Rohe, but taking a harsher, deformalised, more personal and reductive approach. I didn't really understand it at the time, but looking back I can see the link between the honesty of Hunstanton, the Californian Case Study Houses' celebration of standardised factory-produced components, and the architectural language that Norman Foster, Su Brumwell, Wendy Cheesman and I would later develop as Team 4.

Together with other members of MARS (the Modern Architecture Research Group – a younger and more radical English version of the modernist Congrès Internationaux d'Architecture Moderne) – the Smithsons attacked the increasingly formalised international style adopted by the old guard, but also tore into the new contextualism espoused by Ernesto; there was heated correspondence between Ernesto and Reyner Banham, and one of my essays at the AA provoked a frosty response from Peter Smithson for discussing the role of history in modern architecture.

Another challenge to modernism was emerging from the conceptual thinking of Peter Cook, who would become one of the founders of Archigram, and Cedric Price. Cedric was a subtle, radical and considerable

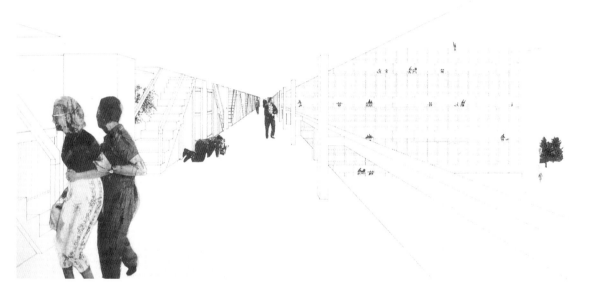

thinker, who overlapped with me at the AA. He saw architecture as a way of responding to the rapid changes of a post-industrial society, teaching a generation to challenge the brief and question what clients really wanted, while trying to find new ways to bring delight, learning, arts and culture to everyone's doorstep. He devised the Fun Palace in the early 1960s with theatre director Joan Littlewood (who had scandalised the establishment by staging the First World War satire *Oh! What A Lovely War* at Stratford East), a mobile home for arts and sciences constructed of moveable and modular plug-ins. Cedric's Thinkbelt project for the declining Potteries area would be a university on wheels, travelling along disused railway lines. Peter Cook's Archigram projects also had a futuristic optimism, in love with the potential of technology and the fast-changing shape of the future, though they had less interest in social or political issues.

Architectural Association – Meeting the Modern in Bedford Square

When I arrived at the Architectural Association School of Architecture in 1954, after a year at Epsom Art School (where I argued about philosophy as much as I studied art), it was the only school of modernist architecture in the UK, and the most important in Europe. Robert Furneax Jordan, my first-year tutor and a former head of the school, had a discursive style, a cosmopolitan and humanistic outlook, and a belief in architecture as a potent force for social and economic change. He invited architects from across Europe, including Ernesto as well as Bauhaus refugees from Nazi Germany and Constructivist exiles from Soviet Russia, to teach and lecture at the school.

The students were almost as impressive as the teachers. Philip Powell and Jacko Moya, designers of the Festival of Britain's Skylon and the Churchill Gardens estate in Pimlico, had left a few years before I arrived, and the year above me included Peter Ahrends, Richard Burton and Paul Koralek, who would go on to design the Berkeley Library at Trinity College, Dublin, and the Keble College, Oxford, extension. One of the finest talents was Ed Reynolds, whose radical forms were far ahead of their time, but who never had the chance to develop his talents, as he died of cancer at the age of thirty-two. They were in their final year when I arrived and were already developing groundbreaking plans for social housing, reflecting the generally leftist and socially engaged atmosphere at the school. Intellectual and political debate was the lifeblood of the AA. Many nights at Epsom Art School had been spent debating how to change the world with Brian Taylor, a good friend and brilliant artist, my girlfriend Georgie Cheesman,

Top left: The Smithsons' Robin Hood Gardens in east London, a magnificent housing scheme completed in 1972 that has been allowed to deteriorate and is now scheduled for demolition.

Mid left: The Smithsons' unrealised 1952 design for Golden Lane, central London, showing the sociability and spaciousness of their 'streets in the air'.

Left: Alison and Peter Smithson at work.

41

and her sister Wendy. So this ambience of debate and discussion at the AA's Bedford Square premises seemed like a natural progression.

Georgie and I had met at Epsom, where we became inseparable. She started at the AA the year after I did, despite opposition from her father, a Lloyd's insurance underwriter who absolutely loathed me, threatening to sue me and chasing me out of his house on multiple occasions. She was a great intellectual influence, and her help with my drawings was probably the only thing that stopped me from being thrown out of the AA (and was not the last time she would rescue my career). She was vivacious and intelligent, with a wild spark. After highs and lows, we separated at the end of my third year at the AA but stayed friends; she worked briefly at Team 4, and later on the landscaping outside the River Café and on the roof terrace at Royal Avenue.

Georgie Cheesman (later Wolton), my first great love. We met at Epsom Art School and studied together at the AA, where she helped rescue many of my drawings.

My initial reports at the AA were dreadful. My drawing had failed to improve, and my ability to express myself in writing was poor. I had to repeat my fourth year. Reports from Michael Pattrick, head of the school, acknowledged my enthusiasm, but gave me little basis for believing that I could succeed as an architect. He even suggested that I move to furniture design – ignoring the fact that draughtsmanship was as important for a furniture designer as it was for an architect, if not more so.

But by my last year, something changed, or several things did. Peter Smithson was my tutor, and became very supportive (once he had got over my endorsements of Ernesto's belief in historical continuity), alongside other excellent teachers like Alan Colquhoun and John Killick. There was also the sense that the post-war cultural freeze was finally thawing. We were inspired by *This is Tomorrow,* the 1956 Whitechapel Gallery exhibition that featured the Smithsons, Richard Hamilton and Eduardo Paolozzi. My drawing had improved too, with Georgie's help, and I wrote my first essay on the future of cities.

My final-year project, which appealed to Peter's social instincts, was a school for children with special educational needs in Wales, which used locally grown timber, and was designed so that the children could participate in building. The school reflected a budding interest in social architecture, in the process as well as the result of construction. Smithson's report on my scheme referred to my 'capacity for worrying about the effect the building will have on people and a concern for shape on the inside', and awarded me the final-year prize.

Meeting Su Brumwell

I met Su Brumwell in Milan at the end of my third year. She was beautiful, intelligent and sophisticated, and catapulted me into a milieu of left-wing politics and modern art in Britain. Su's mother Rene was a Labour councillor from a long socialist tradition. Her father Marcus was a remarkable man. He headed an advertising agency (which he said bored him), chaired the Labour Party's Science and Arts Committee, and had founded the Design Research Unit, the team behind the Dome of Discovery at the Festival of Britain.

Marcus and Rene were strong supporters of Ben Nicholson, Barbara Hepworth, the potter Bernard Leach, and other artists of the St Ives School. They seemed to have met every other artist who passed through England in the post-war years, from Piet Mondrian to Naum Gabo. One painting, which Mondrian gave Marcus to pay off a £37 debt, was later sold to fund the construction of Creek Vean, one of Team 4's first projects.

The late 1950s was an exciting time, with the beginnings of the space race and huge technological advances, but also a frightening one. Su and I joined the Easter 1958 Aldermaston March against nuclear weapons. It was snowing, and we planned to throw it in after one day's marching as it was so cold. But the next day we saw the press, which was full of vicious lies about 'hooligans' and 'commies'. This bore no resemblance to the very orderly civilised march we had been on, so we re-joined the march, and returned in subsequent years. I shall never forget the passion of the marchers, or the kindness of the Quaker families who gave us food, lodging and plasters for our blistered feet, any more than I will forget the venom of the press and some of the bystanders.

We moved in together in Hampstead, and we married in August 1960, while she was completing her sociology degree at the LSE. I went to work at Middlesex County Council, designing schools, drawn to work with Whitfield Lewis, a senior architect for the Alton Estate in Roehampton. Every local authority had an architecture department and some of these were huge: in 1956, the London County Council Architects Department had 3,000 employees, and was led by Leslie Martin, the architect of the Royal Festival Hall, a leading modernist thinker, and a friend of the Brumwells, who helped me maintain confidence a few years later when I was worrying whether I was cut out for architecture. A sense of social responsibility made it seem natural for the majority of young architects to work for the state rather than on the private commissions that dominate today. The focus of architectural training and practice was on public and civic buildings – schools, health centres, concert halls, new housing developments. It is time we returned to that socially driven model.

We took a cargo boat to Israel during our honeymoon – still a young country and looking like a socialist utopia, creating orange groves out of the desert – where we worked on a kibbutz and met some of the state's founders. We hitch-hiked back through Syria, Lebanon and Turkey to Europe, finding unbelievable kindness wherever we went, with the poorest being the kindest of all; hearing we were on honeymoon, people plied us with food and drink. It was a real cultural eye-opener. We came back through Paris, where we saw Pierre Chareau's stunning Maison de Verre, crafted in the 1930s from glass bricks, to allow in light without revealing the view of a blank wall.

New York – The Athens of the Twentieth Century

Arriving in New York was one of the greatest shocks of my life. Su and I left Southampton on an autumn day in 1961. As our ship, the *Queen Elizabeth,* pulled out of the port, we looked down on grey two-storey houses, and men in cloth caps cycling along the quayside of a city still scarred by wartime bombing. Five days later, we woke to see Manhattan towering above us, an urban island with buildings and canyons that dwarfed the ship. That image, and the sheer excitement of seeing those glittering towers for the first time, is still with me. The New Haven local paper had sent a reporter out on the pilot's boat to interview us, as a young couple arriving fresh in New York, and we felt self-conscious, almost like ambassadors for the youth of Europe.

We were on our way to Yale. I was taking up a Fulbright scholarship to study for my master's degree, and Su had a scholarship to study city planning. After the AA, I had been torn between applying for a scholarship in Rome, which I knew and loved, and going to America. But I knew deep down that Rome was the past; America was the future. Yale looked close enough to New York, offered a Louis Kahn building even if Kahn himself had moved on, and was on the sea. Or so we thought – the sea was completely blocked off by industry and naval yards. I never even saw it in the year I was there.

New York had an incredible energy, richness and vitality in the early 1960s. It was the Athens of the mid-twentieth century, the epicentre of modern art, of modern architecture, of modern music. We listened to jazz,

Left: Su and I on 42nd Street in New York in 1961, the year after we married. We were photographed like celebrities by the New Haven local paper on our way to Yale.

Right: Louis Kahn in his Yale Centre for British Art Building.

blues and rock and roll – Charlie Parker, Dave Brubeck, Miles Davis, Modern Jazz Quartet, Elvis Presley – exciting music that seemed a world away from English jazz or skiffle. We saw works by Robert Rauschenberg, Jasper Johns, Jackson Pollock, Willem de Kooning – the artists who were changing painting around the world. We read Marcuse's critiques of consumerism and Adorno on commodified culture. England had only finished rationing a few years earlier, was adapting painfully to its post-colonial future, and felt austere in spirit if not in policy. By comparison, the vigour and prosperity of America, where a 43-year-old John F. Kennedy had just taken office as President, were palpable. The streets were full of people from every country, as London's are today. It was clearly the capital of the world.

After a few days of being escorted round New York like minor celebrities, we made it to Yale's campus, where I had two less pleasant shocks. The first was that the campus was designed as a strange pastiche of a Victorian Oxbridge college, with Gothic revival buildings arranged around grassy quadrangles, and strange secret fraternities for the privileged few. This was a complete contrast to the rest of the town, which was a study in urban dereliction, with the worst poverty and drug problems of the east coast. Town and gown seemed to be forever at each other's throats. It was only when it became clear that the state of the city was pushing faculty and students away that Yale started to embrace rather than ignore its urban setting.

The second shock was delivered by Paul Rudolph, the professor, when I met him on the stairs on my first day. I introduced myself. He looked unimpressed: 'We are already four days into term. Your first assignment is due in ten days. You need to pass it, or you're out.'

After the ruminative intellectual atmosphere of the AA, the relentless pace at Yale showed us what hard work architecture could be; 80- to 100-hour weeks, working through the night, grabbing a few hours rest on the battered leather sofa in the studio. There were 13 of us in the class – about two-thirds American and one-third British – and we would be there day and night. It was an architectural boot camp; students did not so much fail as physically collapse.

Rudolph's early work in and around Sarasota, Florida, had drawn me to Yale. These delicate lightweight houses and school buildings, inspired by his experience as a naval architect during the war, used materials minimally and made the most of natural lighting and ventilation. Rudolph taught us for the first semester. He had a brilliant analytical mind, and influenced all of us, Norman Foster in particular. He also kept late hours; he was busy designing his brutalist masterpiece, the Yale Art and Architecture Building, at the same time as teaching. He drove himself every bit as hard as he drove us.

Top left: Paul Rudolph, our professor at Yale, standing in front of the rough concrete wall of his Yale Art and Architecture Building.

Left: Rudolph's 1953 Walker Guest House on Sanibel Island, Florida. Before coming to Yale, Rudolph was a leading light in the 'Sarasota School', whose delicate architecture drew me to study with him.

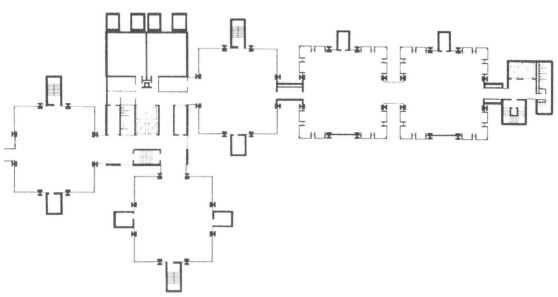

It was an introduction to the different pace of American life. People took pride in not having holidays or stopping for lunch, in contrast to Europe, where everything used to shut for several hours at lunchtime (Renzo Piano told me plainly when we first met, 'I don't talk work when I'm eating.'), and for the whole of August.

It was also a complete contrast to the theoretical ambience of the AA. There was little time for that in Rudolph's world; it was all about production, and about appearance. On one occasion we were discussing cars, and I was debating how they could safely share streets with pedestrians. Rudolph felt I was missing the point; he was more interested in how the cars looked, and the composition their different colours would create when viewed from above. The contrast between the English and American approaches found expression in friendly rivalry between the students too. The Americans put up a banner saying 'Do More'; the English contingent responded with one saying 'Think More'.

Yale opened the door to new influences, both inside and outside the hothouse atmosphere of the Arts Building, temporary home of the architecture school. This concrete and brick building, with services integrated into its honeycombed ceiling, was one of Louis Kahn's earliest commissions. It had a confidence and weight to its concrete floorplates, its handling of geometry and order, and its elegant central staircase.

We went to see Kahn himself lecture in Pennsylvania, where he had moved a few years before. Kahn's poetic sensibility set him apart from the previous generation. He was the first great post-war architect, and a huge influence on Norman Foster and me, an inspirational lecturer and a great teacher. He talked poetically of the nature of materials and the respect that architects owed them, of the relationship between architecture and music, of space and silence, of asking a brick what it wanted to be in a building. His intellectual analysis of the distinction between served spaces, the functional rooms and spaces of buildings, and servant spaces, the spaces and rooms that support them (staircases, toilets, ventilation ducts and so on) made a deep impression on me. His best-known buildings came later, and at their best – the Richards Medical Research Laboratories in Philadelphia, for example, and the Salk Institute for Biological Studies in California – they were stunning.

James Stirling also came to lecture at Yale, and became a close friend. Jim was the bright hope of British modernist architecture and the first to emerge from under the shadow of giants like Aalto, Mies and Corb. We had good architects, but we'd never managed to develop a distinct architectural movement. Working with James Gowan, Jim devised a modernist British vernacular, combining standardised industrial materials – red

Louis Kahn's Richards Medical Research Laboratories at the University of Pennsylvania in Philadelphia. The laboratories are the clearest expression of Khan's distinction between 'served' and 'servant' spaces. The three laboratory towers have open, unobstructed floors and windows to let in natural light. They are grouped round a central service core housing air intakes and elevators. Each laboratory tower is also supported by air extractors and stairways, contained in external shafts.

49

brick, standard window sections, industrial glazing – structural inventiveness, and a sense of architectural rhythm and lightness that brought life to the façades of his buildings.

Stirling and Gowan's designs for Leicester University's Department of Engineering felt like an explosion of new language. The department had a legible 'engineered' structure – you could read what the elements did in supporting the building – but also had a sculptural, almost constructivist aspect to its plant and façade. It was expressive and eclectic, but also clearly modern. Sadly, after he split with Gowan, Jim's buildings lost their lightness of touch and their humour, but he was a huge influence on all of us at the time, as well as a hugely exciting, big presence when I was at Yale. Jim attached himself to our little gang of British students; Norman, Eldred Evans (who was the most talented of us all) and I visited New York with him, enjoying architecture and cocktails at the Four Seasons. (Jim thought he had escaped notice while slipping their elegant ashtrays into his pocket, only to discover them appearing on his bill when we left.) We shared an apartment for a period, hosting the most riotous parties, with plates thrown out of the window to save on washing up, and regular visits by the police.

For my second semester at Yale, Serge Chermayeff, who was a professor at Harvard, took over from Paul Rudolph. Chermayeff had escaped from Russia to England in the 1920s, where he worked with Erich Mendelsohn on projects such as the De La Warr Pavilion in Bexhill-on-Sea and the Hamlyn House in Chelsea, but moved to the United States in 1940. He took a more intellectual and European view of architecture than Rudolph in books like *Community and Privacy,* looking at the balance between the public and private realms, and at how distinctions and transitions between them could be preserved in a modern world that seemed intent on blurring them. Chermayeff was a great teacher and an intellectual force and he dominated us completely. I remember thinking that if he had opened a window and told us we could fly, we would have leapt out.

But of all these teachers, Vincent Scully made the deepest impression. His lectures drew students and architects from miles around, and regularly received standing ovations. He would hurl himself round the stage when he was lecturing, once becoming so animated that he fell off and broke his arm. His breadth of knowledge and understanding of the history of art and architecture, particularly of Frank Lloyd Wright and Louis Kahn, was complemented by a deep civic sense of the relationship

Left: The Engineering Building at Leicester University, designed by James Gowan and James Stirling, felt like a new beginning, the emergence of an English vernacular form of modernism.

Right: Gowan (left) and Stirling in front of the building in 1963.

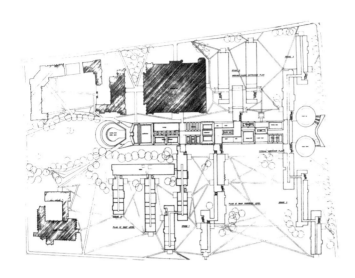

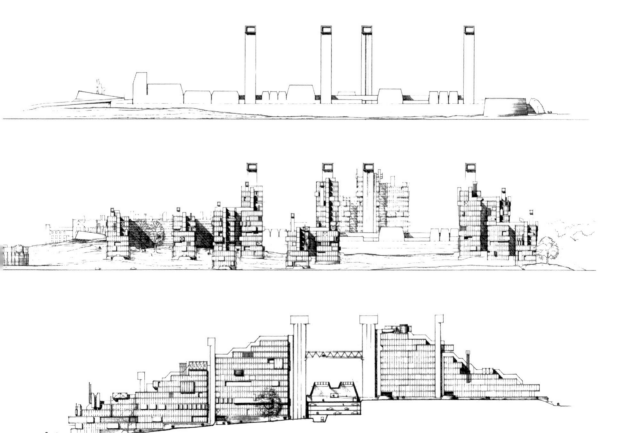

between buildings, people and places (he recommended we read Paul Ritter's *Planning for Man and Motor,* one of the first books to consider seriously the impact of cars on cities).

Vince's lectures opened up new ways of seeing and experiencing buildings, and in particular helped me to understand Frank Lloyd Wright and his ordering of internal and external space. Wright had a profound influence on me. Norman, Eldred, our brilliant fellow student Carl Abbott and I visited every Wright building we could.

Su and I went to stay with the sculptor Naum Gabo and his wife Miriam, thanks to the connections of her father Marcus. They lived about an hour from Yale, in Middlebury, and their house felt like the heart of an intellectual colony: the artist Alexander Calder and the philosopher Lewis Mumford lived nearby. We spent six months there, with the Gabos and their daughter Nina, in this incredible artistic and intellectual milieu, intoxicated by evenings speculating about the future and its possibilities.

Back at Yale, Norman Foster and I began working together closely. Like me, Norman had a scholarship, but his background was as different to mine as could be imagined. He had gone to grammar school before taking a job at Manchester City Council and completing his national service in the Royal Air Force. He managed to persuade Manchester University to take him on as an architecture student, largely on the basis of a portfolio of excellent drawings, and was a star student there.

We instantly struck up a friendship. Norman has a brilliant mind, and an incredibly clear way of explaining and arguing. At Yale, his drawings were already exceptional, while I still struggled, but we connected on a far more instinctive level. For five or six years, we would talk for hours every day, often late into the night, about cities, about architecture, about our practice. It was an intense, verbal love affair, and I don't think I'd ever had such wonderful intellectual discussions with anyone else. We travelled in Carl Abbott's VW to New York, and to Chicago, which we thought of as the Florence of the States, where we visited buildings by Wright and Mies, Louis Sullivan and the early modern pioneers.

Our final-year project (see opposite) was a scheme for science laboratories at Yale. Our design clustered round a central spine, with laboratories down the sides of the hillside site. It had service towers and an expressive structure and its spine followed the line of the slope. At the crit – the formal review of student projects that forms a central part of architectural

Left: Norman Foster's and my student project design for Yale Science Buildings. Heavily influenced by Louis Kahn, our scheme included a central spine of car parking, service towers and lecture theatres along the ridge of the hilly site with laboratories spilling downhill either side.

Right: Norman Foster, me and Carl Abbott, at Yale in 1962.

education to this day – Philip Johnson, the don of American modernism, then teetering on the edge of his descent into post-modernism, snapped off one of the service towers, muttering as if to himself, 'These will have to go.' Looking back, I can see so many of the roots of our later work in that project – the separation of 'served' and 'servant' spaces, the central movement axis, the articulated and expressive towers, the use of prefabrication.

Smoke stacks and case studies

After graduating, Su and I decided to head out west. We had read Kerouac's *On The Road,* and wanted to feel the expansiveness, the sense of space and possibility that America could offer. We relished the way that architects like Neutra, Meier, Schindler and Ellwood had found the freedom to build houses from scratch, and were swept off our feet by the results. Like many young people, we wanted to find our own spirit, our own language, our own technologies to solve the problems of the day.

In particular, we continued to see as many Frank Lloyd Wright buildings as possible. Some architecture, like Le Corbusier's, can be readily understood through looking at façade, plan and section, but Wright is different. His buildings express place and movement. You have to move through them to understand how they work, how they respond to landscape and light, how the relationship between inside and outside is expressed and resolved, how the play of light and shadow changes, brought to life by the sweeping lines of the buildings. We wanted to develop a language that could respond to Wright's ideas – about light, landscape and movement – without simply mimicking his particular style or his forms. We preferred his earlier, more contextual work, though his more sculptural later buildings (like the New York Guggenheim Museum) have proved an equally powerful inspiration for architects like Frank Gehry, Amanda Levete, Jan Kaplický and Zaha Hadid.

The other influence from those early road trips was the industrial architecture around Long Island and New Jersey – the pipes, tanks, girders, gantries and towers of the refineries, factories and processing plants that spilled out around the city, the water towers and grain silos that rose from the flat countryside of the Midwest. England had great industrial and technological architecture from the nineteenth century, from Brunel's bridges to Paxton's greenhouses, but American industrial structures were on a scale that I had never seen before. They were the undiluted and unornamented essence of functional expression. But they could also be visually exciting and even romantic, lit up at night or shrouded in smoke.

Su and I bought a Renault Dauphine, a wreck of a car with some disturbing habits. On one early journey, we were sitting in the front seats,

Left: The muscular industrial architecture that inspired us on our road trips across the USA.

Following page: Frank Lloyd Wright's Robie House, built in Chicago in 1909–11, is one of his finest 'Prairie School' houses. Their horizontal lines and organic styling evoke the flatness of the Midwestern landscape.

and had picked up a hitch-hiker who was sitting in the back. We weren't going very fast, but suddenly we realised the back seat was empty. The engine, at the back of the car, had caught fire, as it tended to do whenever you reached a certain speed (we later realised that the fuel line leaked over the exhaust pipe the more you put your foot down), and the hitch-hiker had opened the door and leapt out.

We travelled across the country, wondering at the sense of space, but also at the poverty and intolerance that persisted in the segregated southern states, where even the smallest gas station would have separate bathrooms for blacks and whites. The discrimination was shocking, and the civil rights movement still in its infancy – it is amazing to think that it would be another 50 years before the USA would elect its first black President.

Somehow, we made it to San Francisco in the Renault without too many fires, where the Federal Housing Authority employed Su, and I took a job with Skidmore, Owings and Merrill. Being at SOM was an amazing experience, though I quickly came to realise that working in someone else's architectural practice was not for me. One day, I was on the twenty-seventh floor of their offices and heard fire engines. Looking out of the window, I saw that the car had burst into flames again.

It was the Case Study Houses that drew us to California. The Houses were commissioned from 1945 to 1962 by *Arts & Architecture* magazine's editor Esther McCoy as prototypes for post-war family housing, 'conceived within the spirit of our time, using as far as is practicable many war-born techniques and materials best suited to the expression of man's life in the modern world'. They were to reflect the spirit of the age.

The Eames House, almost improvised by Charles and Ray Eames and enhanced by their beautiful furniture, was a revelation. But it was Rudolph Schindler and Raphael Soriano who particularly made their mark on me. Schindler had been a student and colleague of Wright's, and worked on the Imperial Hotel in Tokyo. He took Wright's design sensibilities and translated them from concrete blocks to a carefully considered mix of materials, including plastic panels and lightweight steel frame constructions.

Soriano was unusual in that he used absolutely standardised components – plywood, I-beams, tin roofs, cork tiling, Formica – in his 1950 Case Study House, and had started his career building cheap housing for workers. He was one of the first architects I met whose design was not just modernist in style, but seemed rooted in the possibilities of the modern industrial age. Where Mies was essentially a superb modern classicist who built scale mock-ups of his buildings and for whom structure was expressive, Soriano, who later became a close friend of mine, simply used components to structure the building; there was no artifice.

Top left: The Eames House, designed and built by Charles and Ray Eames in Los Angeles in 1949 as part of the Case Study Houses programme, using standardised windows and doors chosen from a catalogue.

Left: The interior with Charles and Ray Eames surrounded by furniture made to their designs, and their collections of art works and folk art.

Left and above: Rudolph Schindler's 1926 Lovell Beach House in Newport Beach, California, shows the influence of Frank Lloyd Wright, with whom Schindler had worked.

Right: Raphael Soriano's Case Study House, 1950, which used standardised steel components to create an extendable and open structure, would influence Parkside, the house I built for my parents in Wimbledon.

We raced around California, seeing as many of the Case Study Houses as possible. I had written my thesis at Yale on Schindler, so felt like an expert when I went visiting. In one, an older woman let me in, and I told her enthusiastically all about Schindler's architecture, his wild life and his many affairs. She listened to me politely, and then said, 'I know. I was his wife.'

We returned to New York, and considered staying there. But we were enticed back to England by the prospect of working on Creek Vean, Su's parents' house in Cornwall. They had commissioned designs for updating their creekside holiday home from Ernst Freud and sent them to us in New York for our views. We delivered a fairly tough critique – this was a job that required fresh thinking and a younger architect! – Marcus Brumwell suggested that we take over. We came back from California in the summer of 1963 (we were also expecting our first child by then), and Norman returned shortly afterwards.

3 The Language of Architecture

From the primitive hut to the soaring skyscraper, architecture seeks to solve problems in three dimensions. It combines scientific analysis with poetic interpretation, using technology and order to create aesthetic impact and functionality. It transforms the ordinary and the mundane by giving order, scale and rhythm to space. Renzo Piano described it as the most public and socially dangerous art: we can switch off the television or close a book, but we cannot ignore our built environment.

Parkside: Adaptability, Transparency and Colour

Parkside, the house that I built for my parents in 1968–9, was the first fluent expression of an architectural language that had been evolving since I arrived at Yale nearly ten years earlier. Its transparency, its use of colour, its industrialised construction and its flexibility set the scene for much that followed. The house, which I designed with Su and my long-term collaborators and partners John Young and the engineer Tony Hunt, is situated on the edge of Wimbledon Common, shielded from the road and the Common by a mound of earth, designed so that only the rooftop is visible.

Parkside was a considerable refinement of our architectural idiom, reflecting how new techniques and materials had transformed our design approach over a decade. It was a prototype of a flexible building type that would adapt to multiple changes in use, family structure and ownership, but was also an intensely personal project, reflecting my parents' characters, lives and values. And it was the last domestic project we would build before the maelstrom of the Pompidou Centre engulfed us.

My father was retiring from full-time medical practice, and my parents wanted to move somewhere that would enable him to continue to see some patients, but would also be single-storey, close to local shops

Above left: With my mother on a site visit at Parkside in 1968. The three steel portal frames of the lodge are in the foreground; the five that would form the main house are beyond where we are standing.

Left: Viewed from the side, you can see Parkside as a series of slices, capable of endless extension.

63

and Wimbledon Common, and easy to maintain and flexible as they got older. The brief combined his rational approach to ageing with my mother's delight in views, in colour, in light, and her growing interest in pottery.

The structure is essentially very simple. Parkside is a discontinuous transparent tube, supported by eight 45-foot steel portal frames (five for the main building, three for the lodge). It is a tunnel of light, connecting its gardens to the beautiful open space beyond. The house mixes mass production with traditional on-site building techniques (we had hoped to prefabricate the whole structure but planning and building regulations made it impossible). Glass panels demarcate 'inside' and 'outside' space – the main house, the garden designed by my childhood friend Michael Branch, the lodge – but also blur the distinction, creating the impression of a sequence of spaces, like a procession of courtyards or patios, rather than of fixed boundaries. The structure is open-ended; the central courtyard could be enclosed with the addition of two more portals, or the building could be extended, repeating its pattern out into the Common beyond.

The external walls were formed of two-inch-thick 'Alcoa-brand' insulated aluminium panels normally specified for refrigerated trucks, joined together with neoprene. As we experimented with new construction materials, John Young kept up subscriptions to numerous industrial magazines, and the inspiration for these panels – lightweight, highly insulated and mass-produced – came from one of them.

The succession of spaces in Parkside expresses a fundamental facet of architecture – the interplay of light, transparency and shadow. A famous essay by Colin Rowe and Robert Slutzky distinguishes literal transparency of light passing through glass or a void, and phenomenal transparency – the layering and organisation of built elements, light and shadow to create appearances of texture, of space, of continuity, of singularity – when light falls on them. The first is a transparency of seeing; the second a transparency of reading, of interpretation. As the visitor's gaze passes through Parkside, these two forms of transparency – layering and penetration – coincide and contrast, creating a dialogue.

I love this play of transparencies. The special glass John Young developed with Pilkington for the Lloyd's Building makes the light sparkle, breaking up the blackness of plain unlit glass, brightening the aspect from the outside, but providing privacy for those at work within. The Pompidou Centre turns expectations inside-out, its structure transparent and legible on the outside, but also enabling light to penetrate deep into its floorplates (the space available for use on each storey).

Pierre Chareau's 1931 Maison de Verre in Paris lets light in through translucent glass bricks, creating a glowing wall, but only reveals its

A concept sketch of Parkside, completed in 1969, showing (from top left), Wimbledon Common, the road, the mound, the lodge, the courtyard, the house and the garden.

structure when you enter through the simple sliding glass door. The building was rediscovered in the 1950s. From the first time I saw it, I was captivated by this magic lantern off the Boulevard St Germain, tucked in under an existing building, and wrote my first article in *Domus* about it. Later I got to know the Dalsace family, who commissioned the building as a home to display their wonderful collection of modern art, books and furniture, with consulting rooms for Dr Dalsace on the ground floor. The interior of the building is even more radical than its steel and glass-brick exterior. Among its many magical and inventive elements was the beautiful steel staircase that led from the entrance to the double-height living space, its banisters leaning away from the stairs themselves, like a cow-catcher on the front of a train. The collaboration between Chareau, Dutch architect Bernard Bijvoet and skilled metal worker Louis Dalbet created a building of carefully designed moving parts, with sliding screens and shelves adapting the house for different times of day and functions. The spaces and craftsmanship have influenced everything from the Pompidou Centre to the interiors of my house in Chelsea, and Renzo Piano's Maison Hermès headquarters in Tokyo.

This play of light and shadow creates scale, and all scale ultimately comes back to human bodies, to the fingers, hands, forearms, feet and strides that defined standard measurements in the pre-metric era – when man was literally the measure of all things.

Scale helps a building to communicate. I have always wanted to make the signals given off by buildings clear and unambiguous, to enrich the enjoyment of users and passers-by alike, to express buildings' role in city and community. These signals should help people to understand the process of construction, navigate buildings and places, see the potential they offer for private and public life. All elements should give order, nothing should be hidden, everything should be legible – the process of manuacture and erection, the role everything plays in the building, how it can be maintained, changed, demolished, and what the building itself does or could do. Parkside has this simple expression – you can see the steel portals that hold up the house and the joints connecting the aluminium panels.

Parkside is also suffused with colour. The insulated aluminium walls are white, the internal walls are yellow and lime, as are the steel portals that form the heart of the structure. In post-war England, it sometimes felt as if colour itself had been rationed, and that only shades of grey and brown were permitted. In this monochrome world, my mother stood out; she had always dressed in bright colours – much to my embarrassment when she dropped me off at primary school. But she clearly made an impression on me. Later, in 1957, when my father had asked Su and me

Left: The Maison de Verre, designed by Pierre Chareau and Bernard Bijvoet, epitomises inter-war modernism in its transparency, its industrial quality and the craft of its construction. The house, tucked beneath an apartment occupied by a recalcitrant tenant, was completed in 1932. I wrote my first published article, for *Domus* in 1966, on the building; its transparency, its flexible use of space and its beautiful staircase all made a lasting impression on me.

Following pages: Parkside viewed at dusk from the courtyard when my parents were living there, the steel frame and aluminium panels clearly visible.

The dining table and chairs designed by Ernesto Rogers, with the open kitchen to the left, and furniture by Le Corbusier and Charles and Ray Eames behind.

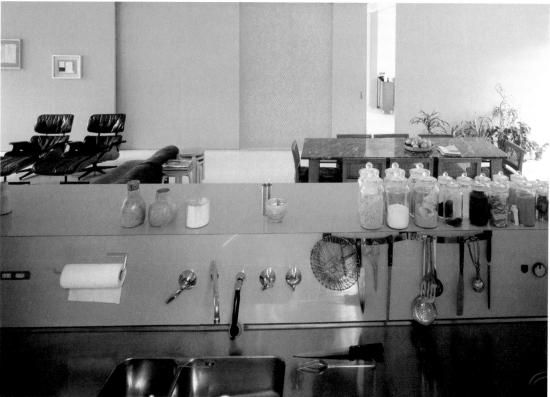

Above: Reflection and transparency: my mother's mirrored dressing table in the bedroom, with the door open through to the kitchen and living room beyond.

Left and above left: Inside Parkside's bright living space, looking out from the open kitchen, with bedrooms and the library beyond the central dining space. The steel portal frames are visible as slices in the ceiling. In the upper picture, my mother's beautiful pots are arranged in 'villages' on the kitchen counter.

Right: My mother in the study at Parkside.

to help decorate the doctors' dining room at St Helier Hospital, where he opened the renal unit and brought the first kidney dialysis machine to the UK, we choose bright yellow, bright green, bright blue and bright red, each wall painted a different colour. These were the colours of cubism, of the work of Mondrian, Matisse and Picasso that had seemed so bright in the gloom of post-war England.

Travelling round the USA and Mexico, I had seen the bright colours of California, of the Case Study Houses. I had seen how colour was used in industrial architecture, to indicate function, distinguish components, or signal hazards. It seemed natural to bring all this back to London, as an additional layer of meaning – a different way of making buildings legible and transparent in their functions – but also as a form of play, a way of lightening and clarifying the formalism of imposing structures. Ancient buildings – from the Acropolis to medieval cathedrals – were much more colourful than their bleached stone tells us today. Using modern industrial components frees you to experiment with colour too: plastics are whatever colour you choose to make them. I sympathise with Gropius who, when asked his favourite colour, replied, 'All of them!' People are frightened about choosing the 'right' ones, but I don't worry about following rules. Green can go with red or pink; if a colour is beautiful, it will go with another beautiful colour.

Parkside originally included a consulting room for my father to continue medicine, and the separate lodge included a carport, and a studio for my mother's pottery. The focal point of the house was an open-plan kitchen. Cooking and entertaining had always been the heart of our family life and bringing the kitchen into the living space made cooking a social activity, not a segregated chore. Over the years, my mother cooked for so many of my friends, and instilled a love of Italian food not only in Ruthie, who went on to create the River Café with Rose Gray, but in Georgie and Su too, and my sons, who are all really good cooks.

On the other side of the kitchen counter, the house made room for the beautiful 1930s modern furniture that my cousin Ernesto had created in Italy as a wedding present for my parents. My mother's pottery was on shelves, and walls were hung with paintings by Ben Nicholson and Patrick Heron – and a prized Picasso print.

Over time Parkside has adapted and evolved: the carport and pottery became a flat for my brother Peter, then for John Young, then the design studio of my son Ab, who moved into the house when my mother died. When Ab moved out, we gifted Parkside to Harvard, as a residential centre for their Graduate School of Design, led by Mohsen Mostafavi. Each year, six research fellows will live in the house, which has been reconfigured by Philip Gumuchdjian, who co-wrote *Cities for a Small Planet* with me when he was working at RRP, pursuing research into urban development, and it will also host lectures and other events. It has changed with the times, accommodating different needs and uses rather than constraining them, reflecting the architectural philosophy later summarised as 'Long life, loose fit, low energy'.

The Limits of Traditional Technique – Creek Vean and Murray Mews

Su and I began work on Parkside in 1968. For five years, first with Norman and Wendy Foster, and then with John Young and Laurie Abbott, we had been working towards a new architectural language, feeling our way along a path without knowing clearly what the destination would be.

When we returned from the USA in 1963, Norman, Su and I had set up Team 4 with my ex-girlfriend Georgie Cheesman, and her sister Wendy. At first, we worked out of Wendy's bedroom in a two-room flat in Belsize Park. Frank Peacock, who had studied with me at the AA (literally along-side me, as our surnames made us neighbours in every class), and was a brilliant technician and draughtsman, built a box to put over Wendy's bed, so that we could use it as workspace during the day. When clients visited, friends would be roped in to pose as architects, to make Team 4 look like a larger concern than it was.

As neither Norman nor I had completed our training, we were not entitled to call our-selves architects. Georgie had qualified and gave Team 4 some legitimacy, but she quickly saw that Norman and I were going to be impos-sible to work with, so moved on. The core of Team 4 was Norman and Wendy (who fell in love with each other and married), and Su and me. Norman and I did man-age to complete our registration, but only after being summoned before the Architects Registration Council for practising without a licence.

Norman Foster and Wendy Cheesman, who married in 1964, at Team 4's offices.

Team 4's first commission, Creek Vean, was both Parkside's twin and its opposite. Like Parkside, it was for our parents – in this case, Su's, Marcus and Rene Brumwell. Like Parkside it has now been listed as Grade II*. Like Parkside it presents a deceptively blank face to the road outside. But there the similarities end.

Marcus Brumwell had asked us to look at the plans for renovating his holiday home on the banks of a Cornish creek by the Fal estuary. We soon decided, and persuaded our client, that he needed to demolish the existing

house and start again. Our designs set up a dialogue between light and shadow, between the geometry of concrete blocks and soft contours of a creekside, between modern materials and sense of place.

Our final design had two axes: the living accommodation was arranged along the contours of the site. A double-height living room, dominated by a hanging Alexander Calder sculpture, and kitchen face out towards the Fal estuary; three bedrooms are angled in towards views over the creek to the hills beyond. A stepped path separates the living room and the bedrooms, bridging over a glass-roofed gallery that forms a connecting corridor and housed the Brumwells' collection of St Ives School art. The path leads down from the road to the creek itself, where we spent many happy days sailing with Marcus and Rene – and our children and grand-children still return there to sail every summer.

The buildings hug the hillside, and have over time been softened by the vegetation that grows over and around them (the planting was designed by Michael Branch), but their form is uncompromising, and you can still see the powerful influence of the Frank Lloyd Wright buildings that we had visited while driving around the USA only months earlier. The house was designed so that it could be extended: the wall at the end of the bedrooms was intended to be a pause not a terminus, a semicolon not a full stop.

Working with Tony Hunt and Laurie Abbott, we used carefully specified concrete blocks for the main structure. But rather than letting them dictate the geometry of the building, we cut them to shape like lumps of cheese, so that they could follow our unconventional contoured plan. We used neoprene, a type of rubber that was a new technology at that time (I think we were among the first to use it), for the joints between blocks and glazing.

At the same time as Creek Vean, we were working on three houses at Murray Mews in Camden. We were exhausted, putting in fourteen-hour days, seven days a week. It's not a good way to work, but we were young, and it was the culture we were used to from those late nights at Yale. I remember saying to Su that I didn't expect to ever have a whole weekend free, but that it would be nice to have just one Sunday off, maybe every other month.

Where Creek Vean was exciting and tiring, Murray Mews was dispiriting. The clients had very different requirements or changed these over time: one of them, Naum Gabo's stepson Owen Franklin (our GP), wanted

Left: Marcus Brumwell, my father-in-law and Team 4's first client, with Creek Vean, completed in 1967, on the hillside behind. The double-height living space faces the Fal estuary; the lower living spaces overlook the creek.

Right: Team 4 at our Hampstead Hill Gardens office in 1963 or 1964. The way we were posing like a pop group, not an architecture practice, convinced John Young to apply for a placement with us.

Above left: The plan for
Creek Vean, showing
the stepped path leading
down from the roadside,
the two wings either side
of it and the glazed
gallery connecting them
under the path.

Above right: Zad, Ben
and Ab on the steps.

Above and right: The
concrete stepped path
now softened by vege-
tation, leading down
between the two wings
of the house.

Left: Pill Creek Retreat,
which we built near
Creek Vean as a summer
house – and a refuge for
the client to escape from
his architects.

a bachelor pad full of art and sculpture at the outset, but had married and had children by the time the house was finished. His needs had changed, but the building had difficulty meeting these.

The budgets were very low and the contractor was incompetent and keen to cut corners: everything leaked, walls weren't square, we discovered a small river running through the sunken dining room in Owen's house, and chimneys missed fireplaces. I remember one horrendous site visit with one of the clients. First of all he poked at a piece of what looked like asphalt, to discover it was just a copy of the Daily Mail painted black. Then we went downstairs, where the U-bend of the lavatory was visible. The owner hit it to make a point, and it broke, showering him in sewage. Charlie Chaplin couldn't have done better. John Young, who had just joined us, prepared intricately detailed plans for tiling the bathrooms, showing how every tile would fit. These were ignored, and used to wrap fish and chips. I walked off site one day and went to sit under a tree on Hampstead Heath, and burst into tears. I wondered, not for the first or last time, whether I was really cut out to be an architect.

At Creek Vean, we were luckier with our builders; their work was excellent, though their attitude was pretty laid-back. If the weather was good, they would down tools and go fishing. This was one of the reasons, though not the only one, that it took the six of us the best part of three years to complete Creek Vean.

From Classical Temples to Friendly Robots

We couldn't continue to work like this. Creek Vean and Murray Mews pushed us to fundamentally rethink our approach to technology and the process of construction. Technology is the raw material of architectural expression, the equivalent of words in poetry. Without a proper understanding of words there is no poetry, and architecture starts from an understanding of technology, materials, the process of construction and a sense of place. Norman and I were modernists, but were inspired by the amazing heritage of early industrial buildings, from the world's first cast-iron bridge at Coalbrookdale in Shropshire, to the incredible lightness and delicacy of Brunel and Paxton, who used iron, steel and glass – the high tech materials of their day – to create great station sheds, bridges, glass houses and crystal palaces.

In the twentieth century, technology had continued to transform our cities: it was the steel frame, the telephone and the elevator that freed buildings from the ground, enabling Chicago to build the first skyscrapers. At the same time, the Model T Ford had shown what could be achieved on

Above left: The kitchen-dining room, the heart of Creek Vean, looking out towards Falmouth.

Left: Inside the gallery, a flexible space for displaying works by Barbara Hepworth, Ben Nicholson and other artists of the St Ives School.

production lines, and so technology had also created an economy of manufacture. Norman and I had studied the use of manufactured components in Buckminster Fuller's work, in Soriano's architecture and Paul Rudolph's early designs, in the open-ended architecture of the Eames House in Los Angeles, in Jean Prouvé's prefabricated steel structures, and in modern industrial buildings and machinery.

Though industrialisation had created countless new possibilities for building and construction, many of the buildings we saw in 1964, and see today, still use tools and techniques – bricks, mortar and timber frames – that have been used for 500 years or more. As Peter Rice, the Irish engineer who became an indispensable partner on the Pompidou Centre and so many other projects, liked to say, traditional techniques have been used so many times that you don't give them any thought; radical architecture has to start from first principles.

I have never liked the label of 'high tech' architecture that is sometimes applied to people like Norman Foster, Nicholas Grimshaw and me, but I do believe we have a similar approach in that expressing the process of construction is an important part of our architectural language, something to be celebrated as it was by Paxton and Brunel, not to be hidden away behind the romantic stylings of neoclassical and neo-Gothic façades.

All good architecture is modern in its time, reflecting both changing technology and the spirit of the age, the zeitgeist. Architectural language needs to evolve with the times, just as painting, music, fashion, even the design of cars does. It is from the interplay of function, technology and zeitgeist that good architecture emerges, with a tough beauty that contains bitterness as well as sweeter flavours.

Our experience with Creek Vean and Murray Mews had shown the limits of traditional technologies; the challenges of working with 'wet trade' contractors – those deploying traditional techniques of bricks and mortar on site – even when they were competent; the time taken, and the risks of constructing fixed buildings for clients whose needs changed over the years. In 1969, a few years after we had completed these projects, I wrote a manifesto arguing for change. At a time when we needed 400,000 houses a year in the UK (a curiously similar challenge to the one we still face nearly 50 years later), it made no sense that it had taken six architects four years to build four houses. We wanted to create buildings that took advantage of industrialised technology, that were general purpose not tailor-made, so that the same shell could cater for different clients' needs or for one client's needs changing over time.

We had to go back to the system-built structures that had inspired us, assembling components not stacking bricks, creating lightweight vessels not heavy-boned buildings. Essentially, the modern building site should be an assembly site, leaving the manufacture of components in the workshop. Using industrial components and systems, our architecture could be based on an interchangeable and adaptable kit of parts, not the creation of a perfectly formed doll's house. It would not be frozen classical music, but jazz, allowing for improvisation, propelled and supported by a regular beat.

Buildings should not rigidly determine the way they are used, but should allow people to adapt and interact with their space, to bring their own character, to perform freely inside and out, to bring life to and complete the expression of the building. Our buildings would not be classical temples where (to use the Florentine architect Alberti's phrase) 'nothing could be added or taken away or altered except for the worse', but friendly robots, non-deterministic open-ended systems that could respond to users' needs, changing as these changed and allowing for improvisation. The tension between buildings being open-ended and adaptable, and the pressure to fix use and configuration often for reasons of short-term cost savings, persists in architecture today.

Adaptability is even more important, as accelerating technological and social change makes it hard or impossible to predict how we will live and work in the decades to come. If our buildings are to be sustainable, they must cope with radical changes in configuration and use.

Romig and O'Sullivan's graph, published in *Hospital Engineering* in 1982, compares the replacement frequency of parts, systems, buildings and urban infrastructure. Flexible buildings should allow for the replacement of services with minimal disruption to the structure.

Researchers have analysed the differing replacement rates for different parts of the built environment: basic appliances (and nowadays IT systems) have a life of ten years, systems like air conditioning and heating can maybe last 40 to 50 years, buildings themselves can last 100 years or more, while the cities' infrastructure and layout date back centuries.[2] A building's framework should allow for services to be replaced and renewed, with minimal disruption.

Allowing for change in the design and construction of a building is a constraint, but constraints are a critical driver of our aesthetic language. Cost, time, the availability of materials, planning and building regulations, evolving technology, political decisions and clients and users requirements – these all shape buildings. But constraint defines the area of possibility, and gives direction to design. There's a famous anecdote about the seventeenth-century architect Inigo Jones being commissioned to build St Paul's in Covent Garden. The Earl of Bedford said that the cost needed to be as low as possible, saying 'I would not have it much better than a barn.' Jones replied, 'Then you shall have the handsomest barn in England!' You do not have to sacrifice beauty or function to a reduced budget, though money always helps, as my mother used to say.

A Beautiful Barn – The Reliance Controls Factory

The Reliance Controls Factory represented a leap forward both functionally and aesthetically, a shift from the language learned from Wright and Corbusier, to one influenced by Fuller, Soriano and Eames, and by the industrial structures we had seen travelling round the USA. It was the first building that we built using standardised components and systems, rather than the chaotic construction of traditional building techniques. The commission came about when Peter Parker, later to be chairman of British Rail, asked Jim Stirling to recommend young architects who could build an expandable 30,000 square foot electronic component factory near Swindon – to be completed within ten months of the first client meeting, and at a cost of £4 per square foot, a tiny budget even in those days.

The restricted budget and timescale were a liberation and a catalyst. Traditional construction techniques would be hopeless both in terms of time and cost, so we had to think differently. Working with Tony Hunt (the creative engineer whose elegant drawings of engineering options helped to define and refine all of Team 4's work), we created a low-slung shed structure from corrugated steel decking, supported by I-beams internally and by cross-bracing externally, the slender shallow Xs of the steel creating a rhythm in the building's outer walls. Everything was designed with an eye on economy, on minimising the quantity of steel needed for the job.

The building was unusually democratic for its time: the offices and the shop floor were in the same building, workers and managers used the same entrances and ate in the same canteen. Everything was designed to

Top and far left: Reliance Controls, built on time and for a very modest budget in 1967, was Team 4's last project. The factory was constructed from standard components – I-beams, braces and corrugated steel.

Left: Internal partitions were moveable, creating flexible and democratic space – bosses and workers used the same entrances and the same canteen.

Right: The window, added by the factory's occupiers, showed that we needed construction systems that could respond easily to changing needs.

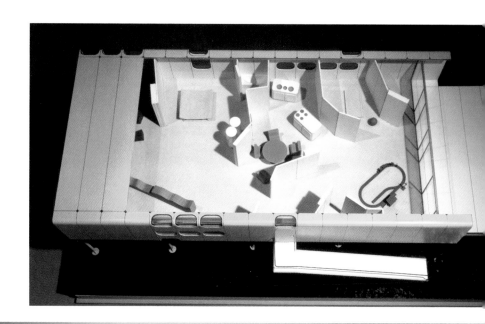

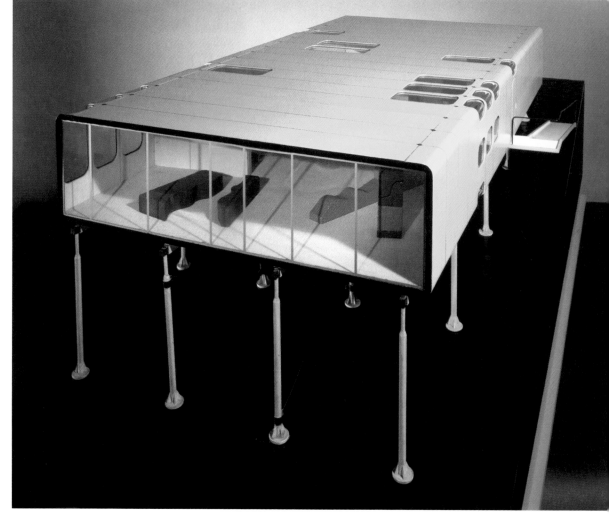

be lightweight and flexible: fluorescent tubes were set into the recessed areas of the corrugated steel roof, internal partitions were non-structural and could be easily moved, and the one glazed wall could be removed to enable future extension.

Some twenty-five years later, in the early 1990s, I had a call from its then owners saying that they were thinking of pulling Reliance Controls down, as the site could accommodate a much taller, denser, multi-storeyed building. There was a small local protest, and I think they were concerned that I would join in and accuse them of desecrating a fine building. 'No,' I said, 'I think that's fine, it's just a shed.' 'But it's a beautiful shed,' they said. 'Yes,' I agreed, 'but it is a shed, it's designed for change.'

Reliance Controls won the Architectural Design Award in 1966 and the Financial Times Award for outstanding industrial building in 1967 (we thought this would lead to a flood of work, but the only query we received was about how the flooring was cleaned). And in 1969 Creek Vean won a RIBA Award for Work of Outstanding Quality, the first time a private house had ever done so.

But by that stage, Team 4 no longer existed. Norman and I had spent four years working furiously hard, constantly pushing each other to think more and do more. But without work the cracks began to show. Norman and I had outgrown each other, and were both struggling for the freedom to develop our own approach to architecture.

The split of Team 4 was painful, but we all remained close and Norman was one of the great supporters of our Pompidou Centre design. We did talk ten years later about re-forming our partnership. But the conversation, in a dreary hotel in upstate New York, came to nothing. Our architectural language and ethos had moved in different directions.

The Zip-Up House

After Team 4 split, Su and I set up as Richard + Su Rogers, and were soon re-joined by John Young, who had joined Team 4 for a year out before returning to the AA to complete his studies. Su's father let us have office space at the Design Research Unit, which he had founded with Misha Black after the war, but we retained a distinct identity.

Following the slow-burn success of Reliance Controls, Su and I wanted to elaborate and extend its language of standardised industrial components. Could we take the use of aluminium panels further, we wondered, and design a house that did away with the need for steel frames and separate roof construction, a structure that would be entirely self-supporting, and could be bought off-the-shelf and assembled anywhere?

The Zip-Up House, initially designed by Richard + Su Rogers for DuPont's 1968 'House of Today' competition – low energy, adaptable and portable.

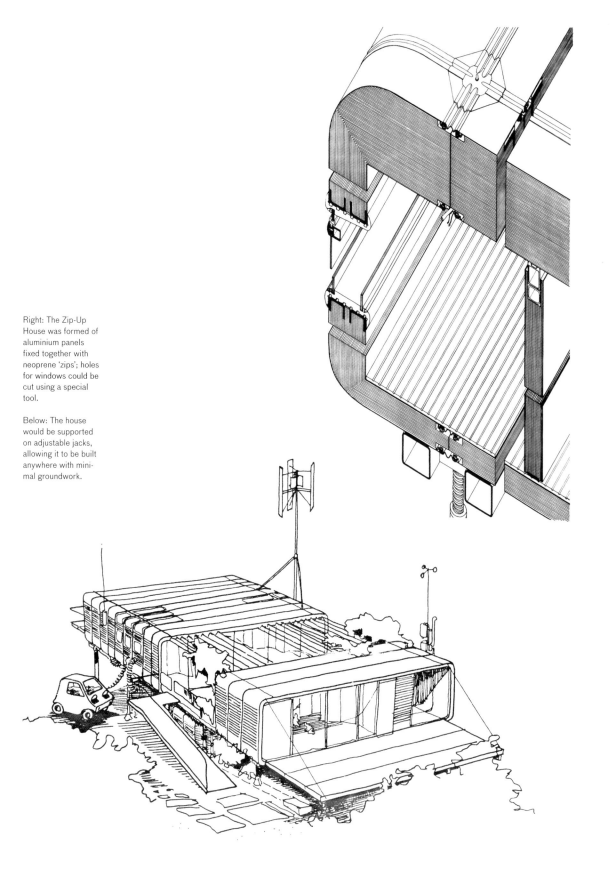

Right: The Zip-Up House was formed of aluminium panels fixed together with neoprene 'zips'; holes for windows could be cut using a special tool.

Below: The house would be supported on adjustable jacks, allowing it to be built anywhere with minimal groundwork.

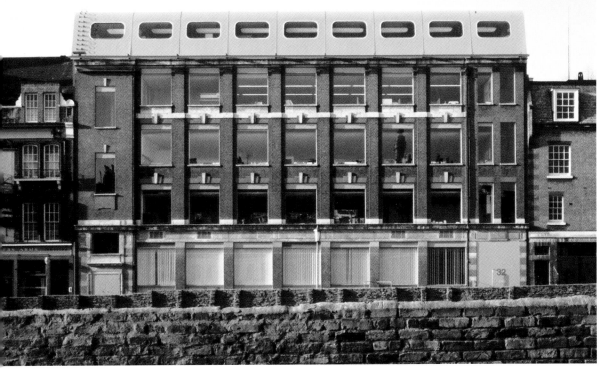

Above: The 'Yellow Submarine' – the roof extension we built for the Design Research Unit where Richard +Su Rogers were based in the late '60s. The construction was inspired by the Zip-Up House.

Right: The Universal Oil Products Factory, completed in 1974, used a prefabricated panel system, but these were glass-reinforced cement sandwich panels, rather than aluminium.

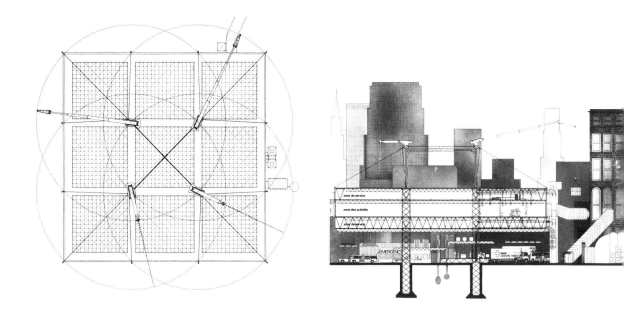

The Zip-Up House, which was an important precursor to Parkside, was designed for the House of Today competition, for the 1969 Ideal Home Exhibition. It was a self-supporting aluminium tube – or monocoque – formed of loops of eight-inch-thick panels that were able to support their own weight. This highly insulated structure meant that the building used minimal heating; one 3kW heater (or the body heat of two medium-sized dogs) would generate sufficient warmth for the standard unit.

The House was additive; the idea was that you could extend it indefinitely, using basic and easily available kit. The customer could buy as many standardised four-foot, self-supporting loops as they wanted, zipping them together with neoprene, and using a special tool (more or less a tin can-opener) to create space for standardised window and door units. The houses would be supported by adjustable steel jacks, which would remove the need for expensive and complex groundworks. The kitchen was on wheels, and services would be brought in through a flexible tube. All the internal partitions could be moved, using inflated inner tubes to create soundproof seals. The house could essentially be assembled anywhere – quickly and without specialist knowledge.

We came second in the competition, but our entry created the most discussion and was later exhibited in Paris by the Arts Council; it also helped establish our reputation after the separation of Team 4. But it was seen as a wild futuristic vision, rather than as a practical, semi-standardised house that could be assembled on site in a matter of days. When we tried to build it on a number of sites, we ran into problems with planning and building control. Looking back, I consider the Zip-Up House to be one of our most radically inventive projects, and its bright yellow model still stands at the entrance to our offices. We went on to use similar panel systems at Parkside, and on projects like the Universal Oil Products Factory in Surrey and the extension (nicknamed the 'Yellow Submarine') that we built on the roof of the Design Research Unit's Aybrook Street offices, where the yellow panels contrasted with the fluorescent pink fire escapes.

Lightness, Compression and Tension

The search for lighter structures goes to the heart of modern building techniques, as does the quest for economical use of materials and environmentally responsible construction. Buckminster Fuller's geodesic domes, and Frei Otto's experimentation with membrane and tensile structures inspired by everything from birds' skulls to soap bubbles to spiders' webs showed how architecture could be formed of light and air, as well as of stone and brick.

The ARAM module, a lightweight relocatable structure, was designed by Piano + Rogersin 1971. It could be built in remote rural areas, war zones or even urban districts. The structure's four cranes would enable it to build itself, with flexible space – for a field clinic, a school, or a civic centre – sandwiched between service floors.

After Wimbledon and the Zip-Up House, we continued to experiment with ways to make buildings lighter, to minimise structure, to maximise space and light, to reduce demands on natural systems and materials. The tensile qualities of steel showed us one direction. Steel can be 30 times stronger in tension than compression; or to put it another way, a single steel cable can support much more than a steel bracket.

In 1971, Renzo Piano and I developed a modular structure for the Association for Rural Aid in Medicine (ARAM), applying industrialised systems and the mobility of the Zip-Up House to the construction of civic buildings. The ARAM Module was designed primarily as a field hospital, but would also allow for other uses – it could be a town hall, a school, a temporary dormitory. It was a portable, democratic town centre. The module would be constructed around a core of latticed steel columns. Using lightweight trusses and steel cables, these would support modules of functional space sandwiched between service floors. The whole structure would hover over any terrain, enabling it to be constructed wherever the steel columns could be sunk into the ground, and it could be parachuted in and erected anywhere, from inner city neighbourhood to developing world disaster zone. Once the columns had been craned into place, each was topped with a smaller crane, enabling the structure to complete its own construction.

The ARAM Module was commissioned by Lalla Iverson, a pioneering American doctor working at Johns Hopkins University. She wanted to bring healthcare closer to the people, to take it out of grand institutions and insert it into the heart of civic and community life. Despite her huge passion for the project, we never raised the funds to build one, though we did detailed studies for a location in one of Philadelphia's poorest districts.

After the Pompidou Centre, in the early 1980s, we built a number of factories that adopted the same cable-hung structure. Fleetguard, near Quimper in Brittany, was a simple steel box, supported by bright red masts and cables. Jean Prouvé, another pioneer of lightweight design and chairman of the Pompidou Centre jury, said it was his favourite of my buildings at that time.

The Inmos Microprocessor Factory in South Wales was the first microprocessor factory in the UK. Designed for a fledgling industry, it needed to be able to accommodate rapid changes in technology and processes, to expand and reconfigure space without disrupting production. It also needed to be built quickly, and to enable complete segregation of the highly controlled 'clean room', where the manufacturing took place, from more conventional offices, meeting rooms, canteens and bathrooms. It also needed to be able to operate 24 hours a day, while accommodating maintenance and upgrades.

The Fleetguard Factory, commissioned by the Cummins Engine Company from RRP and completed in 1981, with a structure suspended on cables attached to slender steel masts.

Above: At the Inmos
Microprocessor
Factory in South
Wales services are
suspended from its
central masts so they
could be easily
adapted to meet the
needs of a fast-
changing industry
without disturbing
sensitive operations.

Left: The central
'street' separates the
clinical conditions of
the clean rooms where
microprocessors are
manufactured from the
offices and support
space in the rest of the
building, as well as
providing a social
space for colleagues
to meet.

Right: Mike Davies,
dressed in red in
the foreground, led
the design team.

Tomigaya was one of a sequence of schemes we undertook for Soichi Hisaeda, a Japanese developer who visited the 1986 Royal Academy exhibition. I visited Tokyo the following year, and was entranced by the city – its vitality and beauty, the mix of old and new, the quality of construction.

Left: Our designs, brilliantly illustrated by Laurie Abbott in a Meccano model, enabled internal floors to be repositioned to create flexible exhibition space (big enough to display a yacht or a small plane), topped with a restaurant and observation tower.

Below and right: The Tomigaya scheme was for a highly con-strained triangular site at a busy road junction. We were allowed to build high but were limited in terms of floor area.

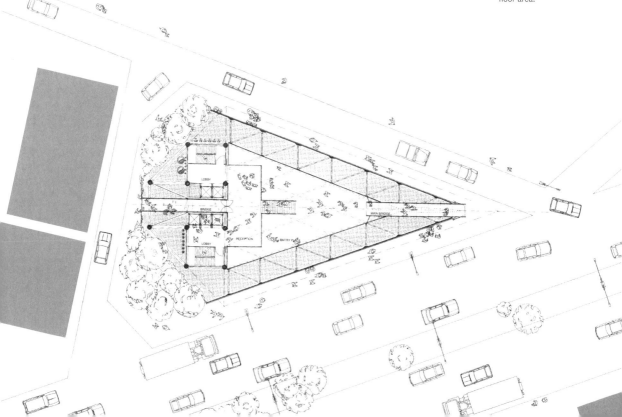

Mike Davies led the design team alongside Tony Hunt, and after some experimenting with separate corridors for the 'clean' and 'dirty' parts of the building, we settled on building two wings either side of a central 'street', which would allow for chance or planned meetings. Steel masts supported air conditioning and other services, and the cables that held up the rest of the building, enabling the workspaces on either side to be entirely column free. The building could be extended without shutting down operations; work could continue behind partitions, while new sections were added.

Despite the sensitive nature of the activities it contains, the building's structure and servicing are completely exposed, celebrated as architectural elements rather than hidden behind façades or in ducts. Reyner Banham wrote that walking along the service deck was the 'most astonishing encounter with the sheer mechanics of truly modern architecture that one can experience' and compared the design to naval architecture, in that it seemed to derive from 'a sense of necessity, a feeling that nothing could be other than the way it is'. The building, completed in 1982, was expected to be made redundant by the technology within seven years, but has adapted to repeated changes in ownership, and was still making microprocessors at the time of writing.

The Millennium Dome, which uses similar cable hung technology to maximise flexibility, is the lightest structure we have designed. In the late 1990s, RRP was preparing a master plan for North Greenwich Peninsula, opposite Canary Wharf in east London. This highly polluted and previously isolated site would be opened up by London Underground's Jubilee Line extension, with government investing to clean up the land. But in early 1996, North Greenwich was chosen as the site for the 'Millennium Experience', a national exhibition celebrating the new century, and the exceptional Gary Withers of the event design firm Imagination approached us to discuss how to fit the exhibition space into the wider master plan. Early discussions focused on 12 pavilions (for the 12 months of the year), with a central arena for performance space, though the government remained unclear what these pavilions would contain.

With only three-and-a-half years to go until the immoveable deadline of 31 December 1999, time was running short. With no specific brief, our solution was to create a huge circus tent, which would be a waterproof umbrella to protect the pavilions and visitors against the English weather. The space would also be highly flexible, to allow the plans for the 'Millennium Experience' to evolve and for the radical changes in configuration that eventually took place. We stretched the tented roof originally proposed for the central arena to cover the whole site, with 12 masts to hold the structure up (while staying low enough not to interfere with City Airport flight

Left: The Teflon skin of the Greenwich Millennium Dome in London, which we built in just over one year. The building was said to weigh less than the air it contained.

Following page: The Dome was supported by twelve steel masts to represent the twelve months of the year, and had a diameter of 365 metres. Electrical and other services were housed in external towers, to maximise flexibility of the internal space, now used as a music and events arena.

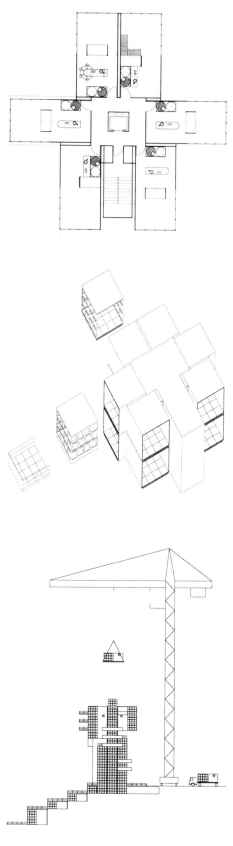

paths), and a diameter of 365m (to match its one-year expected lifespan). Enclosing the whole site under the Dome created neutral space, indifferent to its contents, and the internal pavilions would not need to be weather-proof; they would be sets for a show, not buildings in their own right.

After the change of government in 1997, it was decided that the Dome, while only hosting the Millennium Experience for a year, would be a permanent structure. We had to rethink materials, and switched from PVC to a more expensive (and more environmentally sustainable) Teflon-coated fabric for the roof. The programme had every potential to be a disaster: the deadline was set and there was no room for error. But the construction team did an incredible job, and the Dome was handed over to the client in autumn 1998, work having started on site in June 1997.

After the catastrophic opening night on New Years Eve 1999, when furious journalists and VIPs were left stranded and berating London Underground staff on freezing platforms, the lacklustre Millennium Experience (which lurched unsteadily between didactic and 'Disneyfied') saw out its year. After some delays, the Dome was converted to long-term use as an events arena – one of the largest and most successful in Europe. The building that was a temporary expedient has survived 17 years.

Modular Housing

Since Team 4 built Reliance Controls, the potential of standardised components and off-site manufacture has been widely understood and exploited by commercial developers. Modern office and industrial buildings are almost entirely fabricated off-site, to the highly exacting specifications that computer-aided design and manufacture can deliver. But housing still seems to be stuck with the same basic techniques that we struggled with at Murray Mews.

We have continued to design modular housing, however. In the early 1990s, a Korean manufacturer asked us to prepare designs for a modular system that could deliver 100,000 small studio flats at one-fifth of the standard unit cost. Our design was for single, lightweight stainless steel units, each of 25 square metres, with a flexible layout that could be reconfigured for daytime and night-time use, through folding back individual elements. These would be manufactured offsite, and brought to site on trucks, where they would be fitted into a central core structure (which would also include services). We struggled with the client to allow some variation in units to provide for different family sizes, but they were determined that there would only be one (two-person) module, and the scheme never went into production.

RRP's industrialised housing concept for a Korean client was based on highly flexible steel micro-units for single people, which could be reconfigured for different times of day. The units would be factory-built, brought to site on lorries, and craned into position, plugging into a central service core as a 'kit of parts'.

103

1. Making panels in SIG factory

2. Prior to cladding

3. Applying the cladding

4. Leaving the factory

5. Core assembly

6. Arrival on site

7. Lifting pods into position

8. Zipping up the pods

House-building in the UK is slowed by an outdated delivery model, and the same technology that we were using decades ago. PLACE/Ladywell, shown here, was designed by RSHP to enable off-site manufacture and rapid assembly on site, saving both time and money.

More recently, we have developed with Sheffield Insulation Group a design concept based on off-site manufacturing that produces highly insulated modular housing units, with computer-controlled cutting ensuring that pieces fit together precisely. YMCA London South West was the first client to adopt this technology. Y:Cube is a microflat for move-on accommodation from YMCA hostels. Units are manufactured off-site and delivered fully finished, ready to plug and play. A first Y:Cube scheme of 36 units is complete in Mitcham. Separately, Lewisham Council commissioned a temporary housing scheme using the same process. At Place Ladywell 24 larger family units have been built, each assembled from two modules. Higher-ceilinged ground floor units are dedicated to community uses, retail, offices and a cafe.

We also developed the Tree House concept for the 2016 Venice Architecture Biennale. Tree House uses a timber structure that can be assembled in low-tech factories from locally sourced timber, and can typically be stacked over ten storeys. Each unit has a highly flexible internal layout, and access to private or communal garden spaces on the roof of the unit below. The ground floor is given over to open space and cafes, to encourage interaction and community building. The units support each other and are stacked around a central staircase and lift, requiring minimal preparatory groundwork.

Advances in technology have transformed architecture and construction in the fifty years since we designed the Zip-Up House. But, in the midst of an unprecedented housing crisis, we are still using the same outdated techniques for housebuilding. We need to revolutionise housing, to develop the language and structures that meet the needs of modern society.

The Tree House concept that RSHP exhibited at the 2016 Venice Biennale provides low-cost homes in 75 square metre timber-framed units.

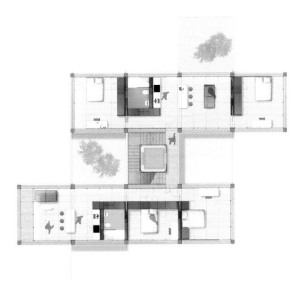

4 Centre Georges Pompidou

Politics hit us fast, the morning after the announcement that we had won the Beaubourg competition. The previous evening, we had been toasted as winners at a glittering party on a *bateau-mouche.* The next day, we went to the Grand Palais, where our designs were exhibited alongside the other 680 entries. The reception at the press conference was unbelievably hostile. There was booing and balls of paper were thrown at us, as we were accused of ruining Paris by desecrating the city with a building completely out of scale with its surroundings. There was not a single positive story in either the French or British press, and even close friends like my former AA teacher Alan Colquhoun joined in the attacks

I had worried about the ethics of the competition from the outset. When Ted Happold from Ove Arup approached us in early 1971 about the project, I was pretty negative. The proposal for a grand cultural centre, in the heart of France's centralised capital, seemed to go against the spirit of the new world promised by the upheavals of 1968. France's Minister of Cultural Affairs André Malraux had made it his mission to decentralise art, building cultural centres in provincial towns and cities, and this seemed like a step backwards, a vanity project for a conservative president. Besides, architectural competitions were rare and risky ways to get work: the winning entry was often chosen by an unqualified jury on the basis of compromise rather than merit, and even then there was no guarantee that it would be built. As a practice we were short of funds and entering a formal design competition seemed like a costly distraction.

There were four of us – Ted Happold, Renzo Piano, Su and I – and we argued it back and forth. The final discussion was over lunch, and I put forward all the reasons we shouldn't get involved. I didn't think we had the staff or resources, I didn't like the look of the jury much (I thought, wrongly as it turned out, that Philip Johnson, who ten years earlier had crushed a

With Renzo Piano in the Pompidou Centre site office (which would eventually become the library) in 1976, trying to work our way through or round one of the many crises that threatened to derail the project.

109

service tower on Norman Foster's and my student project, looked particularly likely to be hostile), and I didn't like the sociopolitical overtones. Ted said that Arup could provide £800 towards the costs of submitting an entry. We didn't have anyone who could work on it full time. Renzo said he would try to coax Gianni Franchini, an elegant and highly skilled Italian architect who he had worked with since they were students, to come over from Genoa. Su, who agreed with me, was called away at the last moment to look after one of our sons, who was being sent home ill from school. When she left, I was outnumbered; democracy prevailed.

Renzo Piano and I had been introduced by my doctor and good friend Owen Franklin, who was Naum Gabo's stepson and a resident of Murray Mews. Owen felt that these two Italians might find each other simpatico. Renzo, like my father, typifies a type of northern Italian man, who dresses more English than the English, in immaculate tweeds with leather elbow patches, and traditional British shoes. Italian architectural training tended to focus on the art rather than the science of construction, but Renzo came from a family of major construction contractors and was incredibly fluent in modern technology, with engineering expertise allied to a truly poetic sensibility: in *The Renzo Piano Logbook* he writes elegantly about the 'magic of the construction site'. My cousin Ernesto had taught him at the Politecnico di Milano, and Renzo had worked with the multi-talented designer Franco Albini in Milan.

I remember walking the streets of Soho with Renzo soon after we first met, talking about the future of humanity, about technology, about sociology, about people, about architecture and what it could achieve – all the dreams and enthusiasms of young men. Our discussions may not have been as intense as my conversations with Norman Foster had been ten years earlier, but they ranged much more widely, with my love of Italy complementing Renzo's love of England.

Renzo has an incredible ability to design from the individual component to the completed structure, while I tend to work the other way round; one of his best books is called *Pezzo per Pezzo* (*Piece by Piece*). His early projects, like the lightweight Italian Industry Pavilion at the 1970 Osaka Expo and his beautiful hillside studio, show the deep understanding of structure, process and poetry that he had acquired from his studies in Genoa.

Renzo, Su and I had formed a partnership the year before the competition, the logic being that three unemployed partners were as good as two. We worked together on the lightweight ARAM Module, on a scheme for the PA Technology Laboratory just outside Cambridge, and on a competition entry for a new gallery for the Burrell Collection in Glasgow. After the Pompidou Centre, we went our separate ways – but we still speak at least once a week, and seek each other's advice on projects. We have become like brothers. Every July we sail on Renzo and his wife Millie's beautifully designed boat around Sicily or Sardinia, and they stay with us whenever they are in London.

Submitting Our Entry – The Gods Aligned Against Us

The closing date for entries was 15 June 1971. The comprehensive competition brief, issued by the Ministry of Culture, in a smart black box, 5cm deep, had been very specific about the drawings to be submitted, and their scales, so that every entry in this anonymous competition would be presented to the jury in a consistent format. It also named every juror and gave their CVs. At a time when architectural competitions were still rare – this was the first major competition since Sydney Opera House in the 1950s – Beaubourg was a case study in how they should be organised (though rarely are).

Design competitions can generate new thinking and ideas, and have helped many young architects to jump-start their careers; before competitions became widespread, the only way to climb the professional ladder was to wait for the boss to die, or at least retire. But the majority are badly run, superficial and exploitative. Clients use them to get a lot of options at a low cost, or even worse to fill in the details of a half-cooked brief. The risk is that hasty choices are made on a purely aesthetic basis, without giving the architect time to understand what is needed or to fully develop their ideas; or that the result is a bureaucratic fudge and the 'safest' option wins. Competitions require a lot of hard work, by clients and architects, to get the right result. They should have a carefully prepared brief with a jury announced in advance, and should be properly funded (half a per cent of the cost of the building as a rule of thumb). [3]

Our work continued right up until the last minute, when we sent Marco Goldschmied to Leicester Square, where there was a late-night post office, so that the drawings could be postmarked and despatched, as stipulated, before midnight. The post office also served as a drop-in centre for drunks and addicts, so was a pretty unsavoury place, with vomit on the floor. Marco took the tube of drawings to the counter, where the clerk told him it was too long to be posted. Marco is very persuasive, but all his arguments fell on deaf ears: rules were rules. So he borrowed a pair of very blunt scissors, knelt on the floor, and cut the drawings down to size, before taking them back to the counter and posting them. (Some time later, Philip Johnson told me that our drawings looked as if a dog had got at them.)

Three days later, the tube of drawings was back on my desk, marked 'insufficient postage'. I was furious – how could they say this when they

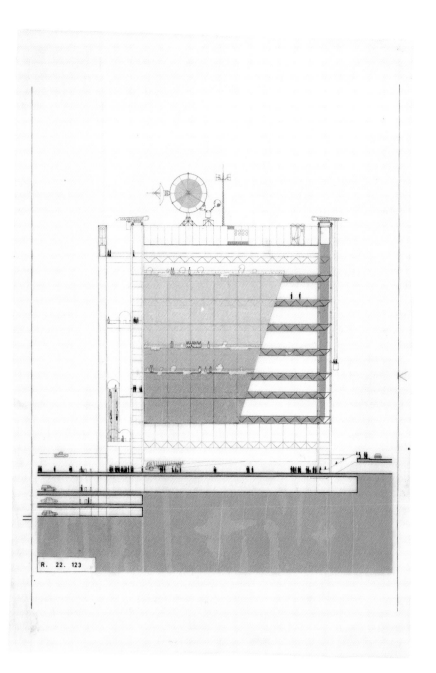

R. 22. 123

The 1971 competition stage section and plan, showing a much taller scheme than was eventually built (58m rather than 28m). Other ideas that were dropped included moveable floors, and the whole building being open at ground level. But the core concepts – of a flexible container offering open floor spaces, a large public piazza and a continuation of the public realm into the building – were already in place.

Following page: The 1971 elevation, expressing the spirit of the age and our concept for a 'live centre of information... and two-way participation', with news feeds, projected images, political slogans, and personal messages. The idea of the screens survived until we told the President that the information displays would be controlled 'by the people'.

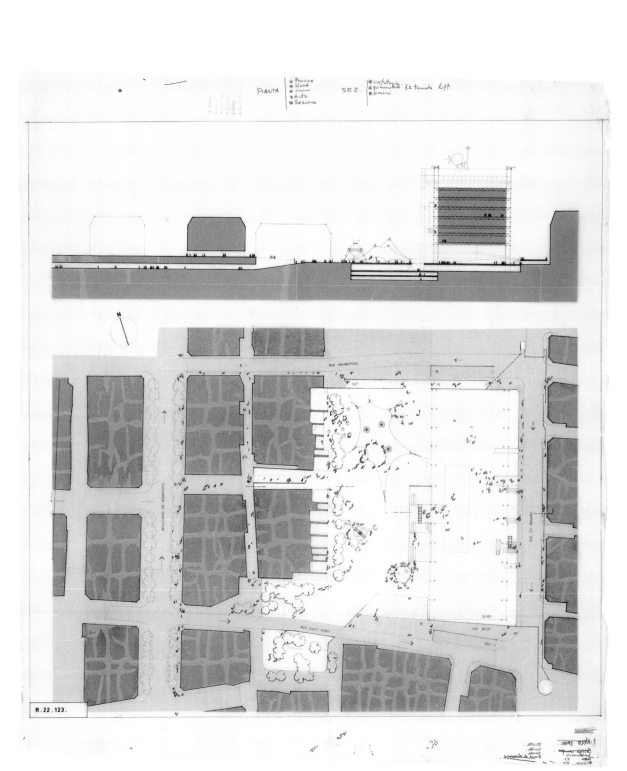

PIANTA
* Pucce
* Nord
* omini
* Auto
* Sezione

SEZ.
* cafeteria
* pianmobil "la tenda left.
* omini

R. 22. 123.

Sezione su la pianta (schizzo)

ANIMATED MOVIES PRODUCTION FOR T

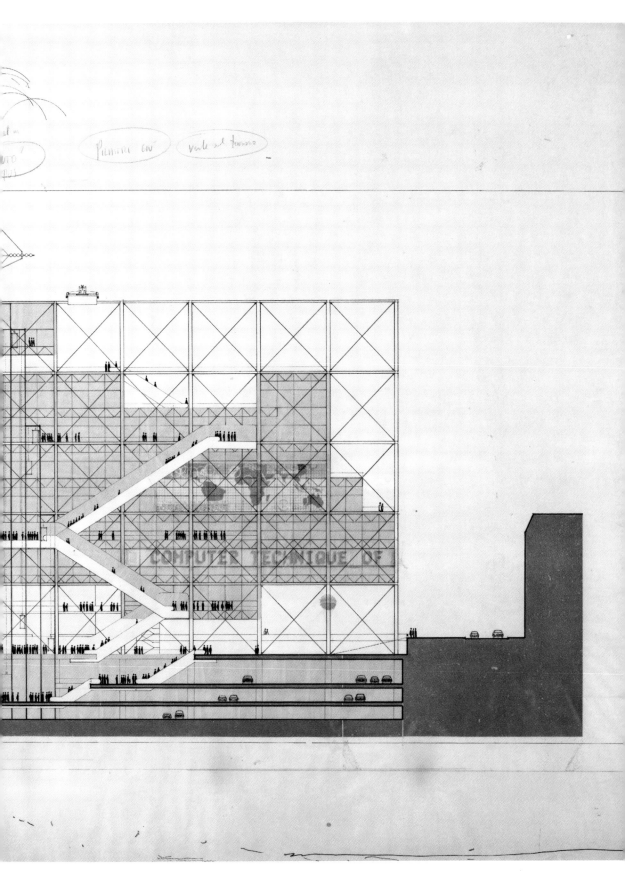

had weighed and accepted them over the counter? I went to the post office to complain. I insisted that they be sent out again, with the vital 15 June postmark. I came up against a brick wall. Postmarks were sacred; they could not be applied retrospectively. Eventually, we reached a very British compromise. The competition rules were very clear that entries had to be postmarked, but there was nothing saying the postmark had to be legible. After some careful smudging, the drawings were sent off again, only to be lost in transit together with all the other British entries. At this point I felt that the gods had aligned against us (I had also just heard we were one of 681 entries), and suggested we give up rather than waste money on reprinting our drawings, but they eventually came to light behind a door in the postroom of the British Embassy in Paris. We never discovered how they got there.

Riots and Red Lights – The Site and the City

If the concept of 'a palace of culture' seemed out of step with the times, and with the new democratic spirit that was spreading across Europe and the USA in the late 1960s, it felt particularly out of keeping in Paris, where *les événements* of 1968 had almost forced de Gaulle's government from power.

When we arrived in Paris four years later, it was still a wonderfully romantic city, with the best food in the world, modern infrastructure, and street life that we could only dream of in England. But the atmosphere was highly charged too: demonstrations, and pitched battles between police and marchers, were still taking place every weekend. One time, when Renzo, Gianni Franchini and I were walking back from a restaurant, police trucks swerved in front of us, and heavily armed riot police leapt out. Some started heading our way, clearly spoiling for a fight. We sat down on the kerb, to avoid looking like a threat, but they nonetheless seized Gianni and beat him quite badly.

Even the concept of 'culture', which has a much broader frame of reference today, then seemed archaic, a hangover from a previous era. One journalist later tried to provoke me by saying that we were building a 'supermarket of culture'. I replied that I had less of a problem with 'supermarket' as a concept than I did with 'culture'. It is not an answer I would give today, but then the idea felt alien and elitist.

Reclaiming the city was central to the demands of the soixante-huitards: the city should be a place for protest, for celebration, for public life, not for squares built like parade grounds, filled with monuments to long-dead generals, religions and capitalists, and lit by the neon signs of advertisers. This mood – captured by the situationist slogan 'sous les pavés, la plage!' ('underneath the cobbles, the beach!') – infected our approach to the competition.

The site identified in the brief was the Plateau Beaubourg, a grotty car park in the centre of Paris, sandwiched between the dense and run-down medieval streets of Le Marais (the old Jewish quarter), and the beautiful old market of Les Halles (which we later fought to save). The area was very poor and was the heartland of Paris's red-light district. In the 1930s, using disease control as a pretext, the authorities had tried to 'clean the area up' by demolishing the brothels around the site, but the prostitutes just moved one street further back. The women were still there, leaning out of windows to greet us.

Renzo and I visited Paris to develop our ideas at the beginning of the competition, and the first thing we did was to walk the streets of Le Marais and Les Halles. We were immediately struck by how little public space there was in the neighbourhood. What Beaubourg needed was not so much a lofty palace of art, but a forum for public life, for the day-to-day meetings of people that animate cities, for rendezvous between friends and lovers, for spontaneous performance and demonstration, for parents to bring their children to play, for anyone to sit and watch the theatre of city life unfold.

So our designs started from the outside in, with public space. In the early sketches, we placed the building in the centre of the site, and surrounded it with public space. But this broke the street-line of one of the longest roads in Paris, leaving space that would never be a great piazza, and making the building the centre of attention, a 'palace of culture' – traditionally institutional, pompous even. We wanted to create a modern building, but one that fitted with the complex fabric of the city, rather than seeking to obliterate it, with the contempt for traditional street patterns seen in utopian plans like Le Corbusier's Plan Voisin. And we wanted the culture to be on the street as much as inside the building.

We relocated the building to one side of the site, so the other façade continued the street line of rue du Renard, and gave the other half of the site over to a public piazza, which continued under the building, and also ran up its outside, where escalators and corridors – our 'streets in the air' – would mix with live information displays, channelling anti-war and revolutionary messages from around the world. The building itself would be lifted on piloti (Le Corbusier-style columns) to make it lighter and free it from the ground. It would hover above a sunken piazza surrounded by shops and cafes, con-nected to the public life of the city, but also connected to a world that was on the verge of transformation by information technology.

The brief, drafted by the Ministry of Culture, was well-written but highly specific, setting out how many bookshelves, how many seats, how

much space for galleries, how many meeting rooms. But there was also a small phrase that gave us the confidence to go beyond these stipulations. The building would not be extended, but 'the Centre's internal flexibility should be as great as possible. In a living and complex organism such as the Centre, the evolution of needs is to be especially taken into account.' This was all the licence we needed to think beyond the detailed schedule of floor spaces and subdivisions that we had been given, derived from surveying existing buildings, curators and librarians. We knew that the whole idea of a library would be transformed in coming years; we could not predict the future, but we could perhaps create a space in which it could unfold.

We saw Beaubourg as a node in the networked society, describing it as a 'live centre of information... a cross between an information-oriented, computerised Times Square and the British Museum with the stress on two-way participation'. It would be a place for all people, all races, all creeds, for the poor as well as the rich. It would be a flexible container, fixed but not determinate, brought to life by flows of information and people across its façades and in its spaces. As Renzo puts it, we wanted to challenge the idea that culture had to be built out of marble, and instead wanted to create an urban machine with moving parts. Nothing would be hidden; everything would be expressed. You would be able to read in every component the process of manufacturing and construction, and the part it plays in the building.

Inside, unobstructed open floors (each one the size of two football pitches) would provide flexible and adaptable space for the library, gallery and research centre, allowing programming to change over time, spaces to be reorganised, free movement of people, and penetration of natural light throughout the building. These floors would essentially be open space, 'pieces of the ground' as Renzo used to call them, where anything could take place – a museum, a market, a political meeting. It would not be a frozen temple of culture, but something that could evolve and adapt, like the ARAM Module, or the glass-and-steel tube that had formed my parents' house in Wimbledon – but on a dramatically different scale. The structure and services – ventilation, heating, water, goods lifts – that would normally take up space on every floor, would be removed to the exterior, providing a richly coloured and textured façade along the rue du Renard, and five unobstructed floors with views out over the piazza.

The Pompidou Centre expresses the belief that finite, closed buildings constrain both their users and passers-by. The fewer constraints that a building places on its users, the better its performance and the longer its life. Our proposal was for an open system, a kit of parts, a framework that would integrate user requirements, ideology and form. Buildings are theatres

The Pompidou Centre's services, viewed from the tight-knit medieval streets of Le Marais.

119

for public life; the Pompidou Centre would allow people to perform freely inside and out, with the stage extended up through the building's façade, so that their performance could become part of the expression of the building.

Knowing Your Jury – The Art of Competitions

In any design competition, the jury is crucial, not only for the decisions they will make, but for the signals they send out about a client's commitment to design. Analysing the jury and their likely interests is a vital part of preparing a submission. A jury of middle-ranking bureaucrats says clearly that the competition will be judged on cost, on feasibility, on financial standing, on almost anything apart from the quality of design.

The jury for the Beaubourg competition was the opposite – probably the most impressive that I have dealt with in my career, and almost as daunting as it was encouraging. About half were architects or curators, and Jean Prouvé – the brilliant French engineer known for his commitment to prefabrication, systems building and standardisation – was elected by the others as chair. The architects included Philip Johnson and the Brazilian Oscar Niemeyer. They were joined by Frank Francis, director of the British Museum, and Willem Sandberg, former director of the Stedelijk Museum in Amsterdam. Su and I had met Willem, who was regarded as the leading curator of his time, when we were staying with Naum Gabo in New York.

Philip Johnson made one politically astute suggestion, as the jury met to consider the 681 submissions. In most competitions, there was no guarantee that the winning entry would be built. Often the winner would be seen as too bright, too complex, so the second-placed design, perhaps from a local team, would be brought forward, or the second-placed team would be appointed to 'work with' the winners. So Johnson proposed that rather than awarding a first, second and third prize, the jury would award a first prize, and then twenty-nine 'thirtieth equal' prizes. This still did not guarantee that the winning entry would be built, but made its replacement by a 'second best' option a lot more difficult.

The jury's formal report praised our proposed public space (amazingly ours was the only entry to create a piazza) and the interplay it would create between the institutions and the culture of the streets. They also commented on the ease of circulation, the connections to the neighbourhood and the flexibility of internal space. 'The winning project,' they wrote, 'has been conceived with a great simplicity and a great linear purity . . . but everything is done to draw out, to stimulate, to keep life there.'

Philip Johnson later told us that one of the reasons that we won was that every head of department (of the library, of the museum, of the

The team at the hastily arranged winners' ceremony: Renzo Piano, Su Rogers, me, Ted Happold and Peter Rice.

121

industrial design centre) could see precisely the space that they wanted to see on the plan. We hadn't even tried to dictate who would go on which floor, let alone the precise layout for the library, the art gallery or the performance space. The building was fixed (though we did have early plans for moving floors up and down), but not deterministic. Buildings should liberate their users, not limit them.

Until the final decision, the competition entries were anonymous. When the jury had voted eight to one in favour of Project 493, the names behind it were revealed. At first there was alarm; nobody had heard of Piano + Rogers. When it was revealed that we were 'in consultation with Ove Arup and Partners, Consultant Engineers', I am told there was an audible sigh of relief.

The President, the Chairman and the Move to Paris

Looking back, it is clear that we had no idea what we were taking on when we arrived in Paris in July 1971. Renzo and I were in our thirties and had only built small domestic and industrial projects. An experienced person would have looked at the scale of the project, especially in a foreign context, and thought, 'This is too much for us!' It was our naivety, and our confidence, that made us think we could solve whatever problems the project threw at us.

Following our noisily hostile reception at the Grand Palais, we met the man who was to make the project happen. Robert Bordaz had been appointed by the President to head the Établissement Public du Centre Beaubourg, the public body that was responsible for the competition, and ultimately for delivering the scheme. He was a senior judge, a big man with white hair, who seemed ancient to me then, though he was only in his sixties. I asked him how many construction projects he had been involved in. He replied that he hadn't, but that he had been with de Gaulle's Free French government in 1943, and had organised the French withdrawal from Vietnam after their defeat at Dien Bien Phu. I wasn't sure how relevant this was at first, but in the months and years that followed I would value his tough but canny, battle-hardened approach to solving problems. He understood how naive we were, and stood by these young foreigners, when everyone else – the press, the French architectural establishment, community groups – seemed lined up against us. He knew how to work his way round the intricate bureaucracies of the French state, and generally got what he wanted through charm and intelligence. Without him, the Pompidou Centre would never have been built.

We had our first meeting with President Pompidou a few days later. He was immaculately dressed, patrician. I remember being intrigued by the deep shine on his shoes. We were still wearing the same clothes we had travelled over in – Renzo in a baggy tweed jacket, me in a denim suit and bright-coloured shirt. I think John Young was wearing a Mickey Mouse T-shirt and jeans. The only respectably dressed person was Ted Happold of Ove Arup, who was wearing what he used to describe as his 'engineer's suit'.

The meeting seemed positive. The President spoke at length about the importance of the project, but we were still unsure whether we would actually be able to pay our hotel bills, let alone complete our designs. We prepared a list of twenty demands, for a contract, for an office, for an advance on fees. To our surprise, when we presented this to Bordaz, he agreed to almost everything. He had seen Pompidou immediately after us, and had been instructed to make the Beaubourg project happen. 'Ça va faire crier,' the President had said ('That'll make them yell'), and he was right.

At the outset of the project we tried to run it by travelling back and forth from London – where my three sons were – to Paris, staying in a flea-bitten hotel that doubled up as a brothel, many of the architects sharing beds. One day, when we had just flown back to London, we were greeted by a telegram from Bordaz: 'If you are not back in Paris tomorrow night, you are fired.' For a few months we continued to commute from London, as Ruthie (now my partner) was working at Penguin Books, designing book covers with David Pelham. But in summer 1972, we made the commitment to move to Paris. Her sister Susan, an artist who was living in Paris at the time, had found our 50 square metre flat in the Marais, four floors up with no lift. Renzo joined us for lunch in the apartment pretty much every day, cementing our friendship and avoiding, at his insistence, any discussion of work.

Ruth Elias had come over from the USA in 1967 with a group of students, some of whom had left the States to avoid being drafted. She had taken a year off from Bennington College, a leading liberal arts college in Vermont, where she had been heavily involved in the free speech and civil rights movements. We met at a dinner party, soon after she had arrived and begun studying graphic design at the London College of Printing. Some time later we met again, and fell in love.

Our wedding at Ruthie's parents house in Long Island in November 1973 was very low-key. Her father Fred was a doctor, and about as near to being a communist as it was possible to be in the USA without being arrested. He was also one of the most charismatic, and culturally and politically sophisticated people I have ever met. I will never forget how warm he and Sylvia – another committed activist, who was writing letters for Amnesty International the night before she died – were to this divorced and largely penniless forty-year-old architect who had fallen so in love with their twenty-year-old daughter.

We returned from Long Island to our tiny Marais flat, but soon needed more space. Roo, our first son together, was born in January 1975 (by sheer coincidence, our doctor in Paris, Dr Vellay, consulted from the Maison de Verre, and was the son-in-law of the Dr Dalsace who had commissioned the building), and my eldest son Ben wanted to come over from England to stay with us for a few months. Later on, Ruthie's sister Susie found a magnificent if very run-down apartment in the beautiful Place des Vosges, with six windows looking south over the square from a piano nobile. We moved in and worked with our friend Judy Bing to convert the apartment into wide open spaces. Though it was completed only a few months before the Pompidou Centre, Ruthie and I have vivid memories of the parties we held there, from Renzo's wedding reception, to our party for the opening of the Pompidou Centre, to the dinner party where we met Ronald Dworkin.

This is how we wanted to live, with Roo riding his little bike round and round the open kitchen, our bedroom on the mezzanine, and a flow of family and friends, coming and going.

We both worked incredibly hard in Paris – Ruthie and I have always mixed work and play. Ruthie began to cook, and we started to explore Parisian restaurants, venturing out every Sunday with other expatriates like Judy Bing, Ed Marschner, Connie and Dominique Borde, and Kirk Varnedoe to discover somewhere new; our chequebook stubs from those years read like a restaurant guide. Whenever we could, we would escape for the weekend, taking the overnight Train Bleu to St Tropez, which still retained its bohemian glamour.

Assembling the Team

Bordaz and his deputy Sébastien Loste were determined we would speak their language, and Renzo and I struggled through contract negotiations that were all in French. Years later, we were having dinner with Loste, and asked him where he had been educated. 'Oxford,' he said. 'So you speak English?' 'Yes, of course,' he replied. I used to think that the English were the most nationalist nation when it came to language, until I met the French. Renzo spoke better French than me, but we often took refuge in ignorance, responding with 'Je ne comprends pas' when we were faced with instructions we wanted to ignore.

After our meeting with Pompidou, and the initial negotiation with Bordaz, our most urgent task was to assemble a larger team in order to

Top: Roo was born in Paris in 1975, and we all lived in the Place des Vosges throughout the completion of the Pompidou Centre.

Left: Ruthie (front row, third from left) came over from the USA in 1967, and continued to be heavily involved in the anti-Vietnam War movement, as well as in support of civil rights and free speech.

Right: Ruthie's parents, Fred and Sylvia Elias.

125

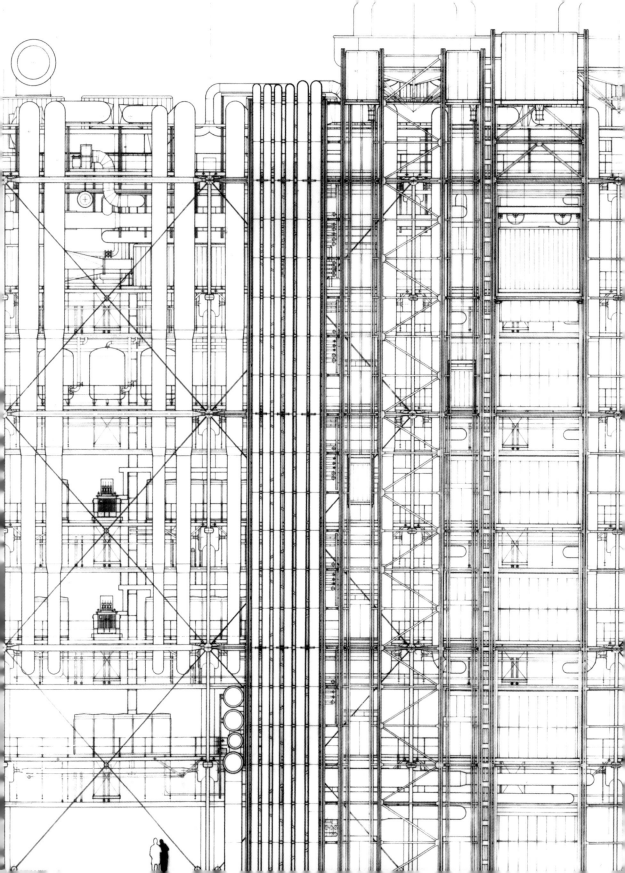

translate our concept designs into drawings and specifications for construction. Su left the practice, returning permanently to London to be with her new partner, John Miller. John Young and Marco Goldschmied took over her role in London, leaving Renzo and me as the principal partners in Paris, with Gianni Franchini leading on liaison with the client and the building's users.

The first person I rang was Laurie Abbott, who had worked with us in Team 4, applying to join the practice in 1964 after seeing drawings of Murray Mews in an architectural magazine. We agreed to see him quite late one evening, and I volunteered to do the interview. Leaving the others in the pub, I returned to the office and saw that the door had been opened. I went inside nervously, wondering whether we'd been burgled, to find Laurie laying out his plans for a 'Sin Palace' in Piccadilly Circus, with his beautiful girlfriend Carol perched on a very high stool in the middle of the studio. We started talking, but I was confused by the fact that every time I stood in front of him, he seemed to look sideways to avoid my glance. It was only later that I realised that his eyes were completely crossed.

Laurie said he had been interviewed 86 times when I called him from Paris, and been turned down by every firm, which said something about the shocking state of our profession at the time, given the brilliance of his drawings both aesthetically and technically. I asked him to join us, and two days later I looked out of the office window to see him pulling up in a car with all his furniture and effects stacked on a roof rack, his wife and kids inside. He had no contract, no agreed salary; he just arrived, and got to work. He assembled a team of Japanese architects, who spoke no English. This suited Laurie; he didn't really want his instructions discussed or debated.

Laurie's drawings were stunning, as good as I've ever seen, despite the fact that he had only trained for two years at Walthamstow Tech, and was largely self-taught (though he later taught alongside me at UCLA). Life is complex, and schools only teach some parts of what we need to know.

Laurie's first love is technology. He often says that he wanted to become a car designer rather than an architect – and he has designed several, including one for Fiat (with Peter Rice and Renzo) later in his career. This passion shone through in his incredibly refined and delicate, but also romantic, drawings, and in schemes like the unbuilt Tomigaya Exhibition Centre in Tokyo, modelled in Meccano and designed with movable mezzanine floors. Later on he tried to train as a pilot, and persisted in taking the test for a private pilot's licence, despite the fact that he had no depth perception in his eyesight, a fairly

Left: One of Laurie's beautiful technical drawings of the Pompidou Centre's services.

Right: Laurie Abbott, one of the most brilliant architects I have worked with (and one of the most eccentric).

Following pages: The colour-coded services ranged across the rue du Renard elevation. After some debate, we chose blue for air conditioning, green for water, red for movement systems and yellow for electricity. They still make the building stand out from the streets of Le Marais.

127

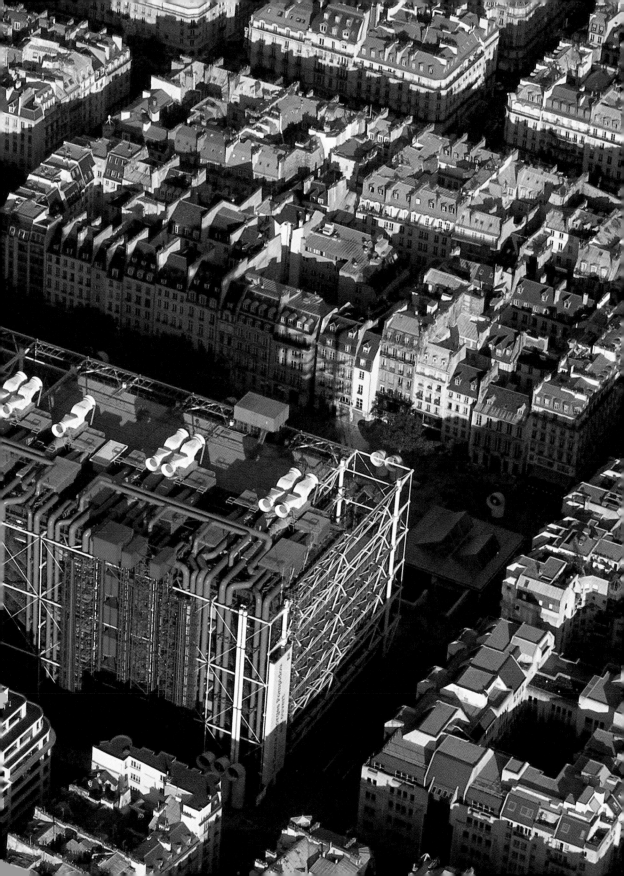

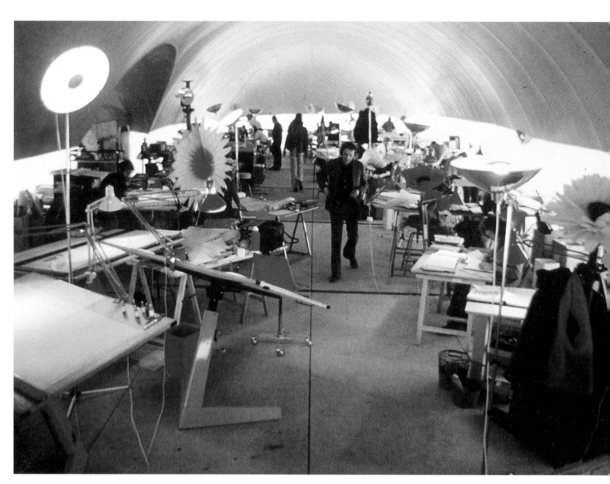

significant drawback. Laurie became renowned in the office for taking the finest-nibbed draughtsman's pens, and sharpening that nib even further, to create his gossamer-light drawings. He is perhaps the nearest to a genius that I have ever known, but he doesn't like the constraints of organisations and workplaces; he has his own way of doing things.

We were also joined by Tony Dugdale, who I knew from my time at the Architectural Association and from lecturing at Cornell. We made contact with three young architects who had founded Chrysalis in California to develop radical lightweight structures – Alan Stanton (who had previously worked with Norman Foster), Mike Davies and Chris Dawson. We were also joined by Swiss and Belgian architects (Prouvé had actually advised us against taking on French architects as their training was so bad at that time).

Ove Arup, initially represented by Ted Happold, had worked with us on the competition entry, and their involvement had reassured the jury. But their partners back in London became very nervous about being party to a contract with such huge potential liabilities, so refused to sign. Piano + Rogers could simply fold if something went wrong; the consequences for a firm of the size of Arup would have been far more severe. We went back and forth in incredibly complex negotiations, far beyond anything we had dealt with before; it was like landing on Mars. I remember banging on Ted's bedroom door in the hotel late at night until he emerged in his pyjamas, so I could plead with him, saying their refusal to sign would kill the project. I phoned Jack Zunz, Arup's chairman, so often that he started refusing to take my calls, though he is now a good friend.

In the end Bordaz took the brave decision to allow Piano + Rogers to sign on their own, but in truth he didn't have much choice. Arup stayed on as consultants to the project, and Peter Rice was joined by Tom Barker, a great services engineer, and Lennart Grut, who later crossed over to join our team. Like Mike Davies, Lennart is a partner at Rogers Stirk Harbour + Partners to this day.

Peter Rice was central to the Pompidou team, and was without a doubt the most creative designer-engineer I have ever worked with. He was gifted not only with powerful analytical skills, but also an Irishman's ability to communicate (and enthusiasm for conversation), and a deep-felt sensitivity to design and to people. He would strip a problem down to its basics, and come up with radical and thoughtful solutions.

Peter had worked for Arup on Sydney Opera House. After Paris, he remained a partner at Arup, but felt like part of Richard Rogers Partnership, working with us on many other projects, attending our Monday design meetings and becoming part of our decision-making process. He

Above left: Our inflatable (and sometimes deflating) office on the banks of the Seine. Ruthie found the paper flowers in a market.

Left: Peter Rice, Renzo Piano and me balancing on a gerberette, with Ruthie looking on.

wouldn't take ideas away and assess options, but engage fully in discussion and debate till he had found the right solution.

Peter became a close friend and collaborator for both Renzo and me. John Young recently reminded me that Peter arrived at one Monday morning meeting having spent the previous week with Renzo in Japan, working on his Osaka Airport project. He said it had been a great trip, but the strangest thing had happened; he had no memory of the trip home at all and felt completely lost. I told him to go to hospital immediately, and that is when Peter learned that he had a brain tumour. His early death in 1992, aged 57, was a huge loss to the practice in the long term, but also had an immediate impact: nobody else had the skill and understanding to implement his plans for Heathrow Terminal 5, so we had to re-engineer them. There is nobody that I miss more than Peter, both as a friend and as a professional genius.

Peter Rice, the most creative designer-engineer I have worked with, drew inspiration from the unexpected, and matched it with a poet's gift for language. He was a critical collaborator on some of our landmark projects – and a dear friend to me – until his early death in 1992.

The Pompidou team was very close – Italians, Swiss, Belgians, Austrians, Japanese, Americans and British alike, we were all strangers in a foreign land. We worked together day and night, ate every meal together, and developed a tremendous sense of camaraderie, though there were some cultural differences between the architects, who were happy with our ramshackle offices, living and working arrangements, and the engineers, who were used to more structured working and living arrangements.

We were constantly looking out for a brilliant project manager to keep this rapidly assembled and immature team together, but nobody ever fitted the bill. So it was down to Renzo's steady and rational manner to see us through both day-to-day business and the intermittent crises that punctuated the project.

Evolving the Design

Our competition entry was little more than a beautifully realised representation of our idea of a centre of cultural information for all, an open-ended structure of steel and glass containing zones for activity, movement and services. We hadn't even built a model when we won, though we had mocked one up to be photographed for the competition. It was a long way away from being a complete design.

In Paris, we began searching for ways to realise our plans, and to respond to the changing constraints and challenges that were thrown in our path – from the site, to budgets, to the demands and instructions issued by the tenant institutions, to popular opposition to road closures, to a kaleidoscope of shifting regulations.

We started elaborating and testing out options for the building's design, with the team getting to know each other in the process, establishing each other's skills and weaknesses, interests and influences. Renzo and I both hated the idea that engineers are brought in at the end of a process to prop up the architects' grand concept. We thought that the relationship between all team members should be more like a multi-dimensional game of ping pong, where you are constantly generating and responding to ideas, adjusting, returning, discussing. This is for me the most intense and exciting period of creativity in the evolution of a scheme.

The basic concept that we returned to was of an open steel framework, with uninterrupted floorplates. Mechanical services, vertical structures, movement systems and all other fixed elements would be placed at the edge of individual floors. This would maximise scope for change, so that any floor could be an art gallery, a sculpture gallery, a library, a restaurant, a classroom, a university, or even headquarters offices. You could add or take away any use without compromising the concept; we would take our cues from modern art and music, allowing for improvisation and change, but using the framework to establish a constant rhythm.

Aesthetically, this concept would give the building a legibly layered exoskeleton of services, establishing a dialogue between these elements and the large floorplates behind. The structure would let in light, express scale, and enable the passer-by to understand the process of its construction and to read the building in many different ways as he or she walked past.

This framework would also form part of the building's public space, the stage on which the theatre of public life would be played out. We described the building as 'an activity container, a strongly layered three-dimensional structural framework with people walking on it and looking down from it, a wide variety of items clipped on it, tents, seating and audio-visual screens, etc.'

Most of the services would be arranged at the rear of the building, facing rue du Renard. The colour scheme was intensely debated: we devised a coding system based on that used by maintenance engineers: water was green, electrical systems were yellow, movement systems were red, air conditioning (for which no standard colour existed) was blue. Bordaz was worried, and asked Pontus Hultén, the curator of the museum, to advise. Pontus suggested a dark brown, like the striking surface of a matchbox. We resisted the proposal, and the debate was only resolved when we agreed to appoint a colour consultant to advise; we found one who agreed with us, so we won the day.

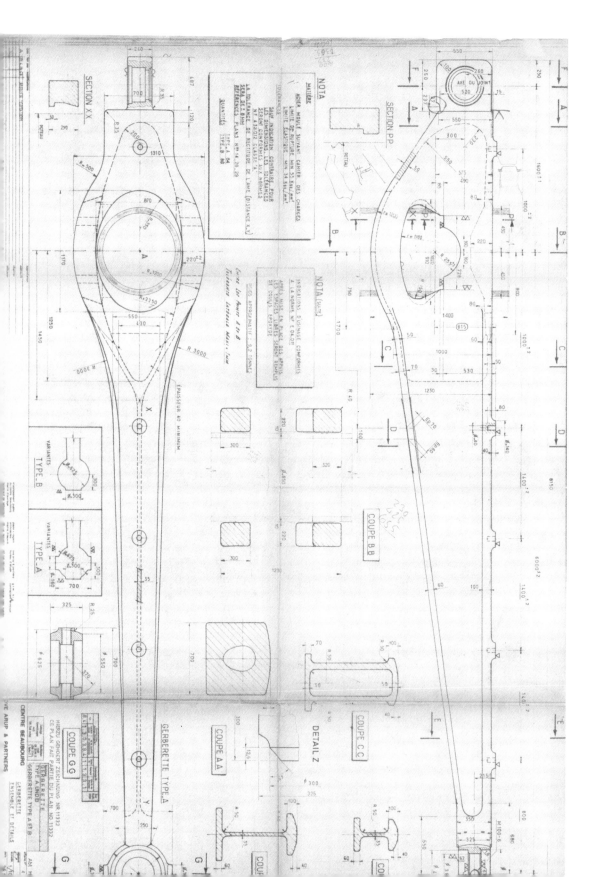

Our concept was straightforward, but the structural engineering was enormously difficult. Each storey had a 48 × 150m floorplate, supported entirely by the building's steel framework. Renzo, Peter, Laurie and I believed that the scale and beauty of a building comes from its detail, that architecture is humanised by the way you order and design its elements. So the structure was not simply an engineering challenge, it was fundamental to the building.

We needed to work out how these open floorplates could be supported by the two rows of columns at either end of the building. With a simple bracket, the inner column would support the entire width of the 48m floorplate and the outer column would simply support the 6m between the two columns. This would mean huge inner columns and girders, and outer columns that were little more than decorative.

Peter worked closely with Laurie and Lennart Grut to develop an elegant solution: a balanced cantilever. At one end, these cantilevers would support the floor trusses, they would pivot around pin-joints on the main supporting columns, their outer arms would be held in tension by external trusses, tying the structure down, sharing the load of the 48m floor, and reducing the depth of girder needed to support it. The bracket was given the name gerberette after its nineteenth-century inventor, Heinrich Gerber. Renzo talked of the assembly of the steelwork as 'Le Ballet Métallique', with workers and cranes creating the structure together.

Crises and Challenges

Resolving the design was only a first step in the journey towards completion. There were more obstacles to overcome, many thrown in our path by the French architectural profession, whose members clearly resented our winning the competition, and who were supported by steel manufacturers, regulators, the media and many politicians. Architecture is not just an exercise in creativity, but also a practical exercise in problem-solving, and navigating the political and practical challenges inherent in a big project. With an exceptional team, and Bordaz's ingenuity, we coped with eight crises, each of which could easily have derailed the project.

1. Site boundary
Almost the moment we won, a pressure group, Geste Architecturelle, had been set up by some French architects to oppose our plans, and threw lawsuit after lawsuit at us. Some of these (like arguing that the jury's decision was invalid as it was chaired by an engineer not an architect) were quickly disposed of. The most serious related to the site boundary. It had

A technical drawing of a gerberette, the balanced cantilever that would support the open floorplates of the building. These huge cast steel hinges would rest on a thick inner column. This would form a pivot, with the load counterbalanced by more slender outer trusses held in tension.

137

no bearing on the building, but work had to stop for 15 days while a court considered the issue. This crisis was very worrying; buildings that stop very often don't start again. However, Bordaz wrote a brilliant report saying that the excavations of the basement had started, and that if we stopped the building work, the sides of the hole risked collapsing. Work started again.

2. Resistance from artists
Jean Leymarie, a noted humanist and scholar who headed the Musée National d'Art Moderne, was implacably opposed to the scheme. This became a big problem when he whipped up opposition among the descendants of artists whose work he had in his collection; in French law, the inheritors of an artist's estate have continuing rights to determine how the art is displayed. Bordaz decided to 'divide and conquer' and approached Brancusi's heirs (probably the most important). They asked that we build a replica of Brancusi's studio in the piazza, and agreed to drop their opposition. The others then fell into line, and Leymarie was moved on, to be replaced by Pontus Hultén.

Renzo and I also met with Sonia Delaunay, the painter and widow of Robert Delaunay, to discuss the hanging of a large collection of works by her and her husband that she was proposing to give to the museum. We were on our best behaviour and were convinced we had charmed her. It was only later that we had a report back: she would rather burn her paintings, she said, than see them exhibited in the space we were designing.

3. The budget
It was only when we submitted our initial designs in spring 1972 (a year after the competition) that costs were discussed. Bordaz told us that our designs and cost estimates were substantially over budget, nearly double. We were taken aback. 'What budget?' we asked. We had never been told of one. 'No,' said Bordaz, 'I didn't want to inhibit your creativity.' 'Well,' I replied, 'you've certainly inhibited it now!'

4. Cracked steel
The gerberettes offered an economical way to maintain open floorplates while minimising the quantity of steel needed. They were a bespoke solution, but one that could be standardised across the building. Peter and Laurie worked with the foundries to develop the gerberettes. Cast steel gave the huge 10-tonne gerberettes a rough, handcrafted look, rather like sculptures. But the first shipment failed testing and cracked, threatening our whole design approach and cost plan. We worried that we would have to start again, but Peter worked with the manufacturers to refine the recipe

and the casting process, and the next batch was a success. There were cheers round the office when they passed testing.

5. Building height and fire regulations

We already had problems with the building height. Paris's highly prescriptive building codes were struggling with our plans; since there had never been another *bâtiment publique de grand hauteur*, there were no rules for it. So rules were invented; we were told that we needed to reduce height so that the top floor was no more than 28m high (the range of fire-engine ladders). Given this new restriction (the original plans had been for a 48m-high structure) and the need to cut costs, we brought the building back down to earth, abandoning our original plan to suspend it on columns above the extended piazza, and made it more compact, reducing the number of terraces above ground and losing a lot of transparency.

6. Steelwork

Finally, in early 1973, with an agreed budget and design, we went out to seek bids from French suppliers for the steelwork. The steel accounted for about 25 per cent of the construction budget, and was the biggest structural steel order that France had ever seen. The proposals came back in around 60 per cent over budget, and all close to each other. It looked like a fix, and the pricing schedules showed clear signs of collusion. There was no way the budget would stretch.

We spoke to Bordaz, persuaded him to declare the bids non-valid, and asked whether we could look further afield. After some consultations with the Élysée Palace and the minister for national production (that is, for French national production), he came back to us with an ambiguous instruction: 'You have to buy the steel from France. I have spoken to the President, and he insists. However, I am now going on holiday for two weeks.'

While continuing negotiations with the French suppliers, we asked around. Nobody apart from us was surprised that the bidding had been rigged – another sign of our naivety – every big steel order seemed to be rigged. Eventually we secured much more competitive quotations from Krupp in Germany, and Nippon Steel in Japan, and took these to Bordaz when he had returned from his holiday. He went through the motions of scolding us, but acknowledged that, as we had secured these bids, he probably ought to show them to his government colleagues.

Bordaz's persuasive skills came to the fore, and Krupp won the contract, working through their French affiliate Pont-à-Mousson. At the last minute, the French suppliers came back with a bid that was identical to Krupp's, but this was handed to Bordaz just as he went into the contract

The assembly of the massive gerberettes, girders and trusses was filmed and named the *Ballet Métallique* after Renzo Piano's original description of the process.

signature meeting and he declined to open it. Once again the project was saved; the French suppliers would have been unable to fulfil the contract at the price proposed, and construction would have become mired in renegotiation. Given the insistence on sourcing steel from France, we asked Krupp to be low-key when delivering to the site. They agreed, and covered up the logos on their trucks, but the tall, blond Krupp workers in their pressed light blue overalls stood out from the largely French-Algerian workforce on site.

7. More fire regulations

Having managed to steer round the French steel-manufacturers' cartel, we faced a new round of negotiation with the Centre Scientifique et Technique du Bâtiment, the French fire-safety authority (the board of which included representatives of the manufacturers who had been outbid for the steel contract). Where they had demanded a partition that could hold a fire back for one hour between the external services and the interior of the building, they now needed two hours. We fought against this new rule, which seemed to have been made up on the spur of the moment, and Laurie produced some stunning drawings to support our case, but eventually gave in. This meant that we had to block up the rue du Renard walls, reducing transparency and natural light.

8. A new president

Then, just as we were preparing for the main structural works, a final (and almost terminal) crisis engulfed the project. Our unlikely champion Georges Pompidou died, and Valéry Giscard d'Estaing took over as President. Why would he have any reason to save a project that was only attracting negative press coverage, and was being built by foreigners? The crunch came in August, when everyone was on holiday, but we were summoned back to Paris (Renzo, on his yacht, was approached by a French naval frigate to deliver the instruction).

We thought the whole project might be cancelled, but the move to rename the Beaubourg Plateau Cultural Centre as the Centre Georges Pompidou was a tactical masterstroke. Cancelling a project named in honour of the recently deceased president would have been almost unthinkable. However, we were told to reduce costs by a third, and to cover up the exposed services on the outside of the building.

These changes would have destroyed our design, but the building was nearly completed, so our room for manoeuvre was genuinely limited. Reducing the scale of the building while still fulfilling the brief was impossible; the cross-bracing and structural design was based on three two-floor

Left: A side elevation of the building, showing how the gerberettes share load between the inner and outer columns.

Following page: The transparent escalator tubes bring the public space of the piazza up the front of the building.

sections. So, unless the building was to be reduced to the height of a suburban hypermarché, there was no way to cut back on the build costs. And covering up exposed services was only going to add more expense, so that idea was quickly dropped. Where we could make cuts, we did; paring down all spending on finishes and maintenance equipment to the bare minimum (which compromised the building from the moment it opened and cost more in the long term).

Sadly, we also had to give up the live information systems on the façades that had formed such a central element of the competition concept of the Centre as a hub for the information age. Alan Stanton and his team had plans for a bright dot matrix screen that would bring the façade to life, but this was dropped after the President asked us who would control what would be displayed. The people, we replied. But which people, he asked again, the left or the right? As he said that, we knew we'd lost the argument.

The cuts also hit IRCAM, the Institut de Recherche et de Coordination Acoustique/Musique, a centre for radical musical experimentation, which was originally intended to form part of the Beaubourg Centre. This project was designed to coax Pierre Boulez, one of the greatest composers of the modern era, back from his self-imposed exile over the Atlantic, where he had been driven by the reluctance of French state radio to broadcast his music. Boulez approached music how I would like to think I approach architecture; he wanted a place where 12 musicians could work alongside 12 acoustic scientists, or 12 sociologists. He resisted closure and classical structures in favour of an open-ended approach.

Claude Pompidou, the president's wife (who later became a good friend and a sparkling presence at dinner parties in our small Belsize Park flat), helped to persuade Boulez to work with other avant-garde composers, like Luciano Berio and György Ligeti, to prepare a brief for the Institut, but it was becoming impossible to accommodate this in the main building – the space requirements were still unclear, and the specific acoustic conditions that the musicians required were at odds with the loose-fit flexibility of the main structure. Another site, formerly occupied by a school, had become available, and it was decided to use it to extend the piazza, and to build the IRCAM space underground.

Mike Davies and his team prepared a range of options, including a structure that would rise from the ground like a gasometer for performances, before sinking back to leave a piazza at other times. The final design was almost fully submerged, a closed box containing performance, studio and workshop space up to 20m under the piazza.

The cuts came at a critical time for IRCAM; excavation had been completed, and an urgent redesign meant that the team actually had to

Visitors enjoy the view towards Montmartre from the escalators, as crowds assemble round street performers in the piazza.

147

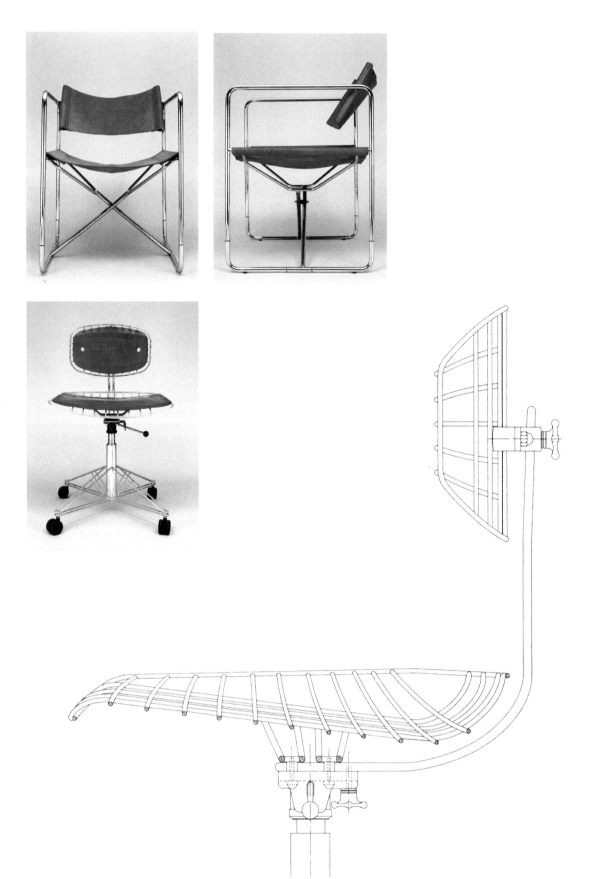

Piano + Rogers also
designed the furniture
system for the Pompi-
dou Centre and IRCAM,
based on simple tubular
steel and leather com-
ponents.

Above: The front ele-
vation of the Pompidou
Centre, designed as
a friendly robot not
a classical temple,
its spaces and struc-
tures adaptable not
determinate.

The Pompidou's open-ended structure contrasts with the exquisite classicism of buildings like Andrea Palladio's Palazzo Chiericati in Vicenza (right), where nothing can be added or taken away without undermining the beauty of the whole.

refill some of the hole they had just dug, at significant cost. However, within the reduced space, the budget cuts actually gave the team the opportunity to work with Boulez to clarify the concept, and to create flexibility through technological innovation and internal flexibility, rather than by including an ever-increasing number of discrete acoustic zones.

Critical Reception – Umbrellas and Brickbats

I vividly remember standing on the piazza, on a rainy day shortly before the Pompidou Centre opened. An elegantly dressed elderly French woman was standing next to me, and invited me to shelter under her umbrella. 'Monsieur,' she said, 'do you know who designed this building?' 'Madame,' I replied, delighted to have the opportunity to take credit for my work, 'it was me.' She said nothing, but struck me firmly on the head with her umbrella, and marched off.

Her silent but eloquent response was typical of the publicity that the Pompidou Centre attracted. From the day we won the competition, we had been subjected to sustained criticism from every angle – from the left, for our collusion with state-backed cultural centralism; from the right, for our desecration of Paris's skyline. One day, in the office, I was shown a petition, which read something like 'We 60 intellectuals wish to express our objection to this horrific and alien steel structure...' I sighed, and was about to put it on the pile of objections when I noticed everyone was laughing. It was a petition that had been presented against the Eiffel Tower nearly a hundred years earlier.

Ada Louise Huxtable and Hilton Kramer, both critics for the *New York Times,* wrote the only positive critiques that I can recall in the seven years of the project, though Kramer was not surprised to be in a minority: 'It simply does not look like anything that anyone has ever seen before, and is therefore especially frightening to people who cannot bear the idea of something really new in the art of building.' Other journalists had already decided on the story, literally in some cases. One *Newsweek* journalist aggressively questioned me about cost overruns. When I produced papers showing the project was on time and on budget, she shrugged, 'I've already filed.'

The process of building the Pompidou Centre had been unbelievably tough. Renzo and I were exhausted and it took both of us months to recover. But for all the changes that the project had gone through, and all the compromises that we had to accept, the Centre had retained its conceptual clarity: a building that incorporated public space, a flexible container for human activity, with open-minded internal spaces that enabled variety and overlapping of uses, an economical and lightweight structure that clearly expressed the technology that created it, a building that added to the richness and diversity of one of the great world cities.

Nevertheless in January 1977, when President Giscard d'Estaing formally opened the Pompidou Centre, Renzo and I had to battle to get invited to the opening ceremony; the nervousness was palpable. But the tide of criticism turned overnight, as reporters saw the queues of people lined up to visit what they had written off as an ugly interloper or a temple to dead elitist culture. Around seven million people came in the first year (more than visited the Louvre and the Eiffel Tower combined), establishing the Pompidou Centre as a modern icon, and fulfilling its promise as a place for all people.

With Renzo, trying out the Pompidou Centre escalators in 1977, before the building opened and the crowds began pouring in.

5 Politics and Practice

The vitality and global importance of London today stands in stark contrast to the drab city Ruthie, Roo and I returned to, from beautiful, romantic Paris, in 1977 after completing the Pompidou Centre. The UK had been on the winning side in the Second World War, but had not seen the post-war investment that had buoyed continental economies.

The British Empire, which had provided London's lifeblood for so many decades, had been all but dismantled, and the city had yet to feel the benefit of international migration or of its membership of the European Economic Community. The only espresso to be had was in Bar Italia in Soho, spaghetti was something that came tinned in tomato sauce, and olive oil was sold in chemists for cleaning your ears out. With the exception of a few Indian and Chinese restaurants, most restaurant food was disappointing at best. The UK was seen as the 'sick man of Europe', and London felt like an imperial capital whose time had passed, looking over its shoulder at cities like New York, while worrying about loss of business to Frankfurt and Paris.

Estates and Activism

Initially, we decided to seek out somewhere even further away from Paris – culturally and geographically – and spent a few months in California, living with Ruthie's brother Michael (a film and TV writer and producer) while I taught at UCLA. We loved the canyons, beaches and palm trees, but I found LA too car-dominated and sprawling, lacking the humanism of more compact cities.

Ben, Zad and Ab were now teenagers, and the Lloyd's competition was looking promising; it was time to come back to London. As the 1970s turned to the 1980s, and the harsh medicine of Thatcherism began to take effect, both Ruthie and I became more involved in the politics and public life of what was now our home city.

In an image that evokes the febrile politics of the decade, the Architects Revolutionary Council, with Brian Anson in the chair, presents its manifesto at the Architectural Association in 1975.

155

More interested in politics and society than in the professional hier-archies of architecture, I had given a firebrand speech at the Royal Institute of British Architects in the late 1960s, demanding that they sell off their beautiful Portland Place headquarters and move to London's docklands, to be nearer the citizens of London. And my stint at UCLA also convinced me that, while I firmly believe that teaching is one of the most important roles in society, I wasn't cut out for it. I preferred the cut and thrust of argument and debate; I wanted to become part of the process of making a better society, not a theoretician or a spokesman for my profession.

I started attending meetings at the Greater London Council, where Ken Livingstone and his Labour colleagues were championing unpopular minority rights causes – feminism, anti-racism, gay rights – that were then derided as 'the loony left'. It was also around this time that I met Anne Power, professor of social policy at the London School of Economics, the heartland of the British Left, at a dinner in east London. She offered to show me round some of the estates in the area, to point out what had gone right but mostly what had gone wrong.

I was keen to take up Anne's offer. *Family and Kinship in East London* by Michael Young and Peter Willmott had been a huge influence on me and a whole generation of architects and urbanists. This masterful study of east London communities examined the close bonds and intricate social structures in the tenements of Bethnal Green – where life was lived com-

munally, on the street (because living accommodation was so cramped and dirty) – and the social and physical disruption many east Londoners had experienced when moved from familiar streets to the post-war new towns built around the edge of London.

Visiting the Isle of Dogs with Anne, and later Tot-tenham in the wake of the Broadwater Farm riots in 1985, I could see how the promise of the brave new world had faltered. Broadwater Farm appeared to have been designed as a ghetto, surrounded by open fields, com-pletely cut off from any sense of the city. In the urgency of housebuilding after the Second World War, planners had lost sight of the way actual people lived, and had left them without any of their familiar social support structures. Combined with high unemploy-ment and heavy-handed policing, the mix was toxic.

Anne's work in the Priority Estates Project became the foundation stone for the National Communities Resource Centre, the charity that she and I set up. NCRC gives people from low-income backgrounds the skills to create and grasp opportunities – the kind of support that had helped me

Left: Professor Anne Power, a tireless campaigner for the poorest in society. Anne and I co-founded the National Commun-ities Resource Centre, which helps people from low income backgrounds transform their lives and their communities.

through my difficult school days. Grand Metropolitan Breweries bought Trafford Hall, an eighteenth-century country house set in beautiful parkland in Cheshire for NCRC, where it offers training to people from across the UK. Most of the accommodation is in 40 of Walter Segal's self-build homes, constructed on wooden frames and insulated with old newspapers. NCRC does vital work, but it struggles for funding.

Anne is committed to society's poorest, and to using her knowledge and her research to make the case for change. Brian Anson, who I had first encountered in the mid-1970s, was an even more radical presence. We met when I was brought in to advise the AA on the final-year project of a group of students he was teaching. These students had not designed buildings, but had proposed a programme of urban allotments on rooftops (inevitably, they were nicknamed the 'Cabbage Patch Unit'). The AA didn't know what to make of this. Brian and I managed to get the project through, and the students got their degrees.

Brian was a great advocate for the marginalised, through his work at the Divis Flats in Belfast, in former colliery villages and in old steel towns, as well as an excellent writer and a great friend to lost causes. When he was out of work, which was often, he would tour the country with the Architects' Revolutionary Council and Planning Aid, talking passionately about how the poor could regain control of the built environment and the political system. He made a huge difference to my thinking and understanding of the social problems that have accumulated in the UK. He was also a far-sighted champion of London's public realm, battling to protect Covent Garden and Hoxton Square from heavy-handed redevelopment and the erasure of character.

Right: Brian Anson, radical architectural activist and campaigner, and champion for London's public realm.

Culture and Civic Life

At the same time as becoming more engaged in politics, I could feel myself becoming more involved in civic life, even embraced by the establishment. We were no longer the 'architectural hippies' who had arrived in Paris in 1971, but had been appointed as the architects of the Lloyd's Building – one of the tallest new buildings in the City of London, commissioned by an institution at the heart of the establishment. Ruthie and I were invited to Windsor Castle for dinner with the Queen and a 'stay over' (the Prince of Wales had yet to share his opinions on architecture with the world at that stage), and in 1980 I was the subject of a BBC Arena documentary – produced by Alen Yentob, now one of my closest friends. The following year, the Tate Gallery's director, Alan Bowness, who I knew through his connections to the Cornish art world (he was the son-in-law of Ben Nicholson and Barbara Hepworth), asked me to join its board.

I didn't initially think I had enough to offer, though art had always been a presence in my life, from childhood trips to the galleries of Venice and Florence, to the Brumwells' artistic connections in St Ives and New York, to my friendship with Philip Guston, to the cultural politics of the Pompidou Centre. But the years spent on the board of the Tate were an education. Fellow board members included Tony Caro and Patrick Heron, two of Britain's most important post-war artists and great champions of art, and we

were advised by the brilliant critic David Sylvester, who became a friend and mentor – I used to visit him at his house on Saturday mornings to discuss art. The highlight of every meeting was the review of potential new acquisitions, and the informed and passionate discussion that this inspired.

It was on the Tate board that I met Peter Palumbo, whose Mansion House Square development I would fight for a few years later. Peter, who became one of our closest friends (and our youngest son

Bo's godfather), was expected to take over as chairman from Lord Hutchinson. However, he made the mistake of criticising Alan Bowness in a newspaper interview, breaking one of the cardinal rules of the British establishment – never attack civil servants, as they can't defend themselves. Peter had ruled himself out and I was asked to take over in 1984.

The Tate had some incredible collections, but there was a lot that needed shaking up. The acquisitions

policy sometimes felt like it was seeking to fill gaps on the wall, rather than select the best of the best. The institution had always been conservative: a great opportunity had been missed in the 1930s, when two board members (one of whom was John Maynard Keynes) were sent over to France with a budget of £3,000. They came back with a few paintings, but half the money unspent. They were congratulated for this, though they had passed up the opportunity to build a collection of significant impressionist art at reasonable prices. When I joined, modern art was still overlooked, and the gallery itself was in a very bad state.

I had seen how museums in the USA were driven by philanthropy and fundraising, with appointments to boards of major galleries substituting for the UK honours system. In France, culture was regarded as a national priority. The Tate seemed to have the worst of both worlds: it still felt and acted like a department of the civil service rather than an entrepreneurial institution, but was viewed as a backwater rather than something vital to the cultural life of the nation.

We began to change things. Peter Palumbo set up a new foundation for private contributions; and when Alan Bowness retired, Arts Minister Grey Gowrie (who later made me his deputy chairman at Arts Council England) and I looked for a more dynamic replacement. Following a brilliant interview, we selected Nick Serota, who had transformed the Whitechapel Gallery, did the same with Tate Modern and would play a large part in the renaissance of the London art world. It was probably one of the best and most significant decisions I have been involved in making.

Cultural conservatism is led from the top in the UK. Margaret Thatcher encouraged our fundraising activity, but was otherwise uninterested. When Patrick Heron, Alan Bowness and I went to Moscow and Leningrad at the end of the Cold War to agree a loan of some Matisses, we were usurped at the last minute by the Museum of Modern Art in New York, who had the White House intervening to press their case; Downing Street did not engage. The civil service mirrored this. Ruthie used to say, of one of the senior civil servants we dealt with, that he had a sort of extra-sensory perception. He could shake his head to say 'No' before you had even started speaking.

A few years after standing down from the Tate in 1989, I was talking to Tony Blair, then newly elected leader of the Labour Party, about renaming the Department for National Heritage as the Department for Culture when he came to power. Tony visibly recoiled from the word, though he did let it through in the end (though as part of a Department for Culture, Media and Sport – only in Britain would these be seen as natural companions).

From RRP to RSHP – Collaboration, Ethos and Conviviality

Richard Rogers Partnership was established when we came back from Paris. The original idea was to adopt a generic name, like Team 4, but Charles Saatchi, then at the head of the world's largest advertising agency and a good friend, said we would be crazy to drop my name just when it was starting to get some recognition. The original directors were John

Young, Marco Goldschmied and me, with Mike Davies joining us a couple of years later. We offered Laurie Abbott a directorship. 'What the fuck would I want to be a director for?' he responded – though he did join the partners in the end. We only had two jobs to start with – Lloyds and Coin Street – and there were no more than twenty of us, all pitching in together on new jobs as they came in, often working sixty hours a week.

Our name was new but our ethos had its roots in the old days of Team 4, in its principles of equal partnership, the mixing of shared hard work with shared relaxation, and a real belief in creating a better society. The constitution that John, Marco and I drew up was based on a commitment to fairness – in distribution of earnings, in benefits and quality of life, in the work we would take on, and in equal treatment for all. We agreed to share profits between all employees and charities, and to limit the pay of the highest-paid qualified architect to a multiple (currently nine times) that of the lowest paid. We still pride ourselves on the benefits we offer, including generous maternity and paternity leave (we were trailblazers in offering the latter), language courses and private health insurance. When we established the partnership 30 years ago, these types of benefits and this type of structure were almost unheard of.

A subsidised canteen at Thames Wharf enabled us to eat together like an extended family (for some years the head chef was Sophie Braimbridge, who was previously married to my son Ab) and we are planning something similar in our new offices. In the summer we play softball against other architects every Wednesday; in the winter we hold parties and play football. We take an annual trip together to see one of our newly-completed buildings and spend a weekend eating and drinking, and thinking about our future. Everyone can use the shared holiday home (Holly Frindle, a Lubetkin-designed bungalow at Whipsnade Zoo, north of London).

The constitution is founded on shared work and shared reward, on conviviality as well as collaboration. Ever since I was a teenager, struggling at school but gathering a gang around me by the village pond in Epsom, I've realised that we work best when we work together. Mutual dependence is not a weakness, but something to be celebrated.

Architecture is very broad. It incorporates people who understand business as well as experts on structure, technicians who keep in touch with the latest scientific thinking, people who understand the materials and process of construction, economists, poets, sociologists, lawyers, artists and engineers. Our office brings together all those skills, and the client's, to develop ideas.

Architects tend to stay with the practice for a long time, some for their entire careers. If someone isn't working well in a particular team, we try to find a different project or role that will suit them better. Usually, two

Top: Laurie Abbott, whose first passion is automotive design, is an unconventional genius who hugely influenced our architectural language.

Left: RRP at our Holland Park studio in July 1983, around the time of my 50th birthday – we could all still fit round a big dinner table.

1. Our Belief

The practice of architecture is inseparable from the social and economic values of the individuals who practise it and the society which sustains it. We as individuals are responsible for contributing to the welfare of mankind, the society in which we practise, and the team with whom we work.

2. Our Aim

We aim to produce work which is beneficial to society. We exclude work related directly to war or which contributes to the extensive pollution of ourenvironment.

3. How We Work

In order to do work of the highest quality, we carefully control the size of the office and the selection of our projects. We recognise that work is not an end in itself

A summary of the RRP constitution, based on collaboration and a commitment to fairness. John Young, Marco Goldschmied and I devised and adopted it in the early 1980s, and it still applies in RSHP today.

and that a balanced life must include the enjoyment of leisure and the time to think.

4. Our Charitable Ownership

Our Practice is owned by a Charitable Trust. No individual owns any share in the value of the Practice. In this way, private trading and inheritance of shares is eliminated and any residual value is returned to society through the Charitable Trust.

5. How We Are Organised

We believe in an equitable and transparent sharing of the rewards of our work. The earnings of the directors are fixed in proportion to those of the lowest paid fully qualified architect. After reserves and tax, any profits are divided between all of the staff and charities according to publicly declared principles. We believe that these arrangements nurture an ethos of collective responsibility to each other, satisfaction in the work we produce and a sense of wider social responsibility.

6. Profit-sharing and Charity

75 per cent of our profits are distributed to partners and staff who have worked with us for more than two years, and another 20 per cent is donated to charitable causes every year, with the remainder being paid to reserves. Each director and employee directs their share of the charitable distribution to charities of their own choice. Over the years, substantial sums of money have been paid to charitable causes.

or three moves can find the right fit: when you recruit bright people, you just need to find the way of using them best, of accommodating personal chemistries and eccentricities, playing to each person's strengths.

The partnership is architect-led, but with a solid core of commercial and management knowledge among the partners. Andrew Morris, who now chairs our board, joined in the early 1980s; his first role was as project architect for our house at Royal Avenue. He now leads the development of the practice as an organisation, its communications, commercial and legal teams, working alongside Lennart Grut and the finance partner Ian Birtles. I've known Lennart since Paris, when he and his wife lived near us, and he led the Arup team on the Pompidou Centre. He joined us in 1986 with responsibility for our overseas work.

Ben Warner has worked with us for 30 years; he set up our office in Tokyo, and now leads our work in the Far East. Avtar Lotay leads our work in Australia, and Simon Smithson, one of our subtlest thinkers, was the project architect during the design and construction of Barajas Airport T4 in Madrid, and now works on schemes across South America. Richard Paul brings knowledge, expertise and energy to complex international projects, such as Tower 3 at the World Trade Centre in New York.

The big change came in 2007, the year that I won the Pritzker Prize. I was in my mid-seventies, and the other two founding partners – John Young and Marco Goldschmied – had left. It was time to think about how the practice would evolve once I stepped back. After some discussion, the partners decided to begin the process of handing over to the next generation, so that the process would be phased and gradual. We added Graham Stirk and Ivan Harbour – two of our most talented younger partners, both of whom had been with us since the Lloyd's Building – to the practice's name: Richard Rogers Partnership became Rogers Stirk Harbour + Partners, with Andrew and Lennart becoming senior partners.

The previous year, I had become engulfed in a controversy that threatened to destroy the practice. We had been asked to hold an event at the office promoting peace in the Middle East. I left the meeting early, but later some speakers had called for a boycott of Israel. This soon got into the papers in London and in New York, where we were working on a project to remodel the Jacob K Javits Convention Centre. There were calls for us to be sacked from the project, and barred from future work in New York. Ruthie and I flew over for a ghastly week of negotiation and bridge-building. We succeeded in stabilising the situation, but it was terrifying to see how quickly a firm's reputation could be damaged by untruths and innuendo.

In 2015, there was another big change when we moved from Thames Wharf to the Leadenhall Building. We were prompted by the new owners of

The RRP directors at Creek Vean in 2003. From left to right: John Young, Mark Darbon, me, Mike Davies, Amo Kalsi, Lennart Grut, Richard Paul, Graham Stirk, Andrew Morris, Marco Goldschmied, Laurie Abbott and Ivan Harbour.

165

Right: With Graham
Stirk and Ivan Harbour
in 2007 when we
re-named the practice
Rogers Stirk Harbour+
Partners.

Below: The growing
team photographed in
front of Wren's Royal
Hospital, Chelsea.

Thames Wharf (it changed hands following Marco Goldschmied's departure from the practice in 2004) wanting to redevelop it. But it was also a logical move, into one of our finest modern buildings, in the heart of the City rather than in an outlying residential district. The new building enables the whole firm to work together on one floor, rather than spread out among the buildings of Thames Wharf.

We have grown from being a practice of fewer than 30 people to having more than 200, which is probably as large as we should be (but I seem to remember saying that when we were 30, 50, 100, or even 12). As we have grown, we have found new ways of working together. When

we started out, we all knew each other well, and could pass work and ideas back and forth, to test, enhance, challenge them, pinning up drawings and reviewing them together in our Monday design forum meetings, working like twelve hands with one brain. We ate and drank together, developing working relationships that were almost as close as family. That informal spirit has been replaced by more formal structures. We have organised ourselves into four teams, three design teams led by Ivan, Graham and me, and a strong corporate core under Andrew and Lennart. The number of partners has grown to 13, with five new partners (Tracy Meller, Andrew Tyley, John McElgunn, Stephen Barrett and Stephen Light) appointed in 2015. And the public profile of the partners is growing, with names becoming attached to specific projects.

The way we work together has undoubtedly changed, responding to growth, partners' preferences and the impact of new technology. Computer-aided design has made a difference, boosting productivity but making design development a more private process than in the days of pinning drawings on walls. Our Monday design forum meetings now focus on managing resources as much as on reviewing designs, and the informal and bohemian culture that fired up John, Laurie, Mike, Marco, Peter Rice and me when we started out, the free flow of ideas and debate, has also evolved. But we have sustained the quality of our architecture; I think our recent buildings are among our best.

HIGH CLASS
SCAFFOLDING
07903 962776
0208 695 6222

6   Building in the City

When I sit at my desk on the fourteenth floor of the Leadenhall Building, I can look across the road to the Lloyd's Building, separated only by 30m and 30 years. I feel I can almost reach out and touch it, as I reflect on the dialogue and contrasts between the two buildings.

Comparing Lloyd's and Leadenhall, and the Pompidou Centre, gives a very clear sense of how technology, architecture and business have changed over time. Pompidou was an open-ended structure, a public fun palace, using as many standardised components as possible. Lloyd's was a commissioned headquarters building, a 'private club', which allowed some flexibility through column-free floors, the open atrium, and the use of external towers for service provision. But it was a much more crafted – almost sculptural – building, carefully fitted to an irregular site, with real attention lavished on its concrete and steel structure.

Today Leadenhall, built as a speculative office building, makes Lloyd's look artisanal. The sophistication of computer-aided design and manufacture means that every piece of steel or glass can be specified and delivered with absolute accuracy, bringing together the aesthetics of craft with the convenience of mass production. The building is smooth in profile, with open floorplates and all services aligned on the one perpendicular edge, creating big, open floor spaces that maximise visual and physical flexibility.

Leadenhall's sloping profile is a response to the constraint imposed by the St Paul's Cathedral viewing corridor, but is also the result of a fundamental rethink of the modern office building. Most skyscrapers are built round a concrete core that contains services, including lifts, staircases and lavatories. You can see the same basic design in tall office buildings the world over; the structure is essentially the same, but clad in different skin. It is a matter of decorative finish, not architecture. This approach has limitations. The layout means that every desk should be in sight of a window, but the core obstructs interior views across the floor to colleagues. The

The Leadenhall Building's distinctive sloped profile ensures unobstructed views of St Paul's Cathedral.

layout also inhibits flexibility; you only ever have about 12m depth of usable space between the central core and the outside wall, so are limited in how many people can work alongside each other, and there is no central shared space for interactions between different teams. These traditional offices cannot meet the fast-changing nature of the modern workplace.

Leadenhall takes a different approach, allowing wide-open rectangular floorplates for occupiers. Since its services (including translucent-walled lavatories) are located on the perpendicular northern edge of the building, every tenant has a view south towards the Thames; there are no columns or lift shafts to obstruct the sight lines. Rather than being constructed around a concrete core, the building is supported by a steel megaframe. This is sandwiched within a ventilated glazed cavity, and divided into seven-storey sections, which create a sense of scale as the eye explores the façade of the building, much smoother than that of Lloyd's or the Pompidou Centre. Plant and event space is housed on the topmost floors, allowing the building to rise to a slender pinnacle without leaving the upper storeys empty.

Graham Stirk, who led the design of Leadenhall, is a brilliant architect. Like Ivan Harbour, he joined the practice when we were working on Lloyd's, but I first remember him working on Paternoster Square, where his focus, his intellect and his attention to detail created the clear geometry that defined our scheme. Graham's intellectual clarity and strategic approach allow him to solve problems down to the most miniscule details of design. You can see it in complex projects like the World Conservation and Exhibitions Centre at the British Museum, and in his own home – a beautiful renovation of a 1960s house in Hampstead completed with his architect wife Susie, which won RIBA's Manser Medal in 2011.

The current crop of tall buildings in and around the City of London is controversial, as tall buildings always have been in London. It's a very English attitude: a new tower would be built, there would be a row, at which point planners and politicians would lose their nerve for years, leaving single buildings standing alone against the skyline. Even today, some critics simply dislike tall buildings, or think them alien to London, recoiling from the 'shock of the new' as Florentines did when the four-storey-high Palazzo Strozzi was completed in the sixteenth century. But skyscrapers work better as a cluster than on their own, even when some of the individual buildings are not as good as they could be. The most exciting element of the World Trade Centre towers in New York, until their destruction on 9/11, was the tautness of the space between them.

As at the Pompidou Centre, we worked with the developer (in this case British Land led by John Ritblat) to 'democratise the brief' of

Above left: RSHP's offices on the fourteenth floor of the Leadenhall Building, where we moved in 2015, with sunlight reaching deep into the open floorplate.

Left: Escalators ascend from the public piazza – a rare civic space in the City of London – to the Leadenhall Building's reception areas.

Following page: A side view of the Leadenhall Building, showing the seven-storey public space, the steel megaframe and the tower enclosing lifts and other services.

171

Leadenhall – to create something of civic and public value, as well as an elegant addition to the skyline. Graham persuaded the client to cut out the lowest floors of the building to create a seven-storey, south-facing public space, with trees, hard paving and seats, and escalators ascending to the reception area above. The building is tall, but its footprint is minimised. Land is valuable in the City of London, and public spaces for lunching or simply loitering are thin on the ground.

Lloyd's of London

Forty years ago, the City of London was a very different place. Many men still wore bowler hats to work, and the skyline was dominated by dull, flat-roofed buildings of middling height, with only Richard Seifert's NatWest Tower standing out from the crowd, looking westwards towards Centrepoint and the Post Office Tower. Social life was confined to gentlemen's clubs for the upper classes, pubs for the workers, and nowhere for women and children. As if to emphasise the City's essentially Edwardian ambience, the city planner wore a tailcoat to work. Dramatic change was around the corner, but it did not feel like that at the time.

Among the most venerable institutions in the City was Lloyd's of London, which had been a centre for insurance trading since its birthplace in Edward Lloyd's Coffee House in 1688. It was the world's biggest insurance market, but felt like a private club. In 1928, Lloyd's had outgrown its base in the Royal Exchange, and moved to a new building in Leadenhall Street designed by Sir Edwin Cooper, then expanded into an adjoining building in the 1930s before moving again in 1950. By the late 1970s this last building, intended to see the market through to the twenty-first century, was also proving inadequate for its rapidly growing business, so Lloyd's was faced with the prospect of a fourth move in as many decades.

In 1977, the Lloyd's board approached Gordon Graham, the dynamic president of RIBA, to seek his advice. They didn't want to spend the next 50 years moving offices this frequently; as they later put it, 'We're in the insurance business, not the building business.' So flexibility was paramount: would their business continue to grow, would Frankfurt become Europe's pre-eminent financial centre, or would the market cross the Atlantic to New York? Information technology was clearly going to have a huge impact (the only machine that I saw on our first site visit was a Xerox copier, and some clerks were still using quill pens), but no one really knew what this would mean in terms of job numbers, floor space, service access and building design.

At Graham's suggestion, and after reviewing an extensive longlist, Lloyd's invited six architects to come forward with ideas for how they could meet their space requirements amid so many uncertainties. This wouldn't be a classic design competition – there was no brief to design against – but a competitive process to select a design team.

Piano + Rogers was more or less dormant at the time, with very little work. The 30-person office that had worked together in Paris had evaporated: I had moved back to London to be nearer my family, and had been teaching at University of California, Los Angeles; Marco Goldschmied had reduced his hours; and John Young was seriously considering retraining as a taxi driver. It was a depressing time: for all the acclaim we had eventually received, our one famous building felt like an albatross around our necks; nobody wanted another Pompidou Centre. Renzo had stayed in Paris.

Lloyd's asked for a building strategy that would last them for the rest of the century, ensure that they could continue face-to-face trading, and enable them to build new premises while keeping working. Beyond that there was still a great deal of uncertainty. As Lloyd's head of administration, Courtenay Blackmore, put it, 'The only thing we know is that we don't know.'

We took this request for a strategy literally, unlike our competitors who jumped straight to design or presented previous projects. For us, there was no point in showing the Pompidou Centre, our only completed large-scale project. Instead we presented twenty-six different scenarios, for adapting, or demolishing and rebuilding, Lloyd's existing premises, with new temporary and permanent structures on rooftops and in garages, to maintain operations. We said little about design, apart from emphasising the need for any new building to work as part of the City of London's tight network of medieval streets, to maintain flexibility and to preserve face-to-face trading. We didn't really expect to win, and I don't think I'd have the nerve to produce such a minimalist response now.

We were called back in early 1978 for a second interview with the Lloyd's redevelopment committee led by Sir Peter Green. John Young, Marco Goldschmied and I were joined by Peter Rice from Arup, and by Renzo. I had bought a suit, and Kirk Varnedoe, the great art historian and close friend (later chief curator of painting and sculpture at MoMA), who was staying with us at Belsize Grove, told me I had to wear a tie. He took off the one he was wearing – blue silk with red dots – and lent it to me; when we arrived at Lloyd's pretty well everybody in the room was wearing one that was almost identical. Perhaps the tie reassured them that we weren't going to build another Pompidou Centre.

Peter and Marco impressed the committee with their analytical understanding of the continuing changes affecting Lloyd's, and once we had been appointed, we began working through the options, to understand the client's needs. Lloyd's wanted to maintain its tradition of face-to-face

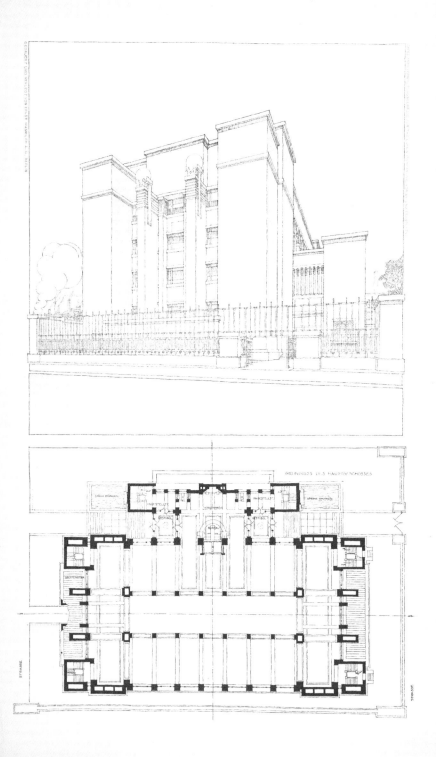

GRUNDRISS DES HAUPTGESCHOSSES

trading, requiring visibility both horizontally across and vertically between floors. It soon became clear that rebuilding the existing offices in pieces simply would not work, and that a new building was demanded. A building structured round a central atrium optimised horizontal and vertical visibility, so we started considering different forms that might fit the highly constrained and oddly shaped site. Following the site boundaries would be expensive and not very efficient, so we reverted to the clarity of a rectangle, with an atrium in the centre and service towers on the outside.

We used these service towers to articulate and give scale to the building, to enrich the skyline, to anchor the rectangle in the site, and to enable easy and non-disruptive replacement and maintenance of everything from toilets, to the cabling that was needed for rapidly changing IT systems – this was the dawn of the digital era. This was especially important as the trading floors were much more intensely occupied than normal office floors, so needed completely different levels of servicing. The toilet capsules, inspired by the sleek metallic lines of Airstream caravans, were to be completely prefabricated, and lifted into position by crane.

The service towers were the most striking element of the Lloyd's design, achieving the same separation of served and servant spaces that had given the Pompidou Centre its open floorplates. Clad in stainless steel, the towers seem to engage in a dialogue with the building as well as defining its profile, referring back to the student scheme for Yale Science Laboratories that Norman and I had worked on in 1961. You could also see the influence of Frank Lloyd Wright's Larkin Building, in the juxtaposition of the service towers and the top-lit central atrium space, and of Louis Kahn's Richards Medical Research Laboratories. Using more expensive stainless steel also reflected the building's status as a headquarters. It is our only major building that doesn't use coloured finishes.

The towers establilsh the building's relationship with the site, and with its neighbours. I wrote at the time that Lloyd's was designed to 'weave together both the over-simplified twentieth-century blocks and the richer more varied architecture of the past'. The building's profile was specifically designed to step down to meet its neighbours, and in particular the Victorian galleries of Leadenhall market. The towers also work with the central atrium and surrounding buildings to create an intricate play of light and

Left and right: Frank Lloyd Wright's Larkin Building was built in Buffalo, New York in 1906. I never had the chance to visit before its controversial demolition in 1950, but its separate service towers, monumental columns and open atrium had a clear influence on the Lloyd's Building.

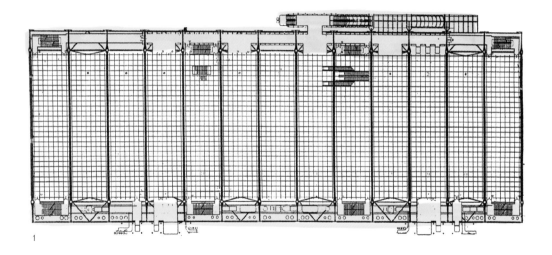

1

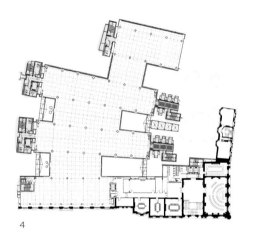

4

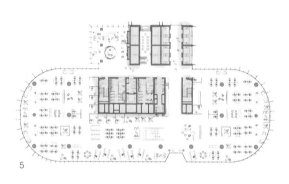

5

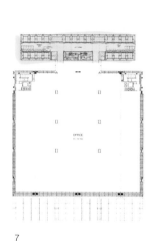

7

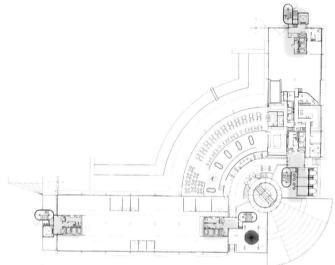

8

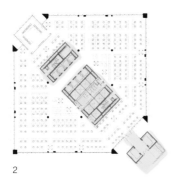

2

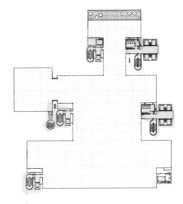

3

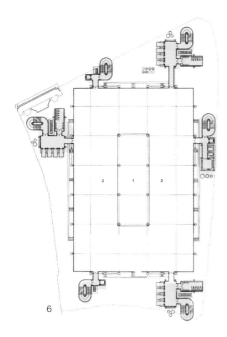

6

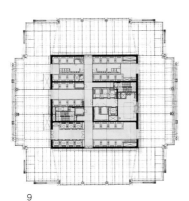

9

These building plans show how removing services from the centre of the building liberates the plan and introduces total flexibility. However, some clients still specify the central service core approach as at 3 World Trade Centre (9).

1. Centre Pompidou, Paris, 1977

2. Torre BBVA Bancomer, Mexico City, 2016

3. 88 Wood Street, London, 1999

4. Lloyd's Register, London, 2000

5. Barangaroo, Sydney, 2016

6. Lloyd's of London, London, 1986

7. The Leadenhall Building, London, 2014

8. Channel 4 Television Headquarters, London, 1994

9. 3 World Trade Centre, New York City, 2018 (estimated)

0   10   20m

Right and far right:
The irregularly-shaped
site of Lloyd's was due
to the unplanned nature
of the surrounding City
streets. We created
a rectangular floorplan
(1) and, rather than
including the services
within it (2), relocated
them on the outside (3).
To everyone's benefit,
and delight, the City
of London didn't count
the services as usable
space, and the size of
the building increased
by ten per cent.

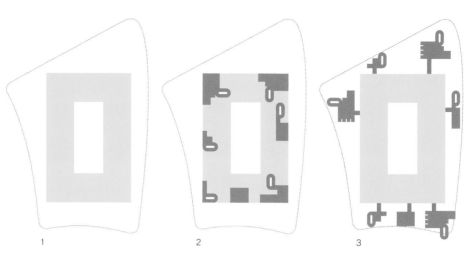

1   2   3

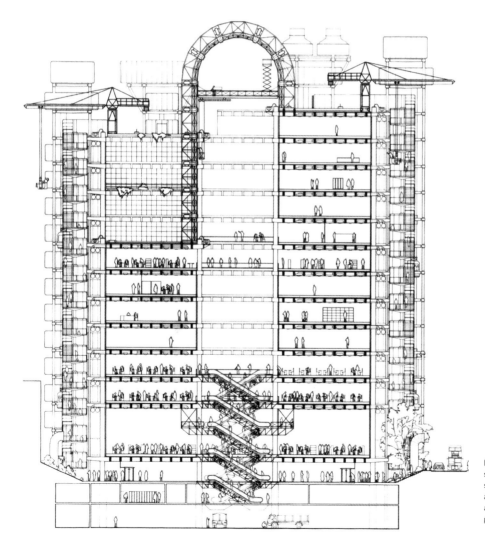

Left: A west-east
section through Lloyd's,
showing the central
atrium, the escalators,
and the barrel-vaulted
glass roof.

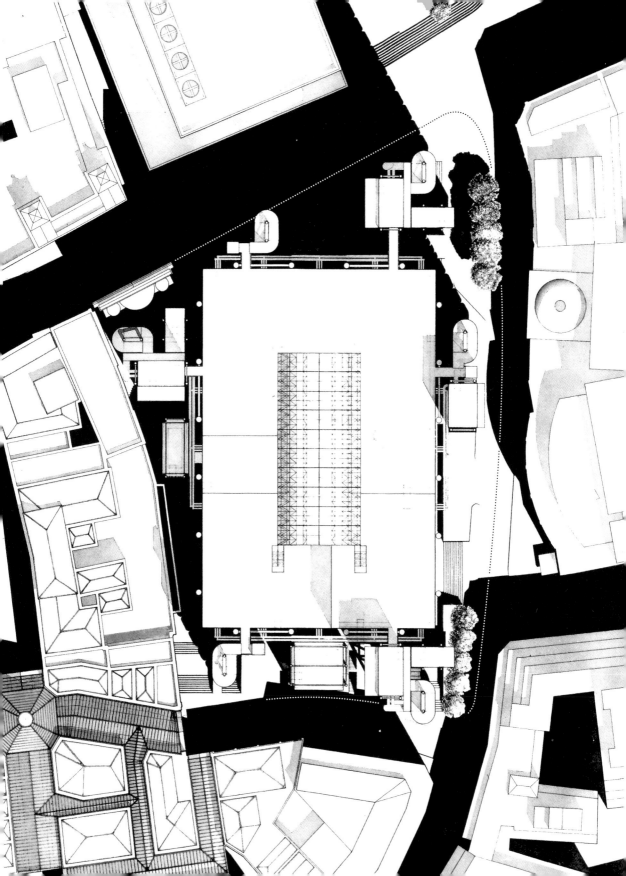

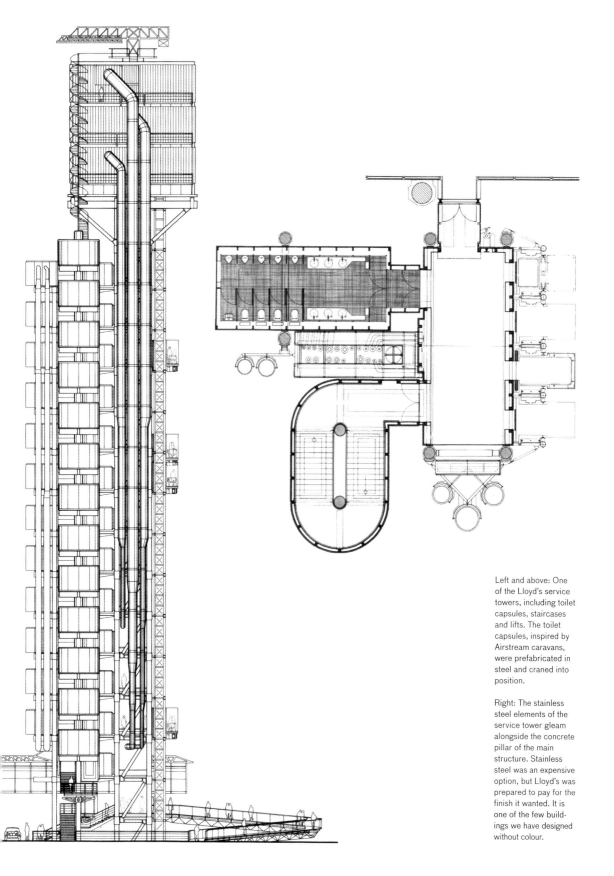

Left and above: One of the Lloyd's service towers, including toilet capsules, staircases and lifts. The toilet capsules, inspired by Airstream caravans, were prefabricated in steel and craned into position.

Right: The stainless steel elements of the service tower gleam alongside the concrete pillar of the main structure. Stainless steel was an expensive option, but Lloyd's was prepared to pay for the finish it wanted. It is one of the few buildings we have designed without colour.

shadow. This is reinforced by the windows' 'sparkle glass', a new product that John Young developed with Pilkington. The glass is slightly textured to provide privacy for Lloyd's workers while catching, reflecting and refracting light to create animation, rather than the dull blackness of unlit glass.

The towers had an unexpected bonus for the client; the size of the building was limited by a maximum plot ratio (plot ratios cap the size of buildings by specifying the maximum floor area a building can contain, as a multiple of the size of the site). To our delight, the City of London agreed that putting the services outside the main building envelope meant they weren't counted as usable space. As a result, we could increase the size of the building by over 10 per cent, which had a big financial impact, and helped convince Lloyd's of the value of our design.

Inside, the trading floors surrounded an open atrium, with the structure supported by four pairs of concrete pillars (the fire regulations made steel impractical, though a return to concrete felt almost like a step backwards after the battle we had undergone to retain a steel structure at the Pompidou Centre). We envisaged the arrangement of space as being like a tide, with Lloyd's occupation ebbing and flowing to use more or fewer floors as business needs changed. The remaining empty floors could be closed off with glass partitions and used as offices by Lloyd's and other tenants.

Above this space, a barrel-vaulted glass roof is an echo, perhaps unconscious, of the nearby Leadenhall Market, as well as the great iron and glass structures of Crystal Palace or the Kew Palm House, or of Milan's Galleria Vittorio Emanuele II.

John Young, who was the lead architect for the project, worked round the clock in his search for the perfect concrete that would create smooth pillars (a source of some tension with the contractor, Bovis, who felt that the detail of concrete pouring was a matter for them not for the architects). He masterminded the designs for one of the most beautiful, and perfectly realised buildings of our career, overseeing the detail of everything from concrete to glass to steel.

John had joined Team 4 in 1966 straight from the AA, where he had completed his first three years of training. Looking for a placement, he said he was searching for a small practice with interesting work and the right ethos. When he saw a photograph of us hanging out of a window like a pop group, rather than posing formally with rimless glasses and bow ties, he knew he had found his home.

Left: A detail from Lloyd's, showing the exquisitely smooth concrete finish that John Young achieved, the sparkle glass that he developed to balance transparency and privacy, and a vent circulating air to cool the triple-glazed facade.

Right: With John Young and a model of the Lloyd's Building in 1983.

The theoretical focus of the AA bored John, and he quickly came back to us after his final year. His grasp of detail and enthusiasm for learning about new technology was critical to our buildings. He is an excellent designer, a skilful and creative craftsman, and a joyful character who quickly became one of our closest friends. For nearly 40 years, his visual sensitivity, his understanding of the nature of materials and his visionary approach made him central to the practice's success. He used to say that he was a details man, while I looked at the big picture. This made us a great team.

John retired in 2003, when he was 60, and his departure left a big hole in the practice; he had been there for me at our highest and lowest points, a constant source of valued advice and friendship. When he noticed that I was sometimes in low spirits on Monday mornings, he instituted our Monday Design Forum meetings, so the week begins with design rather than management discussions (we still have them now), and it was John who worked hard to find ways of making the most of everyone's talents in the practice, moving people two or three times to find the right role for them. Ruthie and I still see him and his wife Tania as often as we can, though we live far apart; they have sold the amazing penthouse that he built at Thames Wharf, but have beautiful houses in Hayling Island in the Solent, and near Santa Fe, New Mexico, where John went to seek out the biggest sky he could find.

Lloyd's was one of the best clients we ever had, and looking back, I realise how fortunate we were. It was the opposite process to the Pompidou Centre, where the specifications had been precisely laid out in advance; at Lloyd's they were worked out through dialogue. We met with the board every month, and they told us when they didn't like a direction we were taking. It's so much easier when clients tell you what they think; there's usually a way round any problem if you consider it early enough. We don't work well in a void; the worst clients are those who are uninterested, or the bullies who throw their weight about without listening.

One day, towards the end of the project, Lloyd's chairman, Sir Peter Green, asked me, 'Why didn't you tell me the building was going to look like this at the beginning?' I answered honestly, 'I didn't know it would.' This wasn't flippant, but a reflection of the way that design translates into reality. Buildings are put together piece by piece, through discussion and clarification of needs and constraints. Each element has an aesthetic as well as a functional role. Architects use models, sketches and computer generated images to bridge the gap between design and reality, but these can be deceptive. They make up for the lack of detail through painterly expressiveness more suited to a chocolate box than to architecture. A building's expression changes as elements are assembled, and it is only when it is complete that it can be fully understood.

The Lloyd's trading floor, with escalators rising alongside the concrete pillars, adding drama and a sense of scale to the atrium space.

The building was the product of this process, not the realisation of a perfect and pristine vision. Epiphanies don't really happen in architecture. There are occasional sparks and moments of inspiration, but if you leap out of bed to write down an idea at 2a.m., it's usually just an indication that you have drunk too much. Designs are developed through analysis and understanding of priorities and conditions, through the layering of ideas and the interplay of disciplines, and through finding aesthetically intelligent ways to meet the client's needs and the site's constraints.

Even so, it was clear that Lloyd's was going some way beyond its comfort zone, and Gordon Graham played an important role in maintaining its confidence. This was a thoroughly conservative institution: the exceptional designer Eva Jiricná, who worked on the design of the interiors and the underwriters' 'boxes', is one of the most stylish women I know, but was told that she couldn't wear trousers inside Lloyd's.

The inherent tension between a truly conservative institution and a modern building came to a head when we were discussing the boardroom. Lloyd's wanted a 'classic' (by which they meant 'traditional') boardroom, and neither John nor I had any idea how to meet this requirement. It turned out that they had previously acquired a complete John Adam room from Bowood House in Wiltshire, intending to reinstate it in their 1958 building, but the dimensions had been wrong and it remained in pieces, in storage. Peter Green suggested we use it in the new building, and we built it as a free-standing 'jewel box' at the very top, surrounded by a promenade. We had even asked the foremost expert on Adam's architecture to advise on the colour scheme, but when I showed Sir Peter Miller, who took over from Green as chairman in 1983, the result, he declared that it 'looked like a Neapolitan ice cream'. He insisted we tone it down with more polite, tasteful shades – making a pastiche out of an original interior.

Public art proved a problem too. I didn't want to clutter the building with poor quality sculpture or hang its walls with second-rate paintings, but we eventually agreed to commission a giant clock. At Ruthie's suggestion, we approached Jean Tinguely, the eccentric but brilliant Swiss artist who had built an abstracted 'Crocodrome' at the Pompidou Centre, which pushed chocolate bars out of its backside, to the delight of visiting children. Pontus Hultén told us that we would only be able to speak to Tinguely between 7p.m. and 8p.m., as he kept his telephone in the oven, and only took it out when he was cooking his supper. Eventually, Ruthie managed to get through to him; he said he loved the Pompidou Centre, loved Richard Rogers' work, loved the Lloyd's Building, and would be very happy to design a clock. He only had one stipulation: the clock must never tell the right time. I pitched this idea to the board at our next meeting, and

The Lloyd's Building, with the steeple of St Andrew Undershaft to the left.

there was a deathly silence before they moved onto the next item of business – a huge missed opportunity.

But the client understood risk – it was at the heart of their business – and were willing to change their mind in the face of careful analysis of particular problems. Courtenay Blackmore, who had been Lloyd's head of administration, and became project director for the new building, was an extraordinary man – warm, loveable and enthusiastic – though we had a particularly tough job persuading him to support our plan for external lifts. The London climate wouldn't allow for them, he said, and nobody would use them anyhow. To persuade him, we found some similar lifts in a hotel in rainy San Francisco, and I sent him a postcard saying: 'Eureka! I have found the lift!' Courtenay and John Young flew out to investigate, riding up and down in the lifts for more than an hour, forging a lifelong friendship in the process.

As with the Pompidou Centre, the building was completed amid eddies of controversy, attacks from inside and outside Lloyd's, anonymous briefings, and letters to the newspapers comparing the structure to an oil refinery. The change of chairman in 1983 totally destabilised our relationships at Lloyd's, not helped by the fact that the new chairman's wife was an interior designer, who brought in classical French interior designers to complete the boardroom and executive offices.

Relations became so soured that I was the only member of the design team invited to the formal opening of the building. At the opening, I found myself sitting next to the dean of St Paul's Cathedral. He asked me whether I was feeling 'beleaguered' – I remember the word very clearly. I said that was a perfect description of how I felt. He told me a story about Sir Christopher Wren, when he was working on St Paul's Cathedral. By the time he had been on the project for thirty or forty years, and had prepared at least three different designs, Wren had become so sick of people interfering and criticising that he built an 18-foot-high wattle fence to shield the building works from prying eyes. It's a situation, and a response, with which every architect will sympathise.

Harmony and Heritage

Lloyd's sought to respond to London's skyline, as well as to intrigue and entice the passer-by. We tested the view from Blackheath in the south and Parliament Hill in the north. From these vantage points the towers and the arched roof of the atrium would be just visible, complementing the spires that still, in the late 1970s, rose higher than the surrounding buildings. The building is designed to be seen in parts, in glimpses, like G.E. Street's Royal Courts of Justice on the Strand, which catch the eye and unwind, opening up terraces, courtyards and a well-defined forecourt as you approach them. As you near Lloyd's, through the winding streets of the City, the form gradually unfolds, the overlapping elements of the façade gradually revealing different spaces and scales. A dialogue is established between surface and depth, between tension and compression, between the horizontal and the vertical.

Urban buildings cannot be designed in isolation; they form part of a tapestry that is forever being rewoven (three-quarters of buildings in the City of London have been rebuilt or refurbished since Lloyd's was completed). But their presence can be more or less harmonious, a critical factor in architecture and urban planning. Harmony does not mean mimicry; buildings should complement, not imitate, each other. There should be a dialogue. We can't freeze architecture at an arbitrary point in the past, requiring all new development to conform to a historicist template, like a heritage theme park. Nor should we insist that every part of a city should be delivered as a perfect composition, like a Nash terrace. A living city cannot purely consist of museum pieces. Above all it is the relationship between buildings and public spaces that matters most. Height, scale and architectural style are all important, but planning should consider the quality and nature of spaces enclosed by buildings as much as the buildings themselves.

Sometimes harmony works through consistency, but sometimes by contrast, by layering and juxtaposing the old and the new. Buildings express their historical context through the technologies and materials that they use. When Vasari repaired and extended the medieval Palazzo Vecchio in Florence, he studiously employed medieval techniques and language in a way that made his additions indistinguishable to most visitors. But when he built the Uffizi Gallery around the corner, he used the most modern design and construction techniques available to him. The Piazza della Signora blends medieval, Gothic and Renaissance to create a harmonious whole. The dialogue across time enriches cities, with styles and historical change merging together like a rich fish stew. In Florence, Renaissance buildings contrast with a medieval background; in central London the dominant background is Georgian, overlaid with countless variations on Victorian and twentieth-century architecture.

Lloyd's was designed to respect and converse with its neighbours. Unlike the Pompidou Centre, Lloyd's profile stepped down to meet the buildings that surrounded it; it was a modern building in its technology and aesthetic language, but it paid close attention to context too. In the intervening years, that context has completely changed. None of its 1970s neighbours are there any more, showing that slavish imitation would have been short-sighted as well as superficial. Cities change, and a new building

is part of a dynamic composition, not a definitive full stop at the end of a work. As soon as it can no longer adapt to the changing needs of its occupiers, it is taken down. This is why so many purpose-built twentieth-century buildings have been demolished.

Mansion House and the Conservatism that Almost Killed the City

By the early 1980s, the City, led by its highly conservative chief planner Stuart Murphy, seemed determined to accelerate its own decline. When I was asked to design a new building a few yards from Lloyd's, Murphy showed me a picture of a romantic Scottish building from the nineteenth century and told me that I should use that as the basis of my design. The financial industry was looking for new large floorplate offices to use as trading floors, but in Murphy's view these had no place in the City; Canary Wharf's construction (in disused former docks) came just in time to save the City from itself. I was critical of Canary Wharf's monocultural office park atmosphere in the early years, but it has improved hugely over time, with shops and bars and life on the streets seven days a week.

Murphy also rejected the Mansion House Square scheme, Peter Palumbo's plan to build posthumously a 19-storey Mies van der Rohe -designed tower near Mansion House in the City of London. Palumbo appealed, and the scheme became the subject of a controversial public enquiry. As an expert witness, I argued that the building was exceptional, would enhance the urban richness of the City of London, and would send out a strong signal that London had the confidence to embrace the new, rather than retreat into a Victorian comfort zone. The proposed building was an exercise in classical elegance, comparable with Palladio and Brunelleschi, though realised in steel and glass rather than stone. I see those who opposed it as vandals, as wilfully destructive as those who bulldoze a historic building.

If executed, the plan would have given London an amazingly beautiful and well-proportioned modern building, and the first and only London building by one of the twentieth century's masters; today we might criticise it for being too short, rather than too tall, given the changing scale of its surroundings. A wonderful new public square – a much-needed rarity among the City's tight-packed streets – would have opened up views of the Mansion House itself, as well as two solid bank buildings (by Cooper and Lutyens) on the north side of the street, and the church of Saint Stephen Walbrook to the south.

The planning inspector decided against Palumbo's scheme on the basis of its impact on its surroundings, and the Secretary of State confirmed the decision. But these surroundings themselves have changed beyond all

Top left: Piazza San Marco in Venice: the classical colonnades, Byzantine church and campanile contrast sharply, but create a breathtakingly beautiful and harmonious whole.

Left: Ludwig Mies van der Rohe's unbuilt Mansion House Square scheme – a missed opportunity not only for a beautiful addition to London's built fabric, but also for a generous public space at the heart of the City of London. Rejecting schemes like this almost destroyed the City, until competition from Canary Wharf forced a change in attitudes.

recognition since then. The buildings to the south and west of the site have been demolished and rebuilt, and the Mappin & Webb building, one of the buildings that campaigners had battled to protect, was eventually (after further planning battles) demolished and replaced by Jim Stirling's No.1 Poultry. The conservationists won the battle, but lost the war. Had the Mies tower been built, it would without a doubt be listed Grade I by now. This appalling lack of vision highlights a contradiction in the role of heritage in planning: new buildings are about the future, but the opinions of those interested in preserving or mimicking the past seem to be regarded as pre-eminent.

All good buildings were modern in their day. Brunelleschi's Duomo in Florence drew lessons from classical Roman and Byzantine architecture, but used Renaissance technology to make an entirely new type of lightweight structure. King's College, Cambridge, one of England's most beautiful sights, blends medieval, Renaissance and classical architecture, weaving together elements that were each once modern to create a harmonious whole. And every time I visit Venice, I marvel at the Piazza San Marco, which combines a zany Byzantine cathedral and palace, with classical porticos and the slim, red brick campanile tower with its bright green roof. Nothing matches anything else, but the composition is harmonious – and heart-stoppingly beautiful.

In the years that followed Lloyd's, there were a number of occasions when we envied Wren his ability to put up a wattle fence against prying eyes. Old Billingsgate Market was the first major heritage project that we were asked to take on. Adapting and upgrading historical buildings is often preferable, cheaper and more environmentally responsible than simply demolishing and replacing them. But you need to be allowed to adapt, otherwise you are left with white elephants. The past is comfortable because it is familiar and holds no danger, but it is sterile too for those same reasons; you cannot progress backwards.

In 1982, Billingsgate Fish Market moved from its nineteenth-century riverside premises to a more easily accessible location in east London's docklands. Two hundred years of market use had taken their toll on Old Billingsgate, but after a campaign led by Marcus Binney of SAVE, it was listed. Citibank took it on, and we were asked to remodel it, so that the trading of fish could be replaced by the trading of shares (which perfectly suited the large floorplate of the old market hall). Our scheme brought light, transparency and modern services into the building, while remaining sensitive to its historic fabric, but the late 1980s recession prevented it from being fully occupied.

Later, we were approached by another bank to make further changes to Billingsgate to meet their needs, letting light into the lower floors by glazing what had once been the openings into the ice cellars. We prepared

Lloyd's Register, completed in 2000, was designed for a sensitive and tight site in the City of London. The building's clear glazing gives transparency and life to the façade, while integrating an existing listed building at ground level.

designs, but planning permission for these was now opposed by heritage campaigners. We were told that we had achieved a perfect balance first time round; nothing further could be added or taken away. As a result, the new owners lost interest, and Old Billingsgate is now used as an occasional venue for parties and product launches. Our alterations would have created a better and more usable building, instead of a beautiful relic preserved in aspic, giving nothing to the city, deprived of its original function, and unable to meet a new one.

Prince Charles and his Carbuncles

While attitudes in the City of London were slowly changing, the knee-jerk heritage lobby had found a champion in a representative of an even older British institution. In 1984, Prince Charles was invited to speak at a gala dinner held at Hampton Court to celebrate the 150th anniversary of the Royal Institute of British Architects. The intelligent and inspired Indian architect and humanist Charles Correa was to receive the Gold Medal, and after a few lukewarm compliments towards him, Prince Charles shared his opinions. There needed to be more focus on rehabilitating buildings, he said, on community planning, on traditional designs. He attacked Peter Palumbo's plans for Mansion House Square as 'yet another giant glass stump, better suited to downtown Chicago than the City of London'.

And he launched a tirade against the Ahrends, Burton and Koralek designs for the National Gallery extension:

> Instead of designing an extension to the elegant façade of the National Gallery which complements and continues the concept of columns and domes, it looks as if we may be presented with a kind of municipal fire station, complete with the sort of tower that contains the siren. I would understand better this type of high-tech approach if you demolished the whole of Trafalgar Square and started again with a single architect responsible for the entire layout, but what is proposed is like a monstrous carbuncle on the face of a much-loved and elegant friend.[4]

This astonishing attack did not only seem rude to the guest of honour and architecturally ignorant, but also denied the very possibility of buildings from different periods co-existing and harmonising with each other as they do in all the greatest historical cities. The Ahrends, Burton and Koralek proposal for the National Gallery was modern in form and in its use of materials. To suggest that the only way to extend the gallery was to imitate its flat classical façade confuses harmony with pastiche, and would have thrown a symmetrical classical building out of balance by dribbling its architectural expression out at one side – anathema to classicism. Were the only options for all London to be preserved intact, or to be systematically demolished to allow for its wholesale replacement on a street-by-street basis? Where was the space for the layering of styles and technologies that gives the best cities their rich texture?

On the way out of the dinner, the Prince stopped to ask me whether I had listened to his speech. 'Yes, I had,' I said, 'but I didn't agree with it. I know you enjoy Wren's architecture, but he was a modern architect in his time. By your logic, he should have built his extension to Hampton Court in a late medieval style to match the Tudor buildings, not in the restrained baroque style that he brought to it. In fact we are standing more or less on the junction between those two sharply contrasting styles, and it seems to me that they have a very successful dialogue.'

That was as near as I ever got to a discussion with Prince Charles on architecture. After his speech, the BBC, RIBA and the Royal Academy were keen to host debates, which would have brought to the surface some of the contradictions in his arguments, as well as some of his more sensible views on community participation. But, Buckingham Palace told us, 'the Prince does not debate'. This seems to be the most serious criticism of royalty to me; that they will not engage in the democratic process of debate that is the foundation of our country.

The Prince continued to intervene. In 1987, we were preparing a master plan for Paternoster Square, an incoherent collection of bleak post-war buildings and spaces to the north of St Paul's Cathedral. We proposed replacing the Underground station, which currently leaves visitors on a pavement with their backs to the Cathedral, with a new station at the centre of the scheme, where a glazed galleria would allow light to penetrate right down to the platforms, and offer passengers an incredible view of St Paul's dome as they climbed the stairs or rode the escalators up to street level.

Soon after the competition sketches had been published, Prince Charles made a speech at the Mansion House. He vigorously criticised the brief and the competition entries, arguing for an approach based on traditional materials and styles, rather than one from 'the age of the computer and word-processor'. He compared post-war architecture unfavourably to the Nazi air force: 'You have to give this much to the Luftwaffe: when it knocked down our buildings, it didn't replace them with anything more offensive than rubble.'

Nonetheless, we thought our design had struck the right balance between a modernist style and palette of materials (though we had included

Making a point: the Louvre entrance, by I.M. Pei, is a simple pyramid made of glass and steel; but the firm, well known for modernist des

The article I wrote for *The Times* in July 1989 was provoked by Prince Charles' persistent attacks on modern architecture and architects, and his refusal to debate or discuss these in public.

Pulling down

The Prince of Wales has attack
modern architects in his camp
human environment. **Richard R**
designed the Lloyd's building an
Centre, rejects the Prince's 'Disn
and argues that architects ar
culprits in the destruction of c

In his sweeping criticism of modernism, the Prince of Wales has failed to recognize that architecture mirrors society; its civility and its barbarism. Its buildings can be no greater than the sense of responsibility and patronage from which they originate. In blaming the architect and the architect alone for the ugliness of our built environment, the Prince exonerates the real culprits, thereby frustrating the very debate he wishes to encourage.

At the heart of the Prince's position is the claim that "our age is the first to have seen fit to abandon the past". This is, to say the least, an eccentric interpretation of the history of architecture, ignoring as it does the great turning points in the course of Western architecture, for example the eclipse of Gothic forms by the Renaissance.

Indeed, if there is any continuity at all in architectural history, it lies not in some illusory aesthetic, but in the fact that all departure from tradition has provoked ferocious controversy and opposition. When the first caveman left the shelter of his solid, waterproof, easily defensible cave for the lightweight, flexible, hi-tech hut (where one couldn't even draw on the walls) he was no doubt stoned for being a revolutionary with no feeling for social and visual tradition.

If the conservative principles favoured by the Prince of Wales and his followers had been applied throughout history, very little of our "traditional" architectural heritage would ever have been built. Most of the great buildings in the classical and Gothic traditions which the conservationists now value so highly were, in their own time, revolutionary. If the height of a new building had to conform to those around it, the great Gothic cathedrals would never have seen the light of day. Likewise, the massive Italian stone *palazzi* of the 16th century, which today can seem the very exemplar of "traditional architecture", dwarfed the one and two-storey wooden medieval buildings surrounding them.

When, three years ago, the Queen opened the new Lloyd's building, the Dean of St Paul's reminded me of the opposition that Wren had met with in the construction of St Paul's. Apparently he had to build a wall 18ft high around the site to prevent his critics from seeing and once more frustrating his plans. Several earlier designs had been blocked, including his 1673 design, of which the "Great Model" can still be seen in the crypt of the cathedral. This is a magnificent project, and had it been built it would have been not only one of the greatest of all baroque masterpieces, but also one of the most

churches, the *palazzi* of Renaissance Italy or St Paul's seem to us to exist in a harmonious relation with their neighbours, it is not because they slavishly imitated them in size, style or material. Rather they embodied new building techniques and distinctive architectural forms quite unlike anything ever seen before. The contextual harmony that they seem to us to enjoy with their surroundings is the result of the juxtaposition of buildings of great quality, clearly and courageously relating across time.

I believe that the new movements in architecture that sprung up around the turn of this century represent an important turning point in the history of architecture comparable to that other great watershed, the development of the classical forms of the Renaissance. Like the beautiful buildings by Brunelleschi or Wren, the designs of Sullivan, Le Corbusier and Mies van der Rohe offer a new aesthetic responsive to the scientific and ethical movement of the times.

Although you would not know it if you listened to the Prince of

Wales, the Modern movement, or at least a great part of it, represented a return to classical principles. It emphasized the integrity of building materials, and it insisted, in contrast to the Victorian preoccupation with historical styles and with surfaces, that architecture was primarily concerned with the relation of three-dimensional form, with the play of light and shadow, of space and mass, rather than with ornament.

Together with these aesthetic principles went certain social commitments. The history of "modernism" had as its starting point the disastrous growth of the 19th-century city, and the spread of slum dwellings. Early efforts in modern design were marked by a concern to develop healthier, greener and more humanitarian environments; English garden cities and new towns reflect this reformist spirit. To the early modernists architecture was not just another money-making business. They sought, in their architecture, to give expression to democratic ideals, to create new public forums and to contribute to freer and more egalitarian ways of

living. Thus from its beginning
modern architecture has bee
most interested in the design of
houses and public institutions lik
schools and town halls and no
like its predecessors, in the con
struction of churches and palace

These classical prin
ciples and progressiv
social commitment
were given a revolu
tionary embodimen
in the buildings of th
early modernists. For exampl
the discovery of relative spac
manifest in the Cubist art, wa
given architectural expression in
greater abstraction of form; i
particular, the newly evolve
steel-frame structural system wa
used to free the walls of a buildin
from load-bearing function, allow
ing greater freedom in plan an
elevation. The possibility of hig
density buildings, including th
high-rise, was explored as a mean
of putting a halt to the spread o
the suburb into the countrysid
and creating sunnier, more sp
cious homes, at a time whe
cholera was endemic in the citi
and the brick back-to-back hous

entered "artfully rendered drawings of a neo-classical mausoleum" in the National Gallery competition

the Prince

Modern masterpieces: buildings such as the Hongkong and Sh
signed by Norman Foster, are "infused with a spirit of innovati

---

the work of
n for a more
ers (left), who
he Pompidou
and approach'
ot the real
city centres

was a symbol of deprivation, not rose-tinted nostalgia. And the democratic promise of mass production was celebrated by the employment of industrial components not only in factory buildings but in furniture and houses.

Also like the architecture of the Renaissance, the buildings of the Modern movement have proved to be not only visually and technically exciting, but capable of existing in a profound harmony with their man-made and natural environment. The Prince of Wales has argued that "architectural adventurousness, producing non-traditional, exciting designs is certainly inappropriate in rural areas". If applied to history this would, of course, have ruled out the work of Palladio or Vanbrugh. But even in the context of the Modern movement, any one who has seen Frank Lloyd Wright's Fallingwater, Mies's Farnsworth House or Alvar Aalto's Villa Mairea, for instance, will know just how absurd it is to suggest that modern "adventurous" architecture is incapable of harmonizing with its natural setting.

The same is true in the case of

the city; buildings like Mies's Seagram Building, Wright's Guggenheim Museum, and Roche and Dinkeloo's Ford Foundation, all in New York, prove that modern architecture can respond to an urban context in a manner that has never been surpassed. Fortunately, Britain is not without modern urban buildings that relate to their situation with a similar sensitivity; Sir Denys Lasdun's Royal College of Physicians, Alison and Peter Smithson's Economist Building in St James's, YRM's own headquarters in the City, and Darbon and Dark's Limington Garden Housing Estate in Victoria, are some examples in London.

From its beginning, modern architecture, like its classical forerunners, has been concerned to incorporate new technology into its designs. Its best buildings have been infused with a spirit of innovation and discovery; they have celebrated the technology with which they are built. The excitement of a technologically adventurous architecture is evident in such modern masterpieces as Paxton's Crystal Palace, Frank Lloyd Wright's Johnson Wax Factory in Wisconsin or Norman Foster's Hongkong and Shanghai Bank.

Today we are living through a period of enormous scientific and technical advance; perhaps a second industrial revolution which offers architects an extraordinary opportunity to evolve new forms and materials. The computer, micro-chip, transputer, bio-technology and solid state chemistry could lead to an enhanced environment, including more rather than less individual control and fewer uniform spaces. The best buildings of the future, for example, will interact dynamically with the climate in order to better meet the user's needs. Closer to robots than to temples, these chameleon-like apparitions with their changing surfaces are forcing us to once again rethink the art of architecture.

alteration in the building's form. But the use and form of modern buildings change dramatically over short periods of time. A set of offices today might become an art gallery tomorrow; a perfume factory may switch to making electronics. And quite apart from the fact that buildings must be able to expand and contract, and change their function, a third of a typical modern office is occupied with technology which will need to be replaced long before the building itself needs to be demolished. All this makes flexibility an essential feature of effective modern design, and renders the classical style quite impractical.

In contrast to the Prince of Wales's historicist architects, who are besotted with a past that never existed, I believe in the rich potential of modern industrial society and my own architecture has sought to respond to the needs of modern institutions by employing the most up-to-date scientific developments and exploiting the visual excitement that is inherent in them. My firm's design represents a search for an aesthetic which recognizes that in a technological society change is the only constant; an aesthetic which allows some parts of a building to be added or altered without destroying the harmony of the whole composition. The Lloyd's building illustrates our approach; it is intended to create a balance between permanence and change; its flexible elements — lifts, internal walls, air conditioning and so forth — permit improvisation within a determinate whole.

Despite its achievements in the past decade, and its future potential, modern architecture has been exposed to a barrage of criticism. It is paradoxical, to say the least, that at a time when the public has expressed a dramatically heightened interest in modern art, and the value of paintings by the modern masters has exploded, the modern movements in architecture should come under such sustained attack. Is it coherent to extol the cubism of Picasso and Braque, while castigating its architectural counterpart in the architecture of Corbusier? Many of the critics of modern architecture now seem to advocate the view that whereas art should be innovative and demanding, supplying new insights into our predicament, architecture should make us feel comfortable with ourselves and the nation we belong to.

The critics of contemporary architecture actually form a very diverse crowd, but while finding little else to agree on amongst themselves they are united on one

Continued from previous page

interior of Lloyd's (up to 2,000 per day), as visit many of our national museums. What then of the public's antipathy towards modern architecture?

This unfounded view that all modern architecture is unpopular is, of course, closely associated with the Prince of Wales. The Prince's contribution to the architectural debate and his intervention in a number of important competitions and public inquiries has been given extensive and often enthusiastic media coverage, but what has been the impact of his involvement?

The Prince's apologists argue that his opinions reflect those of his subjects — the silent majorities — and that his interventions, despite appearances, are thoroughly democratic. Certainly the process by which planning decisions are made is of a forbidding, Byzantine complexity and probably needs reforming. Nevertheless, this slow, expensive, often obscure, haggling between different interest groups — commercial and environmental, national and local — is a rough, if flawed, approximation of democracy. Most of the participants in this process and the decisions they reach are ultimately accountable to one electorate or another; the Prince answers to no one.

The Prince is an advocate of community architecture and he claims that he wishes to see greater openness about the way planning decisions are made; but his own conduct contradicts this public stand. He has, for example, proved rather shy of public debate. On several occasions critics and architects have accepted invitations to participate in a public discussion with him; unfortunately he has always declined to attend. Despite his well-publicized outbursts and his recent television programme, the Prince prefers to exercise his new-found prerogative as the nation's supreme aesthetic arbiter more surreptitiously, by paying secret visits to developers of important architectural projects or talking privately with the juries of major competitions.

In a similar manner we are assured that the Prince's judgements are not amateur or uninformed because he has gathered around himself a royal council of architectural "advisers"; however, he will not publicly disclose the identity of these secret courtiers. Perhaps these inconsistencies point to a deeper contradiction in the Prince's stand. The claim to be defending a democratic approach to architecture does not sit easily

even more dramatic on two o
occasions: Mies van der F
designs for Mansion House
Ahrends Burton and Kora
extension for the National
lery. In both of these cases th
little doubt that the Prince's p
outbursts determined the out
of the relevant planning inqu
Neither does the Prince shov
sign of curbing his undemoc
intervention in the system
public inquiries he professe
admire. In his birthday telev
programme last year, the P
criticized James Stirling's d
for the Mansion House site
the barb that it looked like a
radio; the Prince knew tha
planning inquiry concerning
scheme was at a crucial mom

A familiar theme: most of h
tionists now value so highly,

its deliberations and must
intended to effect its outcom

No doubt the Prince's infl
is usually less direct than i
been on these occasions; how
this only renders it more ir
ous. Rather than risk incurrin
disapproval of the heir appa
architects and their clients no
and guess the Prince's prefer
submitting self-censored de
that they hope will meet
approval.

For example, the Prince's
bunkle" outburst and his
erence for classical re
architecture signalled to th
ganizers and competitors o
second National Gallery com
tion that modern archite
should be excluded from the
list and so pastiche ruled the
The office of I. M. Pei,
known for its modernist des
entered artfully rendered draw
of a neo-classical mausol
This contrasted with its desi
the entrance to the Louv
couple of years later, for Pres.

brick and stone), and a closely contextual urban form. We had not imposed a grid, but had cut into a block, adopting a language of tight-knit winding streets, small alleyways and yards sympathetic to the medieval street pattern. Building materials and technologies have changed dramatically over 3,000 years – only a reactionary would seek to ignore the potential to make buildings that are stronger, lighter, more energy-efficient, easier to use and modify. But the form of public space has changed far less, because people have changed far less. We have an average height just below six foot, we still walk and talk and sit in the same way. The city spaces that worked 500 or 1,000 years ago still work today. The technology with most impact on urban design has been the car, and we are still trying to rebalance our cities, to strike a better balance between the car's demand for space and the needs of people.

When we were first telephoned by Stuart Lipton, who was running the Paternoster competition, he told us we had won, but that we should work with Arup Associates, who had proposed a more classical approach. Then we got another call saying that actually it would be Arup who would lead the project. And after that, our role seemed to get lost in the fog; Arup's scheme was also abandoned, then a neoclassical scheme foundered, and a master plan by William Whitfield was eventually implemented more than 15 years later. A great opportunity had been lost.

As I wrote in a long piece in *The Times* ('Pulling Down the Prince', 3 July 1989), it is a terrible misuse of privilege, or the royal prerogative even, to intervene in public affairs in this way, speaking loftily from the throne but refusing to allow your views to be tested and challenged, while promoting whimsical preferences for decomposed classical columns, pediments and cornices like a modern day Louis XIV. The Prince's outbursts affect people's careers. Ahrends, Burton and Koralek never quite recovered from the Prince's attack on their National Gallery scheme; one of England's best modern architecture practices was held back from completing more of their carefully considered buildings.

Perhaps even worse than the public pronouncements are the private discussions, the whispers and hints, which take place behind the scenes. As well as at Paternoster Square, the Prince may have lost us work at Stag Place in Victoria, and on the rebuilding of the Royal Opera House, where we were congratulated on a brilliant response but told we were 'too risky' and 'had enemies in high places'.

The Prince's intervention was most public in relation to the Chelsea Barracks scheme, which was funded by the Qatari sovereign wealth fund. We had prepared a master plan for the site, for 500 apartments with high levels of affordable housing. To our delight, there was support from most local groups, national consultees and even from historical institutions like the Royal Hospital. But a small local opposition group had emerged, and the Prince of Wales rallied to their cause.

At first, the developers and their Qatari backers stood firm behind the scheme, but shortly before the planning application was considered by the elected local authority, where the arguments on both sides could be aired democratically, Prince Charles intervened. He contacted the Qatari royal family privately to express his concerns and ask for an alternative plan. The Qataris pulled the plug. After two-and-a-half years, we were sacked from the project and the planning application was withdrawn a few days before it was due to be considered. Years of work were wasted, and we had to lay off staff owing to the sudden loss of such an important job.

On this occasion, the Prince's intervention was discussed in some detail in the court cases that followed, but in many other cases, his influence is more shadowy. After the Chelsea Barracks scheme, I asked eight major developers whether they consulted Prince Charles about architects or designs. Only one of them said he actually showed the Prince their designs, but five others said they consulted St James's Palace about a shortlist of architects, to check who would be seen as acceptable to the Prince. As one said to me, 'We're in the risk business, and consulting with St James's Palace is one way we can minimise risk.'

I don't believe that the Prince of Wales understands architecture. He thinks it is fixed at one point in the past (for him, classicism – an odd choice as it is not a style with deep roots in England), rather than an evolving language of technology and materials. But if he is not going to join in debate, it hardly matters whether his opinions are right or wrong. He occupies a privileged position, and he should not use that to damage the livelihoods of people he disagrees with.

7   Humanising the Institution

There is more to justice than the law. The traditional conception of a court-room is one of crime and punishment, of imprisonment and judgment. The stern buildings impose themselves on their surroundings, embodying the authority of the law, protecting their secrets behind thick walls, and putting citizens in their place.

Our designs for Bordeaux Law Courts, which were completed in 1998, started from a different position – we wanted to build a place for learning about justice, where children could be inspired to understand the rights of the citizen, and the philosophical underpinnings of the law. Justice should, in other words, be seen to be done, should be transparent for the plaintiff, but should also be easily understood by the passer-by, the citizen in whose name the law operates.

The French Ministry of Justice had launched a competition for provincial courts across the country, and our entry for Bordeaux brought together our thinking on public space, democracy and transparency and environmental responsibility. Our team, led by Ivan Harbour, built the courts as a democratic classroom, a part of Bordeaux's public realm that could bring the administration of justice out into the southern French sunlight.

Bordeaux is a handsome city that became wealthy through wine and slavery. Today, it also has one of Europe's most progressive mayors – Alain Juppé, the former French prime minister – and has transformed itself into one of the most civilised cities in Europe, with beautiful public spaces along the river and around its great civic buildings, connected by trams and pedestrianised streets.

The site chosen for the courts was on a busy road, next to an existing neoclassical court building, opposite the Cathedral and alongside retained pieces of the medieval city wall. As with the Pompidou Centre, we decided to position the building at one edge of the site, with administrative offices placed along the main road, leaving the courts themselves facing inwards

The Bordeaux Law Courts, completed in 1998, revisited the public character of the Pompidou Centre, but refined and developed the architectural language. Each wooden court is suspended within an open enclosure, bringing the administration of justice into the public realm.

203

towards the Cathedral, where we created a small public square – a place for people, subsequently enhanced by the pedestrianisation of the adjoining street. The building closes off the square in a way that is clearly legible to someone approaching from the Cathedral or the city centre.

The building is open and transparent, light not monolithic. After some experimentation, we built the courtrooms themselves from wood, and suspended them above a concrete plinth beneath an undulating wood and steel roof. The courtrooms are enclosed and calm spaces, drawing on the rich craft traditions of the area, lit from above and naturally ventilated from below.

Six of the seven wooden courtrooms are enclosed but free-standing within a glass box (the other stands outside), and all of them pierce the undulating canopy roof. With the offices providing a backdrop, the courtrooms form elements within an enclosed public space, open to the city, but retaining the segregation and security that the brief demanded. The transparency of the glass box attracts passers-by and contrasts with the wooden courtrooms; light and shadow play over the smooth mass of their structures.

Public access is from the square, up a wide flight of steps and over a pool of water. Plaintiffs and members of the public can access the courts from a gallery suspended above the public circulation space – what the French legal system evocatively calls the *salle des pas perdus* (literally 'the room of lost footsteps'). Judges use separate entrances, as do defendants.

The concrete of the underground car park provides the thermal mass needed to create a reservoir of warmth in winter and cool in summer, and air is also cooled in the summer as it circulates over the pool and cascade in front of the building. The courts themselves use the same approach to ventilation as oast houses, drawing hot air out of the top of the funnel, to be replaced by cooler air from below (the 'stack effect').

Bordeaux represents a development and refinement of the approach to the public realm that we had embodied in the designs for the Pompidou Centre 20 years previously and a new model of transparent civic architecture, blurring the line between public and private, bringing light and air into the closed and dusty world of the courtroom, and creating space for the passer-by as well as for the lawyers and plaintiffs who use the building every day.

It also marked a genuine moment of evolution in our architectural language and in the practice itself, as the older generation (John Young, Laurie Abbott, Peter Rice) began to step back and younger designers like Graham Stirk and Ivan Harbour began to shine. While most of our applicants came from the Architectural Association, Ivan was the first to come

Judges enter the courtrooms via a walkway that runs along the back of the chambers, where there is no public access.

205

from the Bartlett (UCL's architecture school). He joined the firm in 1985 and began his career working at Lloyd's of London. Since then he has demonstrated exceptional breadth and depth; his ideas flow fast and show an incredible fluidity, and he can juggle numerous projects at the same time, with a light touch or deeper engagement as required.

Ivan led the design for the Bordeaux Law Courts, for the Welsh Assembly, for Maggie's Centre and for Barajas Airport Terminal 4, all schemes that show the elegance of his design thinking, and his ability to bring a warmth and humanity even to the most monumental project.

Two Clients for Every Building – Democratising the Brief

For architecture to enhance the city and civic life, it needs to consider more than the client's immediate requirement. The architect must consider the building's users, and the passers-by, asking like Louis Kahn, 'What could this building be? What should it be? What is its essence? What will it add to the city?'

Every building meets the public realm at its entrances – intermediate spaces between public and private, where inside and outside meet. Buildings such as courts and parliaments owe an even greater duty to the public realm. They are not just machines for the administration of justice or the production of legislation; their design should express our shared values. A democratic society deserves democratic buildings, defining and forming part of the public realm; they should be places where all citizens should feel free to roam, learn, and participate. This should apply to train stations, convention centres and airports as much as to courtrooms, parliaments and libraries.

Two Lost Schemes – Tokyo Forum and Rome Congress Centre

Two unbuilt competition entries, designed ten years apart and both led by Graham Stirk, were further elaborations of the idea of democratising types of building that normally retreat from the city and create their own private world, rather than engage with the civic. Looking back I realise how important these schemes were, combining strong forms and structural profiles with a determination to create places for public assembly, not just private meetings.

Convention centres are traditionally huge, blank-walled monoliths, creating an internal 'village' for exhibitors and visitors. We sought to turn this approach on its head, unearthing and reinstating the democratic and

Inside one of the courtrooms in Bordeaux; the roof light allows for natural light and air circulation. Using wood represented a new approach for the practice and created a balance between the formality of courtrooms, and the human scale of crafted objects.

Our unbuilt design for the Rome Congress Centre raised the convention centre in the air, creating an extensive raked public piazza with performance space and informal seating, and offering magnificent views across Rome.

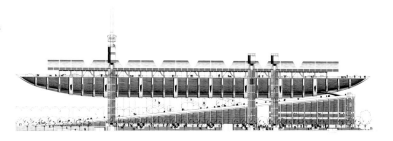

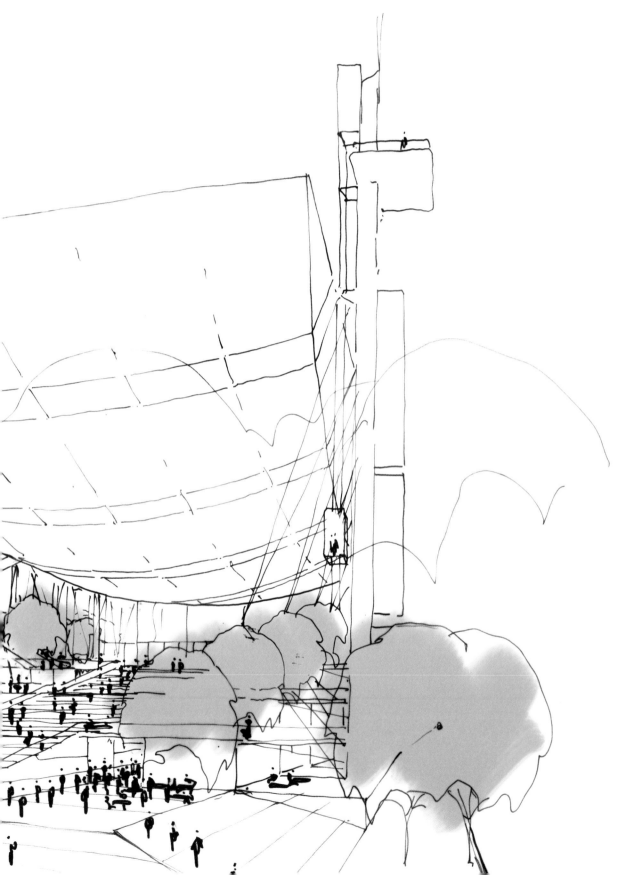

Our 1990 competition entry for Tokyo International Forum raised three huge convention halls in the air, bringing visitors up on suspended escalators and supporting service towers. Below these steel tanks – like great ships' hulls floating in the air – there would be uninterrupted public space, a new piece of city in the heart of Tokyo.

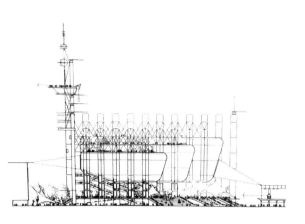

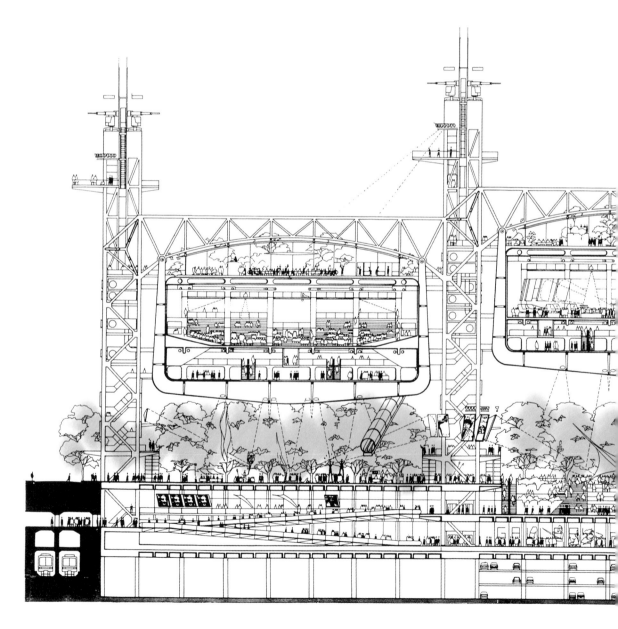

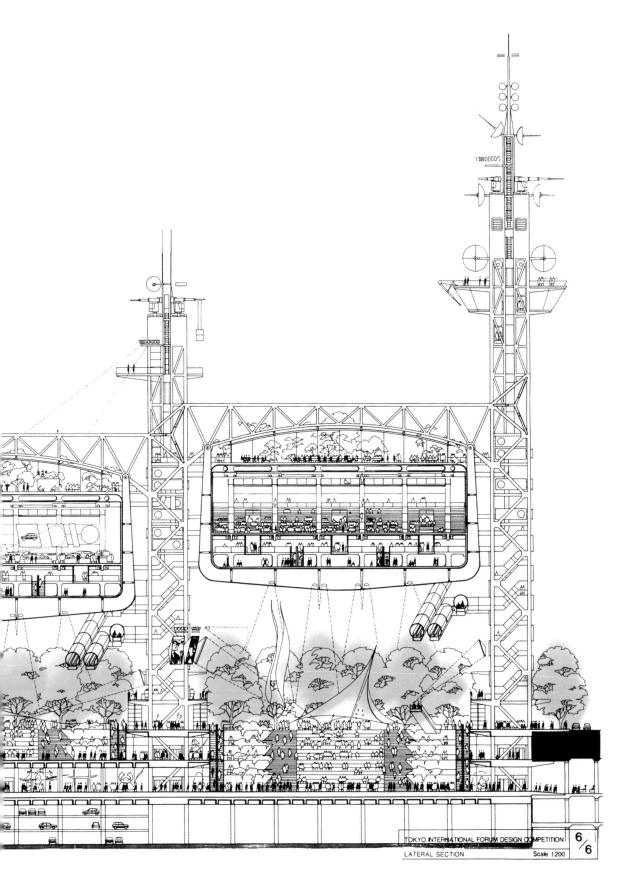

social instinct behind words like 'congress' and 'forum', by creating open-minded public space alongside the highly specified congress halls, building spaces designed to draw in the passer-by as well as the delegate.

The 1989 competition for the Tokyo Forum asked for three auditoria of differing sizes, in one of the densest areas of central Tokyo. Our team, working with Peter Rice, proposed suspending three whale-like steel boxes within a steel portal frame. Underneath the steel boxes, connected by escalators floating in space, was the real 'forum', the public space where people could meet and talk, mingling on their way to and from the adjoining train and underground railway station. Through the use of the steel framed construction, and by suspending the private buildings in space, we were returning to the Corbusian principles of 'freeing the ground', with the services for the auditoria provided within the portal frames.

In Rome, the Congress Centre was to be in the EUR district – the letters stand for Esposizione Universale Roma – which was originally built for the 1942 World Fair. Today it is a quiet suburban area, though still marked by the pompous neoclassical Fascist architecture and urbanism, with piazzas designed for impact and grandeur, not for the everyday meeting of friends and strangers. Our design lifted the convention space up above the ground, surrounding it with an open walkway, and created a new public space underneath, ramping up to a semi-enclosed 2,000-seat amphitheatre, with a hotel beneath it. From this open-minded, indeterminate public space, offering great views out across Rome, escalators would take ticketed visitors up to the wood-clad congress halls. These cantilevered spaces, with service towers to the side, would also provide shade to people enjoying the public space below. Congress halls are traditionally blind boxes; this one would have offered one of the best vantage points over the city.

Airports – New Gateways

When I was growing up, train stations were places of excitement, filled with steam and noise, arrivals and departures, the romanticism of distant destinations. I loved seeing trains in Gare de l'Est and other cavernous stations, bound for Istanbul, Moscow, Athens, Copenhagen. Films like *Anna Karenina*, where the narrative pivots around arrivals and departures in smoke-filled train sheds, deepened the drama. Today, airports play the same role, or they should. In some ways, they are the defining public buildings of the ever-mobile twenty-first century – thresholds for dislocation and discovery, places where families and friends part and are reunited.

But airports are also sites of conflicting priorities. Their operators make most of their money from retail and parking, not from air travel, and even less from romantics gazing out of windows at aeroplanes taking off and landing. Airports are highly functional machines, with requirements that become more complex by the year, but also need to be simple. Millions of us every year pass through layers of check-in, security and shopping to catch flights, and arrive in a new city, disorientated by shifting time zones and changing climates, picking our way through these modern portals to new countries.

Early airports, like Heathrow, Gatwick and JFK in New York, have grown up as haphazard accretions of buildings, parking lots and runways, as blank boxes concerned more with delivering passengers to shops than with helping them to navigate an alien and high-pressure process, or to enjoy the incredible wonder of flying. One of my great pleasures is the view from the plane; I always ask for a window seat so I can look out at the unfolding drama of mountains, lakes, villages and towns, glowing like jewels at night. And I love the luxury of working without interruption. Airports should be able to live up to the drama and delight of air travel.

But whatever clarity and romance airports once had is submerged beneath the detritus of security and retail. This was never truer than at Norman Foster's beautiful Stansted Airport, a poetic lightweight structure, which we studied carefully when we were designing Heathrow's Terminal 5. Stansted is a real gem, but the clarity and legibility of its design has been badly compromised by the shops, security infrastructure and a million other changes that have been thrown at it haphazardly over the years. For their operators, airports may be 'shopping centres with wings', but they should aspire to more than that.

Stansted showed us that anything delicate is likely to be quickly eroded by the assault of changing configurations and demands, so the airports we have designed have sought to create strong statements, to be humane, legible to passengers and usable as public space, and with the flexibility to accommodate ever-changing security and administrative arrangements, without undermining the central organising framework. They also look forward to a time when noise and pollution will be sufficiently reduced for cities to embrace their airports as part of the city, rather than to push them out to desolate peripheral locations.

We began work on London Heathrow Terminal 5 in 1989, the same year that we designed Marseille Airport. But while Marseille was operational in 1992, it would be 19 years before Terminal 5 opened to the public. In the intervening period, we faced endless changes of client, public enquiries, and the tightening of security following Lockerbie and 9/11.

Somehow Laurie Abbott, John Young and then Mike Davies managed to keep the project on track all the way through the process.

Mike is certainly one of the most recognisable partners at the practice – dressed in red, driving a red car with red upholstery. He is also one of the partners with the widest interests – an astronomer and an inventor, and he and his wife Liz are both painters. Mike joined us on the Pompidou Centre, where he quickly found his perfect project in the freestanding IRCAM experimental music centre. He has shaped the practice since then, bringing his endless inventiveness to our architecture.

Barns, Trees and Airport Cities

London Heathrow T5 is a stacked vertical airport terminal. Our original design, led by Laurie Abbott and Peter Rice, was for a more horizontal structure, with an elegant wavy roof modelled on a flying carpet, but BAA (the client) did not have control of all the land, and were already running into planning problems, so we had to think again, to protect nearby villages and waterways. John Young led the evolution of a more compact vertical concept, with an open piazza and a sequence of 'canyons' bringing natural light down to the lower floors, but these restricted flexibility, and had to be rethought as security requirements changed. In order to safeguard our design in spite of inevitable commercial and security interventions, we proposed a building with some very strong architectural fixes, but maximum flexibility within these.

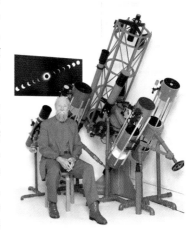

The resulting structure is a lightweight, loose-fit, elegant barn – and one of the largest single-span structures in the world, with a roof stretching over nearly 160m. Inside the structure, but not touching the external plate-glass walls at any point, are five storeys of arrivals, departures and shopping. The two elements are intentionally independent: after the endless planning battle for its construction, the design allows for internal reconfigurations without the need for further planning consents. The airport's operators have already added 250,000 square feet of additional retail space, without touching the external structure at all. These three elements – the vertical arrangements, the space created by the roof, and the canyons that separate the glass walls from the workings of the airport – are critical to the building's success.

Left: Heathrow Terminal 5. Passenger facilities are stacked within one of the largest single-span structures in the world, enabling internal remodelling without affecting the external structure.

Below left: The original design for Heathrow T5 envisaged a much more horizontal structure – similar to that adopted for Barajas Terminal 4 – but planning barriers forced a rethink.

Right: Mike Davies, the unmistakable 'Man in Red', is a wonderful friend and collaborator capable of working with the most difficult clients. He is also an accomplished painter, astronomer and inventor.

Following page: Madrid's Barajas Airport Terminal 4 was designed and built in less than half the time of Heathrow Terminal 5. The coloured roof supports give legibility and a sense of scale to the 1.2 kilometre-long building.

Arrivals and departures are segregated by floor level, as the new security rules required. Departing passengers arrive at the terminal on the fifth floor (crossing over the one remaining canyon – a garden – on the way) then travel down (by lift and escalator rather than endless walkways) to the planes (or the shuttle trains to satellite terminals). Arriving passengers, with less time or inclination to linger, pass directly through the middle floors of the building.

Mike Davies, who took over from John Young after the public enquiry, talks about it being like a Meccano set, with the pieces easily rearranged within a flexible but strong structure, held together by big bolts and brackets, robust enough for the next changes that it will have to absorb as air travel transforms. It is probably one of the most urban airport structures, a five-storey glass pavilion, waiting for a city to embrace it.

Terminal 4 at Madrid's Barajas Airport, which was led by Ivan Harbour, Simon Smithson and Amarjit ('Amo') Kalsi, a great designer who tragically died in 2015, is rather more elegant, perhaps closer to what we originally planned at Heathrow. It took eight years from competition to completion, compared to Heathrow's 19 years. Canyons cut through the middle of what is essentially a four-storey building, bringing natural light into all areas while minimising solar gain from the harsh summer sun of central Spain. There is a natural progression under the oversailing roof from parking and public transport to planes, and back again, with arriving and departing passengers able to see each other, but still segregated in line with the dictates of security.

The 1.2km-long departures pier of the main building, with 40 boarding gates, is given scale and legibility, identity and delight, through the rainbow-coloured succession of 'trees' holding up the steel roof. It's a lot easier and more fun telling a friend that you are by the lime green columns at Gate 25, rather than just giving numbers, and the array creates drama and excitement for arrivals and departures. Above and below these exuberant colours, the use of natural stone for the floor, and the cladding of the roof with sustainable Chinese bamboo strips, creates warmth often lacking in airport buildings.

As aircraft become quieter and less polluting, the role of airports too can change. They can become urban spaces, airport cities where people, friends and strangers can meet, rather than being relegated to the edge of cities. Our recent designs for Mexico City began to explore the potential for this more civic role, and our winning competition entry for Taoyuan Airport in Taiwan takes adaptability to the next level. Its dynamic roof design can quickly remodel interior spaces to enhance passengers' experience, and adapt to accelerating changes in technology, security and mobility requirements.

Inside Barajas T4, the coloured 'trees' give reference points for passengers, while the bamboo-lined roof creates a warm, humane environment.

Maggie's Centre – A Place of Comfort in Crisis

The Hammersmith Maggie's Centre, one of a network of cancer care centres named after the writer and garden designer Maggie Keswick, is a place for people at a very different scale, a haven for people at one of the most difficult times of their lives. Maggie and her husband Charles Jencks, the cultural theorist, were old friends of ours, and I remember Maggie talking about her diagnosis: one moment you are attending a hospital appointment to hear some test results; the next moment, you are told you have cancer, your life has changed, and you are back out on the street. Maggie's can provide a humanising space between.

Maggie's centres are designed to feel like homes, not institutions, medical or bureaucratic. They deal with the person not the illness. In the Hammersmith Maggie's Centre, which won the 2009 Stirling Prize for best building by a British architect, the first thing you see when you open the door is the kitchen with the kettle and the wood-burning stove. There are comfortable chairs, and a view out over a secret garden created in one corner of the busy hospital site. If architects create shelter, then Maggie's is the shelter that we all need at a particularly vulnerable moment. My son Ab is now designing the largest centre in the network at the Royal Marsden Hospital in Sutton, together with his business partner, the architect Ernesto Bartolini.

Ivan Harbour led the team for Maggie's and the Cancer Centre at Guy's Hospital, which takes a similar approach, paying as much attention to personal experience as it does to medical excellence. Patients arrive at an airy and non-clinical welcome zone, surrounded by a cluster of two- to three-storey 'villages', each offering specific services. There are none of the bleak corridors associated with hospitals, and rather than turning away from the city, The Cancer Centre remains connected, using natural light throughout, and providing balconies with stunning views across London.

Central skylights fill the building with natural light, while louvres minimise glare and solar gain from the Spanish sun.

Left and right: Maggie's West London in the grounds of Charing Cross Hospital has at its heart the kitchen table, the kettle and the stove.

Maggie's centres, founded by the late Maggie Keswick, provide shelter and comfort for cancer patients in a non-medical setting.

8 Layers of Life

I am enjoying my life so much more today than in my youth, when I felt isolated and treated as stupid because of my dyslexia. Teamwork and the overlapping layers of work, family and friends have liberated me from this sense of isolation. In the book that accompanied our 2007 exhibition, *Richard Rogers + Architects: From the House to the City,* Renzo Piano said that I could be 'a humanist at 9 o'clock in the morning, a builder at 11, a poet just before lunch and a philosopher at dinner time'. If that's true, then I consider myself lucky.

Ruthie is at the centre of this rich mix of life and work. She is my closest friend and my intellectual partner. We have always worked together – editing books, planning exhibitions, campaigning, getting involved in charitable and community causes – and I count the day a disaster if I don't speak with her at least six times. People see us walking arm in arm at parties, and think that we are inseparable, which we are, though we have to stay close so that Ruthie can whisper people's names in my ear. Following the move to Leadenhall, what I miss most is not working alongside her – the spontaneous cups of coffee at the River Café, asking her over to look at a drawing, visiting the kitchen to taste a soup. But we are still on the phone to each other through the day, talking about changes at the practice, staffing at the River Café, the menu, political protests, plans for parties and charity benefits, potential new hires and openings. Our lives are so tightly twined together.

Royal Avenue

When we found our house on the corner of Royal Avenue and St Leonard's Terrace in Chelsea, it was the view and the light we fell in love with. In one direction was the 'countryside' – the grounds of Wren's Royal Hospital, with the Thames beyond – and in the other the vitality of city life on the King's Road.

With Ruthie on the lightweight staircase leading up to the piazza at Royal Avenue.

The Royal Hospital is an understated English manor house, home for 360 years to army veterans, its yeoman stolidity contrasting sharply with the refined, expressive grandeur of Les Invalides, its Parisian equivalent. Royal Avenue itself was intended to be a grand processional route from the Royal Hospital to Kensington Palace, but it never actually got beyond King's Road. As ever, London resisted grand plans and I like to imagine the eighteenth-century landowner who put his foot down, bringing the whole project grinding to a halt. Ruthie always says that it is fitting that we live alongside a failed urban project.

The house is south-facing, with light flooding in from three sides. Georgian architecture at its best, from cottages to palaces, is strongly articulated, with proportions that support repetition and extension. The regularity of the façades at Royal Avenue allowed us huge flexibility, as we carved out the interior to create something new. Georgian houses are almost a precursor to modern curtain-walled buildings; rather than windows that define the spaces behind them – a big bay window for the living room or a small window above a sink in the kitchen – the same pattern is repeated. Behind the façade, you can put anything you like.

We moved the main entrance from a formal Georgian front door to an inconspicuous side door on Royal Avenue, leading into an internal courtyard, previously a small north-facing garden, which we glazed over. From here you can see the whole five storeys, from the mezzanine and bedrooms above to the basement below. The top of the stairs is an explosion of space and light; the triple-height main room, the 'piazza' as some friends call it, washed with light from twelve traditional full-height sash windows, and the glazed roof over the staircase. After living in the Place des Vosges in Paris, where the main room was large enough for children to ride their bikes, Ruthie wanted the same sense of space in London.

The house is essentially open-minded and social, with bedrooms and bathrooms wrapping round the central space, and guest flats below. A mezzanine – originally designed as a bedroom, but now our study and library – is supported on a T-joint of steel beams painted rich lapis lazuli blue, with high gloss enamel paint usually used for painting helicopter fuselages. Contemporary American paintings hang on the walls; bright-coloured Mexican model animals, and more personal treasures like my mother's simple stoneware pots grouped in their 'village' clusters, are on a low-level shelf beneath them.

There is often a party in the piazza – a friend's book launch, a charity benefit, an extended-family celebration, our annual celebration of the architect of the Serpentine Pavilion in Hyde Park. Like the River Café, Royal Avenue is a place to gather. On quieter days, there may be grandchildren

Left and above left: The double-height living space – our internal piazza – at Royal Avenue, with light flooding in from twelve windows and our stainless steel open kitchen under the mezzanine.

running around, friends visiting, four different conversations taking place in different languages in different parts of the room. At the centre, as at Creek Vean and Parkside, is a stainless steel kitchen – the focus of our family life, where Ruthie and I sit on high stools to talk at the beginning and end of the day. The house has a rhythm: I can see the sun rising as I begin to work in the peace of early morning, and we can watch it setting from the roof terrace in the evening.

Our bedroom is at the top of the house. Every morning we wake to the view over the Royal Hospital. The other bedrooms are at the back of the house – Roo's room still has the Ron Arad chair that he saved up to buy when he was a teenager, and Bo's collection of model aeroplanes is still on his shelves – with a steel spiral staircase connecting them and the roof terrace, which runs over the whole length of the building. From the terrace – the only place in the house where we cannot hear phones or doorbells – we can see Big Ben, Westminster Cathedral, the V&A, the Shard and now Leadenhall.

Ab has worked with us to adapt the house, as it has evolved over the years. Now in partnership with my cousin Ernesto Bartolini, Ab's design practice also worked on both my recent exhibitions – *Inside Out* at the Royal Academy in 2013, and *From the House to the City* at the Pompi-

dou Centre in 2007 – and helped create the visual language of this book too. Like me, he is dyslexic, though his spelling is even worse than mine; I asked once why he didn't use his spellchecking software, and he replied that the programmes couldn't even guess what words he was typing. We talk nearly every day about buildings, art and design.

Below the main living areas, on the ground floor there is a flat that Ruthie's parents, Fred and Sylvia Elias, moved to from New York a few months after we completed Royal Avenue. They lived there for the rest of their lives – independent, but near enough at hand to receive regular visits from their grandchildren and great-grand-children, who were always indulged with love. In the early hours of the morning, Roo and later Bo would come to wake us up in our top-floor bedroom, and would be persuaded to creep down the spiral stairs to see their grandparents instead. As Sylvia used to say, 'It's a grandparent's role to say, "Yes"' – a role we now have with our 12 grandchildren – Eve, Thea, Merle, Rita, Ivy, Asa, Sasha, Ella, Lula, Ruby, Mei and Coco.

Thames Wharf

Upriver is Thames Wharf, an easy four-mile bike ride away, which was home to my practice for as long as Royal Avenue has been home to my family.

After returning from Paris, we had found a Notting Hill office, a beautiful white brick building with its own courtyard in a quiet mews, which had been used as the location for David Hemmings' photography studio in Antonioni's *Blow-Up.* Our original aim was to cap the office size at 30 – the number you could reasonably fit round a large dining table. But by the early 1980s, we had rapidly grown to 60; we were busy with the closing stages of the Lloyd's Building, Coin Street, the National Gallery competition, and industrial buildings for Inmos, the Cummins Engine Company and PA Technologies. We needed more space.

John Young loved to explore London's waterways on his bike, and one day he came across a dilapidated collection of riverside oil warehouses backing on to quiet residential streets, with views of Hammersmith Bridge and the ornate Harrods Repository on the other side of the Thames. John, Marco Goldschmied and I bought the site, and then sold half of it to a developer for housing (which we designed, giving John the chance to build his penthouse flat on the top floor). In this way, we could cross-subsidise the redevelopment and extension of the main block, which would house the practice. Working with Lifschutz Davidson, we created a two-storey light-filled arch on top of the building.

Thames Wharf had been a run-down industrial dead end; we opened it up to the river and the city. Having battled for years for better public space, we finally had the opportunity to create our own place for people. The courtyard garden between the office and the River Café is open 24 hours a day, with a picnic table looking out over the river. It was designed by my old friend Georgie Wolton, not just to enhance the buildings and their setting on the banks of the Thames, but also to act as a safe, enclosed kitchen garden, where children can play while their parents eat, drink and talk at the River Café.

We wanted Thames Wharf to feel like part of the city, not a reclusive enclave like so many industrial buildings were in the past and so many riverside properties are today. And we wanted that spirit of openness and relaxation to permeate our practice inside the building too. Hugh Pearman likes to tell a story about his fellow critic, the late Martin Pawley, returning from visiting us one day. 'How was it?' asked Hugh. 'Oh, you know,' said Martin with an expansive gesture. 'Troubadours strumming guitars in the corridors...' We didn't really have any corridors at Thames Wharf, but it's just about right in other ways.

The River Café

In 1987, as we were finishing the conversion works at Thames Wharf, one of the leases in the building alongside ours came up. Ruthie and I wanted to develop a community with a place to eat together, so we looked at a number of restaurants who wanted to move in, but none of them seemed quite right. The only thing worse than no restaurant would be the wrong sort of restaurant, and in one of those life-changing moments, Ruthie said, 'Maybe I'll do it.' She sought out Rose Gray, whom I had met with Su more than 30 years previously.

Neither Ruth nor Rose had experience in restaurants, but both shared a passion for Italian cooking. Rose had lived for three years with her family in Lucca in the early 1980s and had helped open the kitchen at Nell's night-club in New York, and Ruthie had learned from my mother (an exceptional cook, who had herself only started cooking when she came over to England in 1939) and from spending hours in the kitchen with my family in Florence.

In the beginning, Ruthie and Rose offered sandwiches as well as hot food, taking it in turns to cook the day's dishes using a domestic oven. Some of those – including the grilled squid with chilli, and the pear and almond tart – are still on the menu today. From the beginning they had clear principles: to cook regional Italian food, to change the menu every day, for everyone to participate in the process of preparing and serving meals, to be seasonal and sustainable, and to source the best ingredients. The River Café menu had its roots in Tuscany, though later both menu and wine list extended to other parts of Italy.

Rose and Ruthie in the River Café. From the beginning everyone has worked together to prepare the day's menu.

Thames Wharf was out on a limb, and even London cabbies had trouble finding it at first. The restaurant was also constrained in its opening times by our location in the middle of a residential neighbourhood. The River Café started off by operating only at lunchtime, initially for people working in the warehouses. Then it opened to the public at lunchtime, then in the evening too, first until 11p.m. but now until midnight. Its reputation grew, and after seven years it began to make a profit. Ruthie and Rose became like sisters, finishing each other's sentences, laughing together, and sharing the same blend of warmth towards their team. Their unflinching commitment was to make every dish just as it should be, day after day.

Rose was diagnosed with breast cancer in 2003, but continued to work closely with Ruthie, at the River Café and on their cookbooks. Even

Left: Ruthie by the bright wood-fired oven at the River Café, where everything from turbot to pigeons to langoustines is cooked.

Below: Lunchtime at the River Café.

Right: Thames Wharf, with people eating on the River Café's terrace, chatting in the sunken garden, or just strolling along the river bank.

Above: John Young's beautiful penthouse flat at Thames Wharf includes a sleeping platform suspended above the seating area.

Right: The RRP offices at Thames Wharf, with the roof extension designed with Lifschutz Davidson. I miss the view from the top floor over the Thames.

when she was seriously ill, they would discuss the menu every day, and she would taste and acutely critique dishes that were sent to her. She died on 28 February 2010.

The River Café cooks the Italian food that I love most, and it has a unique ethos and atmosphere. The long room is suffused with light and reflections, at once animated and calm. Outside, on a summer's afternoon, the garden feels like London's best secret: hidden away down residential backstreets, with children playing on the lawn while their parents eat under the trees among the planters filled with fresh herbs and vegetables.

It became a part of the office, a place to have a quiet meeting with partners, to sketch designs on paper table cloths, to meet and talk with young architects who had joined the practice.

Everyone at the café works in daylight and can walk down to the river for a break. If restaurant kitchens have a reputation for machismo, then the River Café is the opposite. It is based on communication and teamwork. When you go there first thing in the morning, the waiters are helping to prepare the food, partly so that they can understand it and talk about it to customers, but also to reflect the spirit of collaboration, of joint endeavour, that Rose and Ruthie instilled.

Left: My son Zad reads 'The 80 Colours of Richard Rogers' at my 80th birthday celebration.

The spirit of the River Café is well-captured in the two films that Zad, my second son, made. Zad is a television and media producer. Together with Harriet Gugenheim, Ben's wife, he made a movie for Ruthie's 60th birthday, which showed the whole family singing together, and wrote a moving and beautiful poem (*The 80 Colours of Richard Rogers*), which he read out at our family celebration of my 80th birthday.

Holidays and Family

Both Ruthie and I love our work, and everything, even holidays, is a continuous part of the whole. I don't garden, cook or have any hobbies; my family is my focus. Now that our sons, their partners and our grandchildren are all gathered together in London, we try to see them every week or two, and speak every day. If Ruthie is away or working in the River Café, I will invite myself to one of their houses for supper.

When the children were young, we took them on adventurous trips – to Moroccan deserts, Mexican pyramids and Nepalese temples – and they've all inherited this spirit of adventure. But over the years it has become more important for us to return to the places where they grew up, and can now bring their own children, and where we have built strong friendships and feel that we are part of the community.

Every August we visit the same farmhouse, converted by Giorgio and Ilaria Miani, two hours south of Florence, which we have rented for the past 20 years. The Val d'Orcia is a Unesco World Heritage Site, a stunning unspoilt valley, surrounded by rolling hills and dominated by the 1,700m Monte Amiata. Val d'Orcia was historically one of the poorest parts of Italy, held back by the heavy clays that formed its soil. The landscape was untouched by man until the 1930s, when Iris Origo, a wealthy Anglo-American woman, came to the valley, set up schools and health centres, and taught the local farmers modern techniques to help them enrich and work their land. Her book, *War in the Val d'Orcia,* is a fascinating account of her life during the Second World War, when she sheltered and helped many escaped prisoners of war.

The house is within 30 minutes of four beautiful villages. Montalcino is a medieval fortress town now known for its excellent wine, Brunello di Montalcino. Montepulciano, which sits on a hilltop full of wine cellars, overlooks the magnificent church of San Biagio, with 'servant' towers that could have been devised by Louis Kahn. San Quirico d'Orcia surprises visitors with its simple high street and beautiful sixteenth-century gardens.

The hilltop town of Pienza is an early masterpiece of Renaissance town planning. It was designed in the fifteenth century, when the architect Bernardo Rosselino (a colleague of Leon Battista Alberti) was commissioned by Pope Pius II to remodel his native village, then called Corsignano. Rosselino devised a beautiful square framed by the town hall, a papal palace, a cardinal's palace and the cathedral, intersecting with an elegant main street, the Corso Rosselino, which runs between the town's two gates. There is a story that, when the work was done, Rosselino apologised to the Pope for not responding to any of his letters. Pius replied, 'If you had done, I would not have had this piece of heaven!'

There is rarely a bed free as family and friends converge, and now our grandchildren visit with their friends. For a month, we enjoy swimming in the pool, long lunches, walks in the cool of the morning, a passeggiata and sunset drinks in a nearby village. Conversations and debates go on long into the evening, and I start each morning watching the sunrise from the terrace, as I work through papers and projects.

In 1993 our love affair with another country began when Ricardo Legorreta invited us to visit Mexico – we were immediately entranced by

its light, its bright colours, its open-minded architecture. We first stayed in a dramatic house overlooking the Pacific, designed and owned by Carlos and Heather Herrera. Since then, we have travelled all round, and in recent years we have more or less settled in Oaxaca, staying at Norma and Rodolfo Ogarrio's beautiful courtyard house in historical Oaxaca City, visiting Monte Alban, and spending Christmases with family near Puerto Escondido.

But there will always be one person missing. Bo, our youngest son, was born in Tucson, Arizona, in 1983. We held him in our arms when he was just 36 hours old. It was one of the most moving moments of my life; though he was adopted, he immediately felt like part of me. From a young age, Bo was passionate about the world around him, in everything from the intrica-

cies of London Transport to the solar system, and had an incredible flair for languages – I remember him singing 'Happy Birthday' in Arabic. He loved school, but he hated exams, was suspicious of any trace of pretentiousness, and sought the company of his family and friends.

Bo worked in my office for three years, alongside his oldest friend Lorenz Frenzen, but began spending more and more time in Vernazza, a beautiful small village in the Cinque Terre on the Italian Riviera, that we have been visiting almost every year for 50 years. Unlike the constant arrivals and departures of Tuscany, Vernazza, which is only accessible by train or boat, is where we go just to be with family and close friends, enjoying the beautiful cliff-top walks to the next villages and the delicious food prepared by our good friend Gianni Franzi. When Roo and Bernie were married in the piazza there, the whole town joined the celebrations.

Bo had settled in Vernazza by October 2011, with his own close-knit group of friends, and was working in his friend Alberto's internet cafe. Everyone joked that 'Rogerino' (as he was known over there) was destined to one day become mayor. But one afternoon after months of dry weather, there was a colossal rainstorm, and a huge landslide, which killed three people. Bo helped people from the water, and was then evacuated by a Red Cross boat (other routes were blocked). I spoke to him that evening when he'd arrived in nearby Viareggio, and was so relieved to hear he was safe. I go over and over that call in my mind, and the terrible call we received from his friend Luna the next morning telling us that Bo had had a seizure and died.

There is no recovery from the death of a child. Death can push people apart or bring them together; we were brought together as a family. At the 'Remembering Bo' memorial at the River Café a month or so after

Vernazza (above left), a jewel in the Italian Cinque Terre, and a treasured place for all the family. Roo and Bernie were married there, and Bo (right) was living there when a landslip devastated the town in 2011 (left).

his death, Bo's brothers and sisters, and his friends from Vernazza, all spoke about their memories of him, and the sadness of a life cut short. His twelve nephews and nieces joined together to sing 'Leaving on a Jet Plane', reflecting his love of travel, and 'I Will Survive', his favourite song.

In November 2012, Ruthie and I spent a day choosing a tree for Bo's ashes, picking an Italian olive, which we planted above his bedroom on our roof terrace in Chelsea. Renzo and I designed a corten steel planter and a white cedar bench opposite it. Ruthie and I often go up there to sit together quietly with our memories, or to say goodbye to Bo when we go away. There are further trees at our dear friend Paddy McKillen's home in Provence, where he had provided us with sanctuary in the weeks after Bo's death, at Renzo' new wing for the Isabella Stewart Gardner Museum in Boston, and on the slopes at Courcheval. Every year on the anniversary of Bo's death, we travel together as a family on the number 19 bus from our house to the River Café, and then come home to talk about Bo, and sing songs around the tree. As a way of honouring Bo and his relationship to Vernazza, I worked with my cousin Ernesto Bartolini and the people of the town on a series of schemes to restore the streets and squares that were destroyed in the landslide.

Writing this book, I have found myself thinking more and more about my own parents, and my brother. Peter and I have become much closer as adults. He was born 15 years after me – a huge gulf when you are

young. I remember my pregnant mother asking me whether I wanted a little brother. I cruelly replied, 'I'd prefer a dog.' I used to say that I was more like my mother, while Peter, the analytical engineer, who co-founded the developer Stanhope with Stuart Lipton, and is now his partner in Lipton Rogers, was more like my father. But now we see more of each other in ourselves. His understanding of the process of building is phenomenal – he chaired Constructing Excellence, the national body dedicated to improving standards in construction – and his attention to detail is the perfect foil to Stuart's exceptional vision and passion for cities.

I have also realised more clearly how huge my parents' influence was. I spoke to Dada every day, and can easily see how her love of art, modernism and colour – embracing rather than recoiling from the new – has informed my choices, but I can also detect, just below the surface, the steel that drove my father Nino to climb mountains and bring his family to England.

My father died in 1993, my mother five years later. Nino lost some of his mental acuity as he aged – a tragedy for someone who set so much store by the power of the human intellect – but Dada remained sharp even at the age of 90, as the cancer that killed her spread. She felt people should age with dignity rather than trying to make themselves look younger, but she remained strikingly beautiful, maybe more beautiful as she got older; when she was in her 80s, Issey Miyake asked her to model for him. When it became clear that death was imminent, I stayed with her at Parkside, sleeping in the same bed, and talking about her life, about mine. Everybody was convinced that I was going to go to pieces when she died, because we were so close, but after the experience of spending that last month with her, I could accept her death peacefully.

In her last days, Dada told Ruthie that she should use more cream on her face and less herbs on her fish. And one of the last, and most characteristic, things she said to me was that the problem with death was that she'd miss seeing the future.

Left: With my brother Peter in 2016.

Right: Our granddaughter Mei using the staircase as a climbing frame.

9   Public Spaces

Nothing gives me greater pleasure than walking and pausing in lively public spaces, from small alleyways to great European squares. Public spaces are places for all people and stages for public life; the public realm is at the heart of our life as social animals; it enables the meeting of friends and strangers, for the exchange of goods and ideas, for political protest and for intimate moments.

Public spaces are the lungs of the city, an expression of society and a force for democracy, the places where there is a mix of activities and people from all classes, all creeds and all races. Whether it is Zuccotti Park in New York, Tiananmen Square in Beijing, Taksim or Tahrir, public spaces are where people can come together to debate, to demonstrate, to demand change. Plaza de la Constitución – known as 'the Zocalo' – has been the centre of civic life in Mexico City since pre-Colombian times. Every parliament should have space outside for public demonstrations; the fact that the UK government seeks to banish demonstrators from Parliament Square is an embarrassment.

Cities are civilised by the treatment of their public domain – their sidewalks, parks and rivers. When we visit a foreign city, these are the places we remember, as much as the façades or interiors of individual buildings. Architecture is not about discrete buildings viewed in isolation, but about the experience of cityscapes, about how buildings respond to topography, frame space and create the structure of cities. I love the way that narrow alleyways, with the sunlight creating a play of light and shadow on buildings, pavements and pedestrians, suddenly explode into the dazzling light of piazzas.

Good architecture should always seek to create well-designed public spaces, filling in and framing spaces so that streets and squares can become living rooms without roofs for citizens. But in today's all-commanding market economy, affordable housing and public space is constantly

Piazza del Campo in Siena, which started as a marketplace between neighbouring settlements, and later became the centre of political and civic life in one of the great Renaissance cities.

under threat – eroded and dehumanised. The architect and his team, the client and the city planner, need to defend these spaces, and champion their civilising effect on the city.

One of my first memories from my pre-war childhood is of looking out from my grandfather's house in Trieste. Opposite there was a cafe, of course, and every morning at about 7a.m., they pulled their shutters up, and would put a table and chairs outside, and a man would come and sit down. He was an accountant, and the pavement outside that cafe was his place of work. I thought it looked like the ideal job: your food and your coffee were looked after, and your customers and friends would come to you. It's the same in Djemaa el-Fna, the huge marketplace in Marrakesh, and in Indian cities, where clerks sit outside with typewriters, helping their clients with forms and letters.

Public space – big or small, noisy or quiet – reflects civic values. Greek and Roman civilisation centred on the experience of citizenship in the agora and forum. As settlements transformed into cities, the spaces of day-to-day activity – from trading goods to washing clothes – became the centrepieces of civic life.

The Agora and the Birth of Civic Life

Though the Renaissance had its roots in Florence, the city of my birth, where Masaccio, Donatello, Brunelleschi, Alberti and Dante flourished, the birth of democracy was some 2,000 years earlier, in classical Athens. Every time I visit the city, I head straight to the Agora, the ancient market-place and historic centre of civic life, to the Acropolis and the adjoining museum. I am always struck by the modernity of culture and philosophy, but also amazed by the public spaces and buildings that stand elevated above the city, built in a dramatic moment of creativity millions of years after the birth of man.

Time does not stand still, however. On 26 June 2016, I went back to Athens, not just to revisit the Acropolis, but also to attend the opening of Renzo Piano's new Stavros Niarchos Opera House and Cultural Centre. This too aspires to be something more than a building, more than just architecture. The building is completely contemporary, topped by a great white horizontal sail, held delicately in place by a perfect steel structure, creating a shaded public space with amazing views out across the city. From its elevated position above the coastal plain, the building looks back at the Acropolis.

The Passeggiata and the Piazza – Public Space in Italy

Public spaces have been integral to Italian cities for centuries, and it is to these streets and piazzas that I return again and again. They are the stage for that most Italian ritual, the passeggiata – the daily parade in the cool of the early evening.

Verona has some of the most beautifully designed pedestrian streets. The same stone is sculpted to fulfil different functions: kerbstones, grilles, drains, low splash panels of shop fronts, planters. The consistency of materials and finish lends a calm and elegant quality, so unlike the frenetic mess of street furniture, paving slabs, tarmac and concrete that disfigures many cities' thoroughfares. I met one man who said he moved from southern Italy to Verona, simply for these exquisitely paved streets.

Many Italian public spaces have long histories as meeting places. The Piazza del Campo in Siena, which today hosts the Palio horse race twice a year, was established at the meeting place of the three hillside settlements that formed the city. It was a marketplace, and then a place where women would gather to wash their clothes in the water channelled through Siena in aqueducts and canals. Its slope still represents the natural topography of the land and water today.

The nine segments of paving that radiate from the Palazzo Publico represent the Governo dei Nove, the merchants who ruled Siena in the fourteenth century. The marketplace was neutral territory between powerful families' strongholds; the centre of commercial and social life grew organically to become a centre of civic and political life, like the Agora in Athens or the Forum in Rome. The Piazza del Campo has been a great influence on my thinking about public spaces, but one that I absorbed almost without noticing it.

The centrality of public space was rediscovered in the Renaissance: more and more private spaces became opened up, like the great parks in London, and the piazzas and streets mapped by Nolli in his 1740 plan of Rome. When Nolli drew his map, around 60 per cent of Rome's footprint was open to the public – markets, squares, parks, churches, baths, theatres. Rome was an open city.

Campidoglio is the site of Rome's ancient citadel, its geographical and ceremonial centre. It remained a centre for government (Rome's City Hall is still at one end of the square), but had become dilapidated by the sixteenth century, when Michelangelo was asked to redesign it by Pope Paul III.

Michelangelo's design emphasised Campidoglio's position as a lynchpin between the Forum of ancient Rome on one side, and 'modern',

Our masterplan for the banks of the River Arno in Florence, the city of my birth, was a precursor to the exhibition *London As It Could Be* (1986). We proposed a linear park, passing under the Ponte Vecchio, with performance spaces, cafes and green spaces, to bring life back to the river banks, cut off by heavy traffic on the embankment. Heritage considerations prevented the plans from being realised.

papal Rome on the other. He remodelled the buildings surrounding the irregularly shaped and sloping piazza, creating a beautiful flight of steps (the cordonata) leading up from papal Rome to the capital, connecting the two cities. The piazza was paved in a stunning pattern of interlocking circles in travertine marble, seemingly an oval but actually egg-shaped to fit in the irregular space. Marking the centre of the piazza is a statue of the Emperor Marcus Aurelius, mounted on a horse. I visited once with the painter Philip Guston, who commented with enthusiasm on the horse's 'stupendous rump'.

Campidoglio is small but exquisitely proportioned. The views west are breathtaking, particularly at sunset, as you see all Roman history laid out before you, linking not just centuries but millennia.

Campidoglio was designed as a totality, but many of our most loved public spaces have been the result of accretion, not creation, growing over time, enriching themselves with new buildings and uses, creating harmony from sometimes startling contrasts. There is no better example of this than Piazza San Marco, whose apparent harmony is actually composed from dramatically different buildings. The square, alongside St Mark's Church and the Doges' Palace, was first cleared in the early thirteenth century, and was enclosed by government and charitable offices on three sides, built over three centuries. These buildings, which have been changed and updated over time, all had arcades and space for shops on their ground floor, giving life to the public space in front of them, and creating a coherence and consistency to the piazza's north, west and south sides.

Later in the thirteenth century St Mark's Church, on the east side of the piazza, was extended and embellished with domes and turrets, and encrusted with marble, amazing mosaics and sculptures. More than a hundred years later, the tall campanile was added, an addition that must have seemed colossal and alien at the time (and would never have received planning permission today), but now looks integral.

San Marco's architecture is an ornate mix of styles, and a living illustration of the point that harmony can lie in contrast as well as consistency, but it suits the city's damp and sometimes grey climate more than Palladian classicism, which needs sunshine to define its sharp lines. It is a tribute to the creativity that city-states can demonstrate, and a symbol of mercantile prosperity; through the window of the smaller piazzetta alongside the Doges' Palace, the piazza looks across the Grand Canal to Palladio's San Giorgio Maggiore, and beyond to the sea – the source of Venice's power.

I have been visiting Venice, the pre-eminent pedestrian city, ever since I was a child, when we used to go with my grandparents. Two of the cafes – Florian and Quadri – are still there today. I remember my grandparents explaining that one was left wing and the other right wing; but I could never remember which is which, and still can't. It is the perfect compact city without trains or cars, where one walks or takes a vaporetto from place to place, shimmering in its mysterious soft blue-grey light. Nowadays, Ruthie and I visit in the winter, when the city is melancholic and wrapped in mist, often to remember our son Bo's birthday. It is never more beautiful than at dawn, or when floodwaters drive tourists away and create reflections of light and buildings throughout the city.

The Erosion of Public Space

In the twentieth century, public space came under attack from two enemies. Urban enclosures privatised what had once been public, and replaced 'open-minded' mixed streets of overlapping functions with sterile, single-use precincts designed simply to maximise consumption and profit – heavily policed and exclusive to those with enough money, the right clothes or the right coloured skin. I was so shocked on my first visit to Houston in 1983, where we had been commissioned to design a new shopping mall. In the heat of a Texan summer, the rich moved from air-conditioned homes, into air-conditioned cars, and then into air-conditioned underground shopping malls with security guards posted at entrances. The poorer people lived above ground in a parallel universe of baking hot streets that were derelict and poorly maintained.

This dereliction of the public realm epitomises J. K. Galbraith's analysis of private affluence and public squalor; social injustice is laid bare. Even in London, which has changed beyond all recognition since I first arrived in 1939, we have only managed to build one major new public park in 100 years, and that took an Olympic Games. Meanwhile, the garden squares of Kensington and Belgravia remain locked, out of reach to everyone apart from property owners, their nannies and children. I argued for this to change when Ken Livingstone was mayor, but to no avail.

The car is the other enemy of our public space, and of cities as a whole. It has destroyed the spirit of community, eaten up the public realm, and demanded that cities be redesigned to meet its needs. Public space became road space, and the meeting places of people were torn up to meet the car's insatiable appetite for ring roads, roundabouts, highways and car parks, ripping the souls out of cities. Great highways severed communities and gobbled up land, occupying up to 60 per cent of the land area of cities like Los Angeles.

In the past 20 years, we have seen a slow revolution, rolling back the dominance of the car, and giving the pedestrian and cyclist, not the motorist, the upper hand. A lot of this is about simple changes to redress the balance: taking down the barriers that pen pedestrians like sheep and allow cars to dominate; creating raised extensions of pavements where these cross roads, so that it is pedestrians who have the right to move around the city smoothly; redesigning our roads to make space for cyclists. It is no accident that the cities voted the most liveable and the most enjoyable to visit are those where the car is controlled and the public can dominate the street.

Beginning to reclaim our cities from cars has already enabled the resurgence of downtown districts, and made our cities cleaner, healthier and more vital. Autonomous vehicles, which are forecast to be commonplace within ten years, will change our cities further, reducing deaths and injuries, transforming public space, increasing productivity and creating new industries.

The Danish architect Jan Gehl has made it his life's work to analyse and understand how people actually use public space, so that we can design streets and public spaces appropriately. His work has transformed Copenhagen, and cities from Melbourne to São Paulo have sought his advice in trying to rehumanise their public spaces. He came to London in 2004 and surveyed a cross-section of streets and squares, including Tottenham Court Road, Trafalgar Square and Waterloo, to see how the congestion charge could be used to create a better city centre for people. London's still fractured governance means that not everything was implemented – and Jan remains very critical of London's public realm – but his recommendations helped to shift the debate, from streets for cars to streets for people.

I have always seen public space as a human right, like the right to decent healthcare, food, education and shelter. Everyone should be able to see a tree from their window. Everyone should be able to sit out on their stoop, or on a bench in a local square. Everyone should be able to stroll to a park where they can walk, play with their children or just enjoy the changing seasons, within a few minutes. A city that cannot provide these rights is simply not civilised. Good public space is open-minded, to use the terminology developed by philosopher Michael Walzer; it does not try to define specific activities, but can accommodate anything – lovers meeting, quiet mourning, children playing, dog walking, political debate, reading, ball games, demonstrations, snowman building, picnics, exercise classes, dozing. Whether large or small, good public space is human in scale; the vast plazas beloved by dictators are designed for tanks and military parades, not civilised human interaction.

Public space is not just a civilising aspect of our cities. It makes a tangible difference to people's lives. Research undertaken for the UK's Commission for Architecture and the Built Environment found that people who could walk in parks or see green space from their windows live happier and healthier lives than those who cannot. [5]

London's Wasted Spaces – Coin Street, Trafalgar Square, South Bank

London has some of the best public spaces in the world, as well as some of the worst. The Royal Parks and Hampstead Heath are some of the most beautiful green spaces of any city, and to walk through them as they are thronged with people on a summer's evening is a delight. Unlike Central Park in New York, which is carved out from – and contrasts with – New York's strict grid system, London's great parks responded to the more human scale of the city, sometimes even creating an arcadian illusion of rurality. There are magnificent set pieces too. One of my favourites is the view from the bridge in St James's Park, with the domes and cupolas of Whitehall sitting alongside Big Ben and the more recent addition of the London Eye.

But for many years, these great parks were the exception. London's street life was as good as non-existent; social life was shut indoors, in smoky male-dominated pubs and clubs, not in the people-watching pavement cafe society of Paris or Rome. Leicester Square, Piccadilly Circus, Trafalgar Square were celebrated in song and popular culture, but bitterly disappointing when you actually saw them – mean gyratory systems for cars and buses.

At London's heart was its most neglected public space – the River Thames. The city of heavy industry and docks barred the public from the riverside. And, while the water quality had improved hugely since the 'great stink' that prompted Joseph Bazalgette to build proper sewers in the nineteenth century, the river was still a dirty and lifeless drain in the 1970s. The Festival of Britain had made a small inroad into the South Bank; its legacy the Royal Festival Hall, later joined by the National Theatre and National Film Theatre. But this remained an isolated glimmer of light, like an enclave or trading post in hostile territory, its back turned on south London. With changes in shipping and industrialisation, cities have begun to rediscover their waterfront. In Barcelona, new beaches were created for the 1992 Olympics. In Sydney, our practice has masterplanned and designed a new urban district on the former docks at Barangaroo, overlooking the spectacular Darling Harbour.

In London, the rediscovery of the waterfront has been a slow process. Our involvement began in 1978, when we were approached by Greycoat Estates, headed by Stuart Lipton. Greycoat had prepared a scheme for speculative offices to run along Coin Street, behind Denys Lasdun's National Theatre and the more nondescript buildings alongside it. The local community was up in arms about the encroachment of offices into their neighbourhood, and the lack of housing provision, and were heavily supported by Ken Livingstone, then leader of the GLC.

The planning application was due to go to a public enquiry in early 1979, where Greycoat's legal team feared it would be turned down, and we were asked (at the suggestion of RIBA president Gordon Graham, who had decided to promote Norman Foster and me as the future of British architecture, and helped both of us achieve some of our most important early commissions) to help develop a design that could get permission. We were tied up with Lloyd's at the time, so we agreed that Marco Goldschmied, one of the three partners at the time, would meet up with the developers to decline politely. He came back saying that he had tried and tried to say 'No',

Right: With Norman Foster at the Team 4 Reunion at the River Café in 2013.

but it had not worked. So, I tried, and got no further; Stuart was very persuasive. I insisted that we be allowed to revisit the balance of public and private space, to connect the new development to the riverfront, to add in housing, to build a bridge over the Thames. To my surprise, they agreed to everything.

I appeared at the first public enquiry armed only with initial sketches. We lost, but Stuart decided to try a second application, with a legal team that included Garry Hart, who I worked with for many years and who later became an adviser to Derry Irvine, Tony Blair's Lord Chancellor. Working with Laurie Abbott and Andrew Morris, we developed plans for a galleria running from Waterloo station down to the river, with shops and public space at ground level, offices above, service towers of varying height providing a new backdrop to the South Bank, and 300 homes for local people on the south side. We also proposed a pedestrian bridge, connecting the development to the north side of the river by Temple, to bring life to the South Bank and create a grand passegiata from Waterloo station to Aldwych.

These plans didn't satisfy the protestors, who only saw the office developments, rather than the revitalised public space that we were trying

Our plans for Coin Street (above) would have created a new walkway from Waterloo Bridge to the Thames, with a pedestrian bridge connecting to the North Bank (right).

Left: The walkway would have been within a glazed gallery, containing offices, shops and affordable housing.

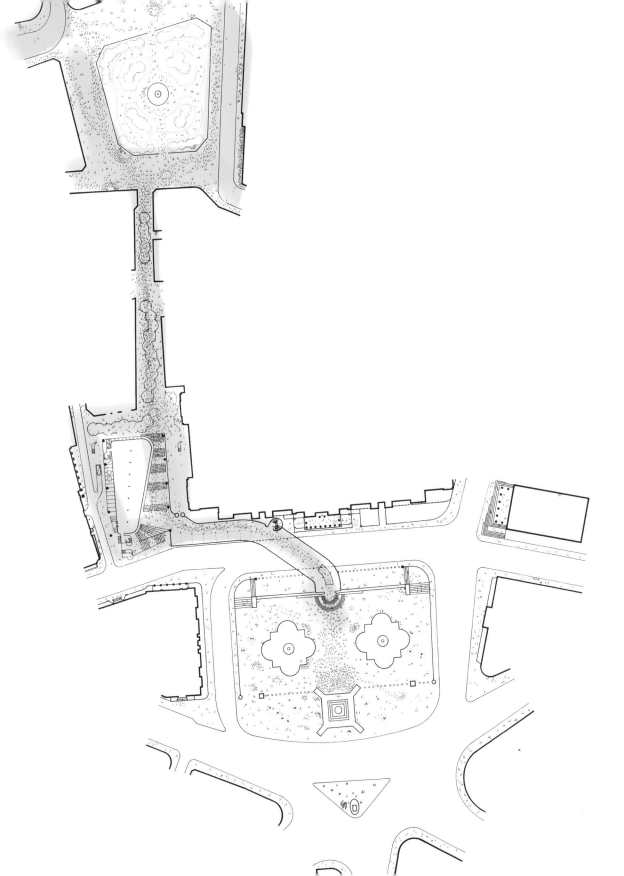

to create or the housing to be built alongside. Coin Street was a flash point in the gradual encroachment of office space outside London's established city centre, into areas that were traditionally dominated by working-class housing. It was an uncomfortable surprise to find myself arguing a developer's case against community groups (supported by Labour GLC leader Ken Livingstone) in the planning enquiry, but I found that I could deal with the cut-and-thrust of cross-examination quite well – a legacy of growing up in a household where debate and discussion were prized. Our practice was moving offices at the time, and the protestors heard about this and came to picket our moving-in party; Ruthie invited them in, and we had a great evening dancing and drinking, before returning to battle in front of the planning inspector the next morning.

Eventually, the planning minister Michael Heseltine granted permission both for our scheme and for the community housing scheme. It seemed a very English fudge, to give two schemes planning permission. I suspect his expectation was that it would only be the developers who could build their scheme. Greycoat Estates, who owned some but not all of the land, prepared to implement their plans, but the GLC intervened, providing the money to enable Coin Street Community Builders to buy the land, and take their scheme forward. This scheme stalled, so Greycoat were approached again, but by that stage Stuart had moved on and they had lost their appetite for the project. Now, of course, the Coin Street development and the Oxo Tower are at the heart of the incredible urban walkway that has been opened up on the South Bank, passing from Westminster to London Bridge, connecting Tate Modern, the South Bank Centre and Borough Market, and thronged with crowds every weekend.

On the other side of the river, Trafalgar Square, once the heart of an empire and strewn with imperial monuments, was essentially a congested roundabout in the early 1980s. Beyond political demonstrations and New Year's Eve celebrations, few ventured onto its pigeon-infested central areas. You had to take your life in your hands to get over the road, and there was nothing to do or see if you made it.

On the edge of this drab gyratory, the National Gallery needed space to expand. But in keeping with the Thatcherite spirit of the age, the additional gallery space was to be funded by building offices, and developers were invited to enter a competition together with architects. Speyhawk approached us, and we developed a scheme that lifted the new gallery space high in the air, with natural lighting above, and flexible servicing from below. Beneath this we showed office space, designed to be detachable, so that it might be replaced by gallery space if funding became available under a more enlightened administration.

Left: Our entry for the National Gallery extension competition in 1982 examined how we could strengthen the link between Leicester Square and Trafalgar Square.

Right: A model of our scheme, showing the public space created underneath the raised galleries, with the walkway connecting through to the centre of Trafalgar Square.

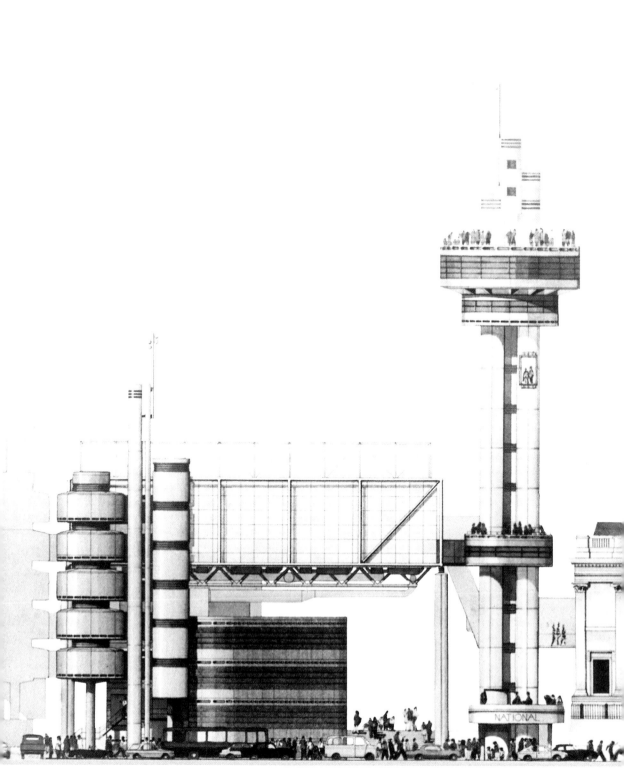

To one side, we placed an observation tower with a cafe on top, offering Londoners a vantage point in the heart of the city, and also forming a counterpoint with Nelson's Column, the classical cupola of the gallery and the elegant spire of St Martin-in-the-Fields. A leader in *The Times* praised our entry as 'large in conception, bold in execution, a gesture of architectural confidence', though talked of 'bathos' in the juxtaposition of a coffee shop with a spire pointing to heaven and a statue of a great war hero. But creating space for all people seemed every bit as important to me as glorifying a deity or an admiral.

We also undertook an extensive study of the local roads, looking to see whether there was any way of pedestrianising Trafalgar Square. We weren't able to justify pedestrianisation to our client, but we proposed lowering the ground under the extension, to create a sunken piazza, with an underground gallery leading south beneath the road into the heart of Trafalgar Square. To the north, we made new pedestrian connections with Leicester Square and Piccadilly Circus. We wanted to give London – 32 towns without a town square – the type of shared civic space that a capital city deserved.

RIBA president Owen Luder described our scheme as 'Sod you!' architecture, a remark that was intended to praise our lack of compromise, though the epithet did us damage in the public debate. Our proposals were more discussed for their striking architectural form than for our attempts to complement the monumentality of Trafalgar Square or to create new walking routes for Londoners. In the public exhibition, we attracted most votes, both for and against, though Hugh Casson, the competition chairman, hinted that we were not popular among some important people.

Our scheme came second to a design by Ahrends, Burton and Koralek, which adopted a similar language, but was never built, following the Prince of Wales's denunciation of it as a 'monstrous carbuncle'. These remarks, which did terrible and lasting damage to the reputation of one of the best studios of our time, stopped the process dead in its tracks. The National Gallery gave up on the idea of a developer-funded extension, and launched a new competition, restricted to architects who might be more acceptable to the heir to the British throne. The result was an extension that politely mimics the main building, but has no connection to today.

Our National Gallery scheme proposed raising the galleries off the ground, to maximise natural light and public space. Below them, commercial offices would be built to cross-subsidise the development, but could be replaced by galleries or other uses over time.

London As It Could Be

I had another opportunity to push these ideas at the 1986 Royal Academy exhibition featuring Jim Stirling, Norman Foster and myself, curated by the brilliant Norman Rosenthal. The three of us were given free rein, but asked to showcase experimental thinking. Jim and Norman exhibited recently completed buildings – Jim's Neue Staatsgalerie in Stuttgart and Norman's HSBC Building in Hong Kong – but I returned to the River Thames, and the strange absence where London's heart should be. The Thames had always felt like a canyon or a barrier, rather than a connector. In the 1960s, all city life seemed to be on the North Bank; the South Bank just had the Royal Festival Hall, County Hall, and old wharf buildings. I visited Lambeth's chief planner, responsible for this area, after I had left the AA, to ask whether we could convert some of the warehouses to homes and offices. He said that there might yet be a renaissance in port activity, so the riverside buildings should be preserved. Once more, the past was proposed as the blueprint for the future.

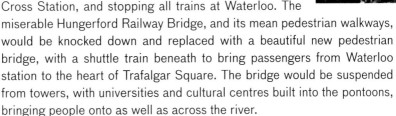

In 1986, we argued that the Thames should be transformed from a social and physical barrier – a canyon – to a connection. We proposed closing Charing Cross Station, and stopping all trains at Waterloo. The miserable Hungerford Railway Bridge, and its mean pedestrian walkways, would be knocked down and replaced with a beautiful new pedestrian bridge, with a shuttle train beneath to bring passengers from Waterloo station to the heart of Trafalgar Square. The bridge would be suspended from towers, with universities and cultural centres built into the pontoons, bringing people onto as well as across the river.

We would pedestrianise the north of Trafalgar Square (going further than we had dared to in our proposal for the National Gallery extension), and link it on a north–south axis to Leicester Square and Piccadilly Circus. On the east–west axis, the Embankment would become a great south-facing riverside park, joining up a series of half-hidden gardens and squares, with walkways, restaurants and cafes, and space beneath for cars to run in tunnels alongside the District Line.

The models made for the exhibition by Laurie Abbott and Philip Gumuchdjian (with whom I later wrote *Cities for a Small Planet*) were beautiful, with a shallow pool of water representing the Thames. One evening, a mischievous Jim Stirling added some goldfish to the water, thinking they would add some amusement the next day. But he had not

Above left: Trafalgar Square in the 1980s; a traffic-choked roundabout unworthy of a great city.

Left: A sketch of the proposed pedestrianisation of the north of Trafalgar Square from *London As It Could Be*, the 1986 Royal Academy exhibition of work by Norman Foster, Jim Stirling and me. Fifteen years later, Norman's detailed designs for the proposal would be realised.

Right: HSBC Main Building in Hong Kong, designed by Norman Foster and completed in 1985. It was exhibited at the Royal Academy in 1986, alongside my *London As It Could Be* plans.

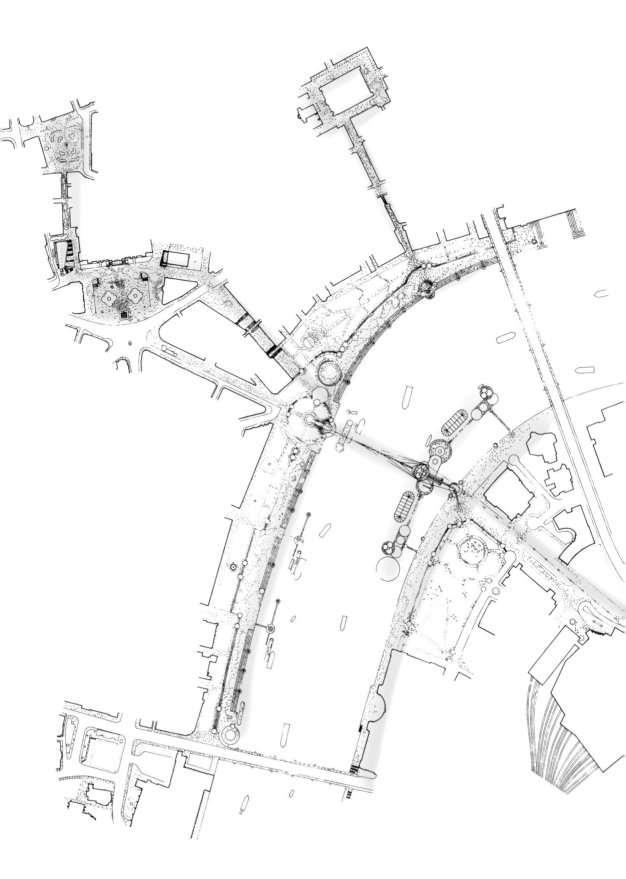

considered the water circulation system, which chewed up the goldfish and spat them out in pieces, making the water more horror film than fairground until it was drained and replaced (the incident attracted a formal complaint from the RSPCA).

London As It Could Be was the most popular architectural show that the Royal Academy had ever held (until *Inside Out* in 2013), but it also illustrated how hard it was to make anything happen in London. We looked at the feasibility of building the new bridge, but discovered that 70 separate permissions were needed to build a bridge over the Thames, any one of whom could stop it. And London's government was fragmenting too: the Greater London Council was in its last days, leaving the city without any strategic city-wide government from 1987 to 2000, by which time some of the ideas we were pushing would start to resurface.

Charing Cross Station is still there, and its rebuilding effectively blocked any plans for relocation, but the footbridge to the South Bank has been improved enormously, and the pedestrianisation of Trafalgar Square has been a huge success. In 1994, we won a competition to revitalise the South Bank Centre, and proposed a new 'crystal palace' – an undulating glass roof, oversailing the 1960s buildings but leaving the Royal Festival Hall rising above it. Alongside new pedestrian connections, this would have created a new mixed-use centre on the South Bank and a shop window for the arts, but the scheme ran into funding and community relations problems and was never completed.

Public Space – London Deserves Better

Many of London's public spaces still let us down. Street life still fights for space with haphazard street furniture, badly parked cars and ugly paving half patched up with great gobs of tarmac. Many of what should be great spaces – like Leicester Square – have been turned into neon-lit outdoor malls. And our incredible heritage of garden squares is still mainly behind lock and key, inaccessible for the citizen and hardly used by the rich whose flats overlook them.

There are pinpricks of light. The Olympic Park in east London has been beautifully landscaped and is gradually finding its long-term function, giving a heart to an area that lacked good green space for many years. It is now home to London's youngest and fastest growing neighbourhoods, connected along revitalised canals to Islington, Camden and King's Cross, where lively new (privately managed) public space has opened up what were once deserted rail lands or dangerous back alleys, for students, office workers and passers-by.

Our 1986 plans for a new bridge connecting Waterloo to the Embankment, flanked by floating islands with new restaurants, galleries and universities. Charing Cross Station would be closed, and a shuttle would bring visitors and commuters over to a North Bank reinvented as a linear park.

The Embankment
reborn as a pedestrian
space, from *London
As It Could Be* (1986).
This terrace, in front
of Somerset House,
would reclaim the river-
front for pedestrians,
with cars and other
motor vehicles buried
in tunnels beneath.
Burying roads in
tunnels seemed like a
good solution at the
time; today the focus
is more on taking more
surface space for
cyclists and pedestri-
ans, with congestion
charging to reduce
car use. Connecting
the linear parks and
public spaces along
the Embankment is still
unrealised.

The South Bank has finally been opened up, offering London's greatest public spaces, enlivened by festivals and thronged by Londoners and visitors all the time. Dedicated cycle lanes have been put in place across the city, and many car-choked gyratories are being replaced by more civilised two-way streets, as at Aldwych, where my daughter-in-law Lucy Musgrave's practice Publica have included this as part of their strategy for the area. All citizens should have the right to space. We are slowly moving forward, but there is so much left to do.

The pedestrian bridge, with monorail running beneath, which we proposed to replace the railways running into Charing Cross.

At the 1986 Royal Academy exhibition, alongside the models for our bridge and floating islands.

MANIFESTO FOR LONDON

THE BATTLE for London is on. It may not be official, but the General Election campaign has already started in all but name, and nowhere will that battle be more closely fought than in London. Seventy-four seats are there for the taking, and Labour will fight hard to increase its holding. To win the election, Labour must win London. If the Conservatives lose London, they almost certainly lose the country.

But for either party to win the votes of Londoners, they must also win the hearts and minds of Londoners. They must learn what are the fears and concerns of the people, what their hopes and desires are. They must do what few politicians do: they must listen.

This time last year they had an unparalleled opportunity to listen. The Evening Standard with the Corporation of London and the Architecture Foundation mounted a series of debates entitled London in the 21st Century in which, for the first time in more than 50 years, Londoners had a chance to express their views on how the city should be run. From professionals and

LONDON IN THE **21st** century

Sponsored by
The Evening Standard &
The Corporation of London

The Evening Standard's conferences on the future of London — launched a year ago this week — were the biggest public consultation about the capital for 50 years. With a General Election just a month or two away, we commend to the politicians the ideas that the debates inspired. **VALENTINE LOW** reports

activists, they all had their turn at saying what sort of city they wanted to live in.

The result exceeded all expectations. The debates — held at Westminster Central Hall after the planned venue turned out to be too small — were packed to the rafters, with more than 2,000 people turning up each time to talk, listen, shout, heckle, clap and even stamp their feet. The atmosphere was electric as a whole range of ideas was exchanged, from the radical and the shocking to ones

platform before. Here was democracy in action, with the knowledge, experience and plain good sense of the people often coming as a breath of fresh air after the safe, bland and empty rhetoric of the politicians.

Not since the war and the publication of Abercrombie's County of London and Greater London Plans in 1943 and 1944 has there been such a wide and open consultation of London's inhabitants about the future of their city.

best what needs to be done to improve our city are those who experience it every day. Who knows better than commuters what the most effective transport systems could be? How better to improve the capital's dilapidated tower blocks than by asking the people who actually have to live in them?

Democracy itself was one of the key themes. For more than 10 years, since Margaret Thatcher abolished the GLC there has been no single elected body to look after the interests of Londoners; one of the highlights of the debates was when Tony Blair put himself firmly behind calls for a single elected authority — and an elected mayor — for London. Those who attended the debates were in no doubt that London needs a democratically elected authority to deal with strategic planning issues. London is the only capital city with no planning authority, even though the Thames, public transport, air pollution, sewage and water are not issues which respect borough boundaries.

It was also clear that something needs to be done about public transport.

10 Citizenship and the Compact City

We couldn't believe our eyes. The vast domed space of Westminster Central Hall was nearly full, and the queue was still snaking out of the building. It was 1996, and I was chairman of the Architecture Foundation, which had planned a series of public debates on the future of London.

While cities across Europe were resurgent, London felt becalmed. Lucy Musgrave, who was running the debates (and later took over from Ricky Burdett as the foundation's second director), had been over to Berlin to see how its Stadtforum brought citizens together with politicians, in order to discuss new ideas and schemes for a city that had just been reunified after the fall of the Berlin Wall. Inspired by this model, we planned a series of debates on 'London in the 21st Century' – on public space, transport, culture, housing, future visions, the River Thames.

The Architecture Foundation had been set up by Ricky Burdett and me in 1991 as an independent centre for architectural debate, events and initiatives, seeking to provide some of the strategic thinking that London and other UK cities lacked. We assembled a brilliant board of political, cultural and design leaders, including the director of the Tate, Nick Serota, the architect Zaha Hadid, the developer Stuart Lipton, planning lawyer Garry Hart and editor and journalist Simon Jenkins. The foundation had run exhibitions and design competitions in Southwark, Croydon and for a 'foyer' (a continental model of residential centre for unemployed young people) in Birmingham.

For the debates, the foundation used its far-reaching network to gather urban thinkers from London and abroad – from the mayor of Barcelona Pasqual Maragall and the German ecologist Herbert Girardet to *The Guardian's* editor Alan Rusbridger and the Labour Party's new leader Tony

Left: The London *Evening Standard*'s report on the debates, held in 1996, about London in the twenty-first century.

Above right: Ricky Burdett, who set up the Architecture Foundation with me in 1991, and now leads the LSE Cities programme.

Right: Lucy Musgrave, who worked with Ricky on the debates, and now runs the urban design practice Publica.

Blair. But we expected the events to be of selective interest, and had hired St James's Piccadilly, a beautiful Wren church with a capacity of around 400 people, to host them. However, board member Andreas Whittam Smith, a founding editor of *The Independent* newspaper, had convinced the *Evening Standard* – London's local paper – to help us with publicity, and within days of launching more than 1,000 people had signed up for each debate, despite our assurances to St James's that these would be low-key events. We managed to switch venue to Westminster Central Hall and around 15,000 people came to the seven debates, with taxi drivers and market traders joining in the conversation alongside architects and planners. It was a powerful rebuke to anyone who claimed Londoners weren't interested in politics or planning.

The debates generated ideas that still influence London today – including an integrated transport authority, more priority for walking and cycling, higher-density housing, reclamation of derelict land, new pedestrian bridges in the heart of London, and the pedestrianisation of Parliament and Trafalgar squares.

I had been pushing the last idea since the *London As It Could Be* exhibition at the Royal Academy in 1986. On the evening of the third debate, with the enlightened Conservative minister John Gummer and the visionary Herbert Girardet alongside me on the panel, I asked the audience of 2,500 to consider the potential of these great civic spaces, and then for a show of hands. There was overwhelming support for pedestrianisation. Subsequently, Gummer, who had ministerial responsibility for London among a great many other things, called together a cross-Whitehall meet-

ing to discuss pedestrianising the squares. This eventually led first to the pedestrianisation of Trafalgar Square, with Norman Foster commissioned to undertake the detailed design, and then to a scheme for Parliament Square, which sadly was dropped when Boris Johnson took over as mayor in 2008.

Perhaps most dramatically, at the debate focused on London's future, Simon Jenkins provoked Tony Blair into announcing that, if he won the following year's election against John Major's

Ecologist Herbert Girardet at the London in the 21st Century debates.

increasingly fragile Conservative government, he would legislate for a mayor of London. After a gap of ten years, subject to a public referendum, the capital would again have an elected leader (as it turned out, the same one who had led the Greater London Council in 1987). Both politicians and the public – it seemed – were taking the state of our capital city seriously again.

The Death and Life of Great Cities

It had all been very different ten years earlier. As the *London As It Could Be* exhibition closed at the Royal Academy, and a centralising Conservative government shut down the UK's metropolitan councils (including the Greater London Council), the outlook for urban areas seemed pretty bleak. Cities were seen as crime-ridden, polluting and polluted. To some extent this was a hangover from the nineteenth century, when urban life had been truly horrific: in 1851, male life expectancy in cities was around 25 years, half that in rural settlements. The Victorian pamphleteer Andrew Mearns, quoted in Peter Hall's *Cities of Tomorrow,* conveys the horror of the 'city of dreadful night':

> To get to these pestilential human rookeries, you have to penetrate courts reeking with poisonous and malodorous gases arising from accumulations of sewage and refuse scattered in all directions and often flowing beneath your feet; courts, many of them which the sun never penetrates, which are never visited by a breath of fresh air... you have to grope your way along dark and filthy passages swarming with vermin... every room in these rotten and reeking tenements houses a family, often two. In one cellar, a sanitary inspector reports finding a mother, a father, three children and four pigs.

The first response to these horrors was the garden city movement led by the visionary Ebenezer Howard at the turn of the twentieth century, and then the post-war slum clearances of the 1940s and the new towns of the 1950s and '60s, the last taking people from inner-city tenements to new suburban homes. But by the 1980s, the cracks were beginning to show in the utopian planned cities and new towns of the post-war era, from Harlow to Cumbernauld in the UK, and from Oscar Niemeyer's Brasilia in South America to Le Corbusier's Chandigarh in India.

Meanwhile negative views of cities – as unpleasant, dangerous and economically outdated – persisted. The computer age would, it was assumed, make commuting a thing of the past as people worked from their suburban or rural home. Inept urban redevelopment schemes bulldozed the layered richness of urban areas and replaced them with highways and single-use buildings. Many cities across the UK and Europe, particularly former industrial centres, were haemorrhaging population, and seemed to be drifting towards the status of their hollowed-out US counterparts, with endlessly sprawling suburbs, and ghost-town centres occupied only by those with no opportunity to move away.

It seemed like a depressing coda to the great history of cities as the birthplace and cradle of classical civilisation, the heart of Renaissance culture, and engines of the Industrial Revolution. Louis Kahn talked of the city as 'the place of availabilities. It is the place where a small boy, as he walks through it, may see something that will tell him what he wants to do his whole life.' That sense of possibility seemed to be in retreat.

Family and Kinship in East London
Michael Young and Peter Willmott

But even as the death of cities was being declared, there were signs of revival, with its roots in a more careful and inclusive urbanism. Willmott and Young's *Family and Kinship in East London,* published in 1957, showed what could be lost in urban clearances, while in the 1960s the American sociologist Lewis Mumford made effective arguments for the 'organic city', where urban planners should consider first the relationship between the city and its occupants. The leading light was American writer and activist Jane Jacobs – a veteran of protests against Robert Moses's plans for slum clearance, grand highways and comprehensive redevelopment across New York. In *The Death and Life of Great American Cities,* Jacobs wrote of the life of New York's older streets, where activities, uses and people overlapped at all times of day and night, and how informal oversight could create security in parks and streets – if only they were designed on a human scale, with space for people to walk, chat and simply sit out and watch the world go by.

Across Europe, a new generation of city leaders were starting to realise that the quality of urban spaces and buildings was itself an asset, for both civic prosperity and urban life. It was an exciting period for me. Cities were in my blood. I was born in what had once been a city-state (as my father, with his studies of Florentine guilds, was always reminding me), I had grown up in London, and I had marked the turning points in my career in New York and Paris.

In Paris, seeing the Pompidou Centre's impact on tourism, culture and civic life, President Mitterrand had launched a programme of major cultural projects (often described as the *Grands Projets*), including I.M. Pei's Louvre Pyramid, Jean Nouvel's Institut du Monde Arabe, and the Grande Arche de la Défense designed by Johan Otto von Spreckelsen and later taken on by Paul Andreu. I had advised Mitterrand on setting up the competitions, and sat on the jury for the Bibliothèque Nationale and the Grande Arche de la Défense, whose inauguration would coincide with the bicentennial of the French Revolution in July 1989. In the latter competition, we were told that we would submit our recommendations to the president, who would then take the final decision. But I stuck my neck out and protested that this was unacceptable: if the president wished to be involved in the jury process, he could join us. Otherwise, we would declare which design we had selected, and he could publicly overrule us if he wished to. To my surprise and delight, Mitterrand agreed to join us, and spent a full day engaged in sophisticated argument and analysis.

In Spain, the death of Franco in 1975 had unlocked a tide of civic pride in Barcelona, whose citizens had even been forbidden from speaking in Catalan under the fascists. Barcelona had a magnificent inheritance in the shape of Ildefons Cerdà's nineteenth-century plan, which laid out a regular grid, with corners cut off each block, to allow for a public space at each intersection. A succession of visionary mayors led Barcelona's post-Franco renaissance, Narcís Serra, Pasqual Maragall and Joan Clos (the three were so close that they often seemed as one – 'The Mayors'.) The Mayors rekindled the dynamism that had driven Barcelona's growth as an

industrial and trading hub in the nineteenth and early twentieth centuries, and used architecture and urban design as a tool to engineer revival. Under Maragall, the city bid for and won the 1992 Olympics, using the event to enhance 100 squares across the capital, to clean up and restore a heavily polluted industrial coastline (used for the athletes' village), and to rebrand the city on the international stage.

I first met Maragall one summer night in the late 1990s. I was visiting the city, and he suggested we meet one evening at midnight, for dinner. I thought I was used to late hours as an Italian, but when I arrived at the restaurant it was just filling up, and we stayed there, eating and drinking and talking, for several hours. Maragall, who became a close friend, had appointed Oriol Bohigas, the masterplanner of the Barcelona Olympics, as head of the urban planning department and councillor of culture; I was asked to join a design review panel, to advise both Maragall and his successor Joan Clos on the design quality of schemes.

In Berlin, the reunification of Germany in 1990 had opened up new possibilities and I had joined a group of designers and urban thinkers for a discussion about the fate of the Berlin Wall. My proposal was a linear public path along the Wall's route; others wanted to obliterate its memory, but I don't believe you can, or should. The following year, we were commissioned to prepare a masterplan for Potsdamer Platz. It had once been the biggest traffic junction in the world, Berlin's equivalent of Piccadilly

Left: *Family and Kinship in East London,* by Michael Young and Peter Willmott, focused attention on the social networks and community life of east London's run-down housing.

Right: I met French President Francois Mitterrand when I sat on the jury for some of his *grands projets.* His commitment to architecture was reflected in the way he spent a day debating and analysing submissions with us.

271

Three visionary Mayors led Barcelona's renaissance in the 1980s and 1990s, following the fall of fascism in Spain. Pasqual Maragall (shown above, speaking at the London in the 21st Century debates) used the the 1992 Olympics to transform a heavily polluted waterfront dotted with slum encampments (above left) to a series of beaches and marinas, with the athletes' village re-purposed as housing after the games (left).

The reunification of Germany offered an opportunity to reconnect blighted urban districts in Berlin. Potsdamer Platz had once been the centre of the city, but was cut in two by the Berlin Wall (above right). RRP's masterplan made Potsdamer Platz a new mixed-use hub for the city (right), linking to Tiergarten and the Brandenburg Gate to the north. But ultra-conservative city planners killed the scheme.

Circus, but had been bombed to smithereens during the war, and then sliced in half and sterilised by the Wall in 1961.

Our plans, prepared for the three largest landowners, were based on two organising principles. We proposed reinstating the historical footprint of Leipzigerplatz. Alongside it, Potsdamer Platz would be revitalised as a new pedestrian hub for a resurgent city. Mixed-use residential, retail and office blocks would fan out from this central point and grow in scale as they moved outwards. Running north to south, a linear park would connect a human-scale piazza, with pedestrian and cyclist priority, to the great park of Tiergarten, the Reichstag and the Brandenburg Gate. But politics intervened in the form of Hans Stimmann, Berlin's arch-conservative chief planner, who said the city should lead the masterplanning. I had some sympathy with his position, but was furious when we were set up at a series of public meetings, where we were subjected to a relentless attack from local politicians, architects and citizens – one of the most unpleasant experiences of my architectural career. Our plans were torn up and Stimmann commissioned a new masterplan from a traditionalist German firm, imposing design codes covering building form, height and materials. A battle ensued between rigid classicism and our more fluid modernism. Renzo Piano later took on implementation of the plan, and we were commissioned to design three blocks, now battling against the irrationally rigid design codes that Stimmann had imposed.

These cities all bore witness to the failures of post-war town planning. Separation of functions, car dominance, out-of-town shopping centres and the displacement of communities to bleak new towns or sprawling suburbs; these were not just failing to revitalise depressed cities, but were actively poisoning them.

The rediscovery of the compact city as the most sustainable and vital urban form was gathering momentum, but London still seemed trapped in old ways of thinking, without the political momentum, the vision or the will to reinvent itself. The ship felt like it was heading towards the rocks, but nobody was on the bridge. In 1994, John Gummer, the Conservative Secretary of State who first realised the damage that out-of-town shopping centres were doing to towns across the country, asked me to join an advisory committee on the River Thames. Given my long-standing concerns about London's neglect of its great river, I was happy to join. But there was still an absence in London where civic leadership should have been. At our first meeting, I asked Gummer who was ultimately responsible for London. 'I am,' he said. 'But you're also responsible for all local government, housing, planning and environmental policy,' I said, 'and for the civil service!' London needed a leader.

Cities for a Small Planet – Defining the Compact City

Looking back over the last 50 years, I would say that the most influential research I have carried out was on the compact sustainable city. My ideas on cities and architecture had been developing in a series of lectures I'd given since *London As It Could Be* in 1986. In 1989, I gave the Smallpeice Lecture at the Royal Society, making the case for modern architecture. I compared the great Renaissance cities to soulless non-places like Houston, Texas, and argued strongly for the power of good modern architecture to complement rather than clash with the historic fabric. I called for more ecological awareness, and for government to give more direction to our cities, rather than leaving them to the mercies of the free market.

These ideas were further explored in my Walter Neurath Memorial Lecture the following year (published as *Architecture: A Modern View*), which also looked forward to a new architecture that could interact more dynamically with its users, as part of a symbiotic and networked society, with art and science harnessed to the service of all. I compared this future architecture to the way that an automatic pilot on an aeroplane can monitor and adjust systems, and quoted a beautiful passage written by Mike Davies about living in the building of the future:

> Look up at the spectrum-washed envelope whose surface is a map of its instantaneous performance, stealing energy from the air with an iridescent shrug, rippling its photogrids as a cloud runs across the sun, a wall which, as the night chill falls, fluffs up its feathers and, turning white on its north face and blue on the south, closes its eyes, but not without remembering to pump a little glow down to the night porter, clear a view patch for the lovers on the south side of level 22, and so turn 12 per cent silver just before dawn.

In 1995, I was asked to present the Reith Lectures, the annual series of radio lectures named after the BBC's founder. For my parents, my being asked to present the Reith Lectures was the ultimate intellectual accolade, far more important than the knighthood I'd received in 1991. For other friends and family members, my subsequent invitation to take part in *Desert Island Discs* – another radio show that has become a national institution – was probably more significant. At the end, I was asked the standard question, 'What luxury would you like to take with you to a desert island?' 'Ruthie,' I replied. 'But you're not allowed to take a person – those are the rules!' 'Then I'm not going!' Ruthie gave the same answer 15 years later when she appeared on the same show.

I was the first architect to give the Reith Lectures, so the content needed to be clear, engaging and accessible. A dry discussion of the evolution of modernism was not the way to win over a radio audience. I worked on the lectures with my colleague Philip Gumuchdjian. Ricky Burdett helped, and so did my son Ben – an elegant thinker and writer who was then working on his biography of the philosopher Alfred Ayer, and has since had senior policy roles in London local authorities and 10 Downing Street, and now runs the think-tank Centre for London. We set up camp in Le Corbusier's Maisons Jaoul on the outskirts of Paris, which then belonged to Peter Palumbo. We decided to start in space, describing how beautiful and fragile the earth seemed in images captured by the

first satellites. I talked about the intense cultural history of our cities, their creativity and power, as well as their poverty, environmental degradation and social alienation, and of their growing importance as the primary human habitat of the twenty-first century.

I argued for a new generation of sustainable compact cities, which respected urban limits, which conserved and generated resources rather than simply consuming them, and which chose densely populated hubs linked by public transport, walking and cycling over car-based sprawl. I drew links between public space and human rights, between civic space and civic values, and spoke of the urban environment's capacity to emancipate and civilise, rather than segregate and disempower. These, I concluded, were the only cities capable of meeting the environmental and social challenges that we faced, including the spectre of climate change, which had taken centre stage since the Rio Earth Summit in 1992. I spoke of our efforts to develop a more environmentally sensitive architecture, of our unrealised plans for London, and of the huge social and political changes that technology would unleash.

My eldest son Ben with his wife Harriet Gugenheim.

The Compact City

The well-connected, live–work, socially mixed compact city remains the only sustainable form of development. The elaboration and realisation of this concept lies at the heart of my Reith Lectures, my work with the Urban Task Force, and my work with Ken Livingstone. More than half of the world's population now lives in cities. To manage urban growth we need to create compact cities, driven by good design, social inclusion and environmental responsibility.

The Compact City

Increase density: density, linked to public transport, brings vitality to communities, is energy efficient, allows people to meet face-to-face, enables businesses to prosper, and makes transport and other services viable.

Create mix: compact cities mix uses, and mix people from all backgrounds, avoiding ghettos of privilege or poverty.

Value public space: from park to pavement, public space is the heart of the city, providing a place for civic life and for the meeting of people.

Re-use land: building only on previously developed land protects green space, prevents car-based sprawl and drives higher density.

Improve transport: make public transport, walking and cycling the most pleasurable and efficient means of transport.

Start from the centre: working outwards, building and retrofitting around transport hubs and corridors.

Ensure the highest quality of architectural and urban design: good design humanises; bad design brutalises.

Minimise carbon emissions and environmental impacts: considering materials, flood risk, natural systems, operating costs, longevity and adaptability.

Pudong Peninsula – A New Town on the Yangtze

One of the examples I used in the Reith Lectures was our strategy for the Pudong Peninsula in Shanghai, which embodied all the principal features of the sustainable city – hierarchies of density linked to public transport nodes, public space for all, a mix of uses and overlapping activities, and urban forms designed to minimise energy consumption through natural systems.

In 1991, Shanghai was expecting its population to rise from nine million to seventeen million over five years, and the mayor had decided that a teardrop-shaped peninsula across the Huangpu River from the Bund, the city's nineteenth-century merchant street, would be redeveloped as a new city satellite for one million people. The scale of the ambition was incredible. A million people was like building Manchester from scratch.

As a port and trading post, Shanghai had always been more open than other Chinese cities, but it felt fairly closed in 1991. Behind the Western buildings of the Bund were mile upon mile of housing estates, and the Pudong Peninsula itself was dominated by low-grade workshops and informal settlements cut off from the rest of the city.

The existing plans were for the worst sort of car-based development, a Chinese Los Angeles; a sea of indistinct, isolated point blocks separated by double- and triple-decked highways, with pedestrians relegated to underpasses and footbridges, with no public space or civic centre. This was seen as modernisation. When I first met the mayor, I commented on the fact that almost everyone was travelling by bike in the city, meaning this as a compliment. 'Don't worry, Mr Rogers,' he replied. 'We're going to ban bicycles by the end of the century.'

Our plan, led by Laurie Abbott working with Ove Arup, was for a mixed-use radial district with new metro connections to central Shanghai, and a local orbital rail system. As at Potsdamer Platz, a large public space would form the centre of the new development, and nobody would be more than five to ten minutes' walk from this central park, or other parks along the riverbank. The six orbital rail stations would form the hubs for the highest-density development, and most movement inside the district would be on foot or bike. Throughout the development, apartments were mixed with offices, shops, cultural centres and schools, and the massing of the buildings was designed like a series of overlapping waves, so that every building could maximise its daylight, and its exposure to cooling winds. This use of natural systems to light and cool the buildings, together with the transport strategy, would reduce energy consumption by 60 per cent, compared to a standard urban district.

Above left: Barcelona, modeled on Ildefons Cerdà's strict grid system, is one of the world's highest density cities, though mainly eight to ten storeys high.

Left: Notting Hill was developed as a suburb in the mid nineteenth century, mixing buildings and green space to create one of the highest-density – and now most desirable – neighbourhoods in London.

279

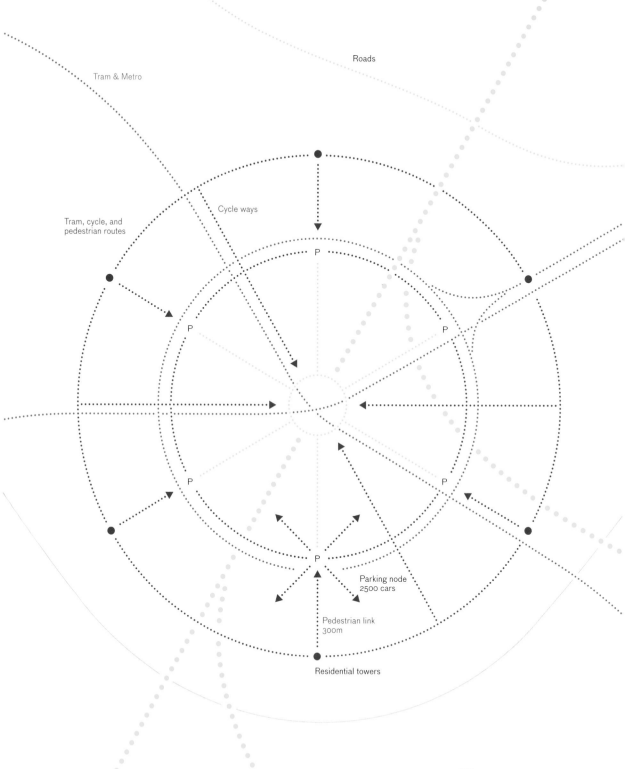

Roads

Tram & Metro

Cycle ways

Tram, cycle, and
pedestrian routes

P

P

P

P

P

P

Parking node
2500 cars

Pedestrian link
300m

Residential towers

River

Tunnels

The masterplan for Shanghai's Pudong Peninsula, a new community designed for a million people, was based on a clear transport hierarchy, with rail (pink), tram and cycling routes (purple), and roads (yellow).

The scheme's highest buildings were grouped around transport nodes, but were also positioned to maximise daylight and views out over the central park or the Huangpu River.

The plan was not a precise blueprint, but a strategy for developing a sustainable district, a comprehensive response to the challenges that climate change posed to traditional urban planning. It remains one of the most powerful diagrams we have prepared, helping to crystallise our urban thinking in the practice, and to develop a template for developing sustainable mixed cities that could be scaled and adapted to different contexts. But the Shanghai scheme floundered: we were repeatedly assured by the city government that it was being followed, but the only thing to prevail was the concentric form. The careful massing and movement strategy that we had proposed was ignored in favour of a ring of whimsical office towers connected by busy multi-lane highways, with a small park marooned in the centre of a gyratory system.

New Labour and the Lords

When Tony Blair committed to giving London an elected mayor at the Architecture Foundation debate in April 1996, he was already seen as 'prime minister in waiting', as John Major's Conservative government tore itself apart. Ruthie and I had become more involved in the Labour Party during the 1980s, as part of the group of artists, actors and musicians who were mocked by the tabloids as 'Luvvies for Labour', and had become good friends with Neil Kinnock, then Labour's leader, and his wife Glenys. Neil seemed to be leading his party out of its early 1980s depression, and it was a real shock when he lost the 1992 election.

I later came to know Tony Blair moderately well and I enjoyed discussing urban and cultural policy with him and other 'New Labour' luminaries, like Peter Mandelson and Derry Irvine (who had been our barrister in the Coin Street public enquiry, alongside the brilliant Garry Hart). Tony was mesmerising in those early days, as he led Labour back to power after the bitter disappointment of 1992. But in spite of his abilities, I will never be able to forget or forgive the way he took us to war in Iraq on the slenderest of pretexts, without even waiting for United Nations approval. It is sad that the second Iraq War tarnishes the whole record of the longest period of Labour government in history.

In 1996, I was approached by Blair's chief of staff, Jonathan Powell, to see if I would be interested in becoming a life peer. I agonised about the decision, as I had always argued for a House of Lords based on democracy, not patronage, but my mother and father encouraged me to take up the offer. They had gently disapproved of my knighthood, which they saw as an old-fashioned bauble, but becoming a peer involved real political power (or at least influence), so shouldn't be passed up.

I made my maiden speech in May 1997, arguing for an urban revolution in how we thought about and managed our towns and cities.

> We can ignore the figures about increasing inequality; but it is harder to ignore huddled figures sleeping in streets and doorways or trapped in decaying housing estates. We may flee from inner-city dereliction and take to the suburbs, but in so doing we extend the urban sprawl into the countryside. We may bemoan the decline in public transport while we sit in our cars and poison the air; but meanwhile, urban air quality continues to decline, one in seven of our inner-city children suffers from asthma.

The House of Lords is very impressive; it's old-fashioned but full of expertise. You have to do your homework before speaking there. (I also keep the only tie I possess on a peg there – you can't go into the chamber without one.) As a revising chamber it can raise questions without imposing a veto, and its deliberations have made a real difference from time to time; parliamentary time is limited, and the government often has to compromise to get its legislation passed. Nonetheless, in my view it should be replaced with a mainly elected chamber; we cannot really call ourselves a democracy when only half the Parliament is chosen by the people. The House of Commons resists reform, because it is worried about losing power to an elected chamber, but effective oversight needs the authority that only election can confer. I have suggested that members of the House of Lords should be allowed only one term of seven years, giving them enough time to make a difference but not requiring them to worry about re-election or to abandon their career outside Westminster. These elected members should sit alongside a number of respected experts, appointed by an independent commission for the same period of time. Such reforms would preserve the best characteristics of the House of Lords – its expertise and experience – without making it another forum for party politicking or a dumping ground for former ministers.

The Urban Task Force – Revitalising Our Cities

I had discussed the Reith Lectures with Tony Blair, and he had mentioned doing something about housing – a critical problem then as now – if Labour came to power. Very soon after the 1997 general election, I had a call from Deputy Prime Minister John Prescott, who told me he had read *Cities for a Small Planet*, and wanted me to chair a task force looking at how to build the housing that the UK needed.

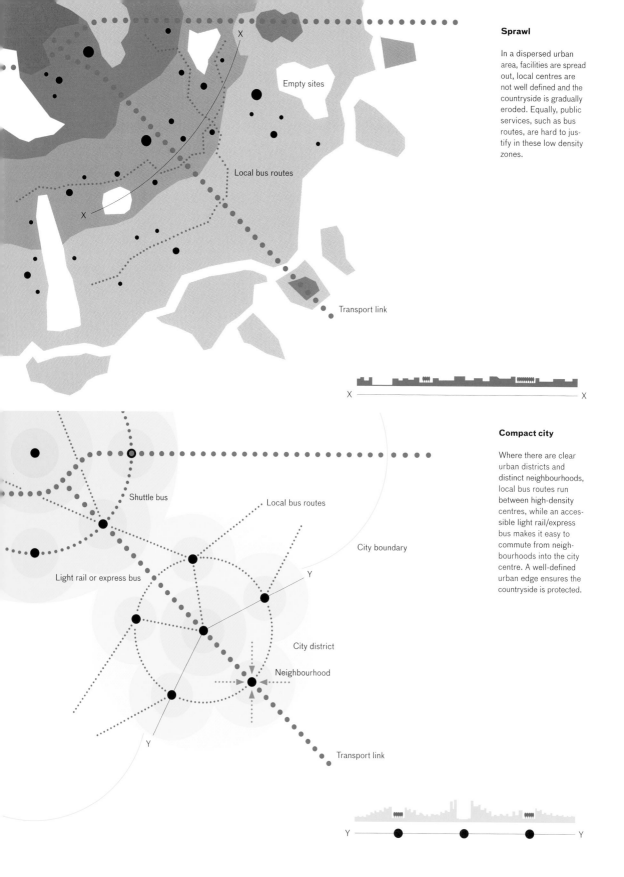

Sprawl

In a dispersed urban area, facilities are spread out, local centres are not well defined and the countryside is gradually eroded. Equally, public services, such as bus routes, are hard to justify in these low density zones.

Empty sites

Local bus routes

Transport link

X — X

Compact city

Where there are clear urban districts and distinct neighbourhoods, local bus routes run between high-density centres, while an accessible light rail/express bus makes it easy to commute from neighbourhoods into the city centre. A well-defined urban edge ensures the countryside is protected.

Shuttle bus

Local bus routes

City boundary

Light rail or express bus

City district

Neighbourhood

Transport link

Y — Y

I've worked closely with two politicians, John Prescott and Ken Livingstone. In both cases, I've been warned what difficult characters they were, but found the opposite to be true. John was passionate, which I like, and never scared. Some politicians will try to manoeuvre, to find compromise, to dodge the difficult issues. John would just go for it. He threw all his weight behind the task force – the power of the Prescott fist. He would brief me in advance of meetings with his officials or fellow ministers, so that I was forewarned about their criticisms, he allowed me to pick most of the task force members myself, and he gave us free rein in developing our report. Every time we mentioned 'beauty', for example, his officials bridled, but John supported us.

Our first big issue was about scope. I was determined that the report would not just be about house building, but also the revival of our towns and cities. Even in 1998 many architects, politicians and planners were still talking in terms of moving out of cities. There was a faltering recovery in some places – the 1996 IRA bomb in central Manchester prompted the city to rethink the future of its declining centre – but these were still the exceptions. Many cities had laid off their architects' departments so that they could continue paying for milk for schoolchildren, or libraries, or care for old people – a grim and unenviable choice.

It was also important to link the physical and the social. Many of the senior people in the Labour Party at the time saw the problems of inner-city deprivation in purely social or economic terms – with community development, training and employment opportunities as the solution. There was some suspicion, perhaps rooted in the depressing results of many inner-city slum clearance projects, about whether the built environment could make a tangible difference to people's lives. I fought that point and won the day, though I can't think anyone expected anything else from a task force chaired by an architect.

John and I appointed Sir Crispin Tickell, former UK Ambassador to the UN and a great advocate for environmental causes, Alan Cherry of Countryside Properties, Professor Peter Hall, Tony Burton of the Campaign for the Protection of Rural England, and Anthony Mayer, chief executive of the Housing Corporation. I was determined that we wouldn't have a civil servant as secretary; Nicky Gavron, chair of the London Planning Advisory Committee, recommended the brilliant Jon Rouse, who was at that time working at English Partnerships (the national regeneration agency). Jon

Left: These diagrams from the Urban Task Force report, published in 1999, showed how a fragmented city could be remodelled as a compact city, with strong connections, and the clear hierarchy of densities that could support local services – from buses and trams, to shops and schools.

Right: Visiting Hull in 1999 with Deputy Prime Minister John Prescott, who backed the Urban Task Force enthusiastically.

managed a complex and intense programme, and pulled together the arguments and recommendations of our final report.

The Task Force met monthly, with an enormous number of working
groups and research trips between meetings. We visited towns and cities
in the Netherlands, Spain and Germany, as well as England. I remember a
visit to east Manchester where industry had moved out of an entire urban
quarter, leaving dereliction and empty space, with four out of five homes
derelict – like an English version of Detroit.

We had agreed an objective – the Urban Task Force would 'identify
causes of urban decline in England and recommend practical solutions to
bring people back into our cities and towns' – and we developed our 137
recommendations on the basis of a clear understanding of what worked

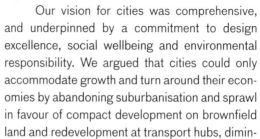

in successful cities, backed by the ten technical
reports that we commissioned.

Our vision for cities was comprehensive,
and underpinned by a commitment to design
excellence, social wellbeing and environmental
responsibility. We argued that cities could only
accommodate growth and turn around their economies by abandoning suburbanisation and sprawl
in favour of compact development on brownfield
land and redevelopment at transport hubs, dimin-
ishing the importance of the car. Neighbourhoods would accommodate the
rich and the poor, and mix uses, with different activities overlapping at different times of day to create a continual animation of place and space.

We established the ideal densities to sustain transport services,
local schools and shops, and looked at how certain street widths could
strengthen rather than sever social networks. High density, we explained,
did not have to mean high-rise. Leslie Martin and Lionel March's land use
studies in the late 1960s and early 1970s had already demonstrated that,
within the right urban grid, mid-rise perimeter blocks could be as dense as
high-rise skyscrapers; Barcelona has as similar density to New York, but
in eight-to-ten storey buildings. Its population is the same as Atlanta's, but
covers one twenty-fifth of the land area. Some of the highest density areas
of London are blocks of Belgravia and Notting Hill, and these are also
some of our most perennially popular neighbourhoods.

We agreed that local authorities should be empowered to lead the
urban renaissance, for design to be an objective for all central government
departments, for new local designations for regeneration areas or places
where councils, businesses and residents could work together to enhance
their environment, for fiscal incentives for recycling and retrofitting old

buildings as well as building new ones, for reduced parking provision, for switching investment from highways to walking and cycling, for tough new targets for brownfield development, and for curbs on greenfield expansion and out-of-town shopping centres.

Good design would be the glue to bind cities back together, blending buildings, public spaces and infrastructure to make places that worked, that could adapt and last. Too often those leading redevelopment projects in towns and cities saw design as something decorative, as a veneer to be applied when the real work was done, like 'lipstick on a gorilla', to borrow one of Norman Foster's phrases. Instead new development should be based on spatial masterplans and properly run design competitions. We recommended extending the model of the Architecture Foundation across the country, to create a network of architecture centres.

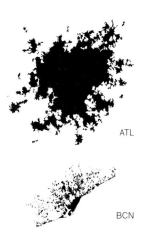

ATL

BCN

Towards an Urban Renaissance was published in April 1999, and secured a significant degree of cross-party consensus. The Commission for Architecture and the Built Environment (CABE) was set up in August to improve design standards. Five years later, densities had risen from an average of 25 to 40 dwellings per hectare; 70 per cent of development was on brownfield land (it rose to above 80 per cent later before falling back, and neared 100 per cent in London under Ken Livingstone); and British cities were regaining population.

But the report's biggest impact was the change in mindset that it brought about. People began to see cities as the foundation stone of civilised life and the dynamo of our economy – an asset to be optimised, not a problem to be tackled or a hellhole to be fled. Planners and developers began to talk the language of urbanism, to think about the quality of place, not just the quantum of development.

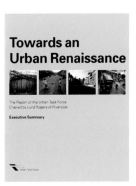

Towards an Urban Renaissance

The Report of the Urban Task Force
Chaired by Lord Rogers of Riverside

Executive Summary

John Prescott was relentless in pushing the report's recommendations forward (supported by Gordon Brown, who went through our report in detail, and Tony Blair, who took more of a 'big picture' approach). He was replaced by David Miliband after the 2005 general election, at which point the usual pattern of British politics re-asserted itself: every time a minister had been in office for long enough to understand the complexities of urban regeneration, he or she was replaced, and four ministers occupied the post between 2005 and 2010, when Labour lost office.

Left: The then Mayor of London, Ken Livingstone, celebrating the first anniversary of the London Eye in 2001.

Above right: Study comparing Atlanta (top) and Barcelona (below). The images, prepared by Ricky Burdett's team for the LSE's *Urban Age* conferences, contrast Atlanta's carbon-intensive sprawl with Barcelona's compact city form. Both cities have a metropolitan area population of around 5.5 million.

Right: The Urban Task Force report – its name echoing Le Corbusier's *Towards an Architecture* – argued that building more houses could only be achieved through the revitalisation of England's neglected towns and cities.

287

Architecture and Urbanism Unit – Design for a Greater London

'I want you to do this in London,' Ken Livingstone said, waving a copy of *Towards an Urban Renaissance* at me. He had invited me to meet him, together with Nicky Gavron, in late 2000, a few months after he had become London's first directly elected mayor, standing as a independent after a botched attempt by the Labour Party to fix their candidate selection process.

I happily accepted Ken's offer; the Greater London Authority had limited budgets and powers, but there was still so much potential. I established a small Architecture and Urbanism Unit, with Ricky Burdett as my deputy (Ricky is now the LSE's Professor of Urban Studies and director of LSE Cities). Richard Brown, the co-author of this book, who had been working in Ken Livingstone's office since the election, was appointed to manage the team, and we set about deciding what to do. We soon recruited Mark Brearley, a talented architect with a real feel for the textures of London's cityscape – the high streets and town centres, the parks and green spaces, the industrial estates and wharves – and a long record of engaging – and often arguing – with planners and developers across the city. Gradually we expanded the team to more than ten people.

Ken was a visionary mayor, who made a big difference for London, boosting cycling and bus use, introducing a congestion charge and increasing the city's confidence. The first London Plan set out a vision for London that reflected Urban Task Force principles. London had started to grow again, and the plan made a commitment that London would accommodate this growth within its borders, and not eat into the green belt or spill over into satellite towns. New-build housing would be at its most dense near public transport hubs, parks and green spaces would be protected, car parking would be limited, and town centres would be the preferred location for new retail and office development.

London would also take a more relaxed attitude to tall buildings. As the economy had recovered from the early-1990s recession, and the City of London realised it had to compete with Canary Wharf, a swathe of applications for tall buildings was being made: Norman Foster's Swiss Re Tower (nicknamed 'the Gherkin'), KPF's Heron Tower, Renzo Piano's London Bridge Tower ('the Shard'), as well as our practice's Leadenhall Building ('the Cheesegrater'). Ken issued early policy guidance supporting tall buildings of exceptional architectural quality, located in clusters to give scale (primarily in the City but also near rail hubs), with public access at ground level and minimised provision for car parking. He strongly supported new schemes in the face of opposition from English Heritage and other conservation groups. I told Ken that I didn't want to spend all my time defending these schemes in public enquiries, but I made an exception for the Shard, Renzo Piano's elegant tower above London Bridge railway station.

The Architecture and Urbanism Unit (A+UU) published design guides, on streetscape, on housing and housing density, on roof terraces and living roofs (which become more and more important in a higher density city where fewer people have private gardens, despite the British planning system's suburban obsession with 'overlooking'). But Ken wanted us to influence more than policy; he wanted us to make things happen. We had no budgets, so we decided to 'catch and steer' (the phrase was Mark Brearley's) what was happening on the ground.

We started out with an objective of 100 public spaces. Transport for London (TfL) was adjusting road layouts and renewing stations across the transport network. Couldn't these projects also create some beautiful public space for people, as well as expressways for buses or forecourts for stations? We helped TfL and the boroughs appoint and manage architects and designers, particularly from smaller emerging practices, oversee-ing the design of new squares and public spaces in Brixton, Dalston and Acton. Other schemes stalled: Stanton Williams won a competition to pedestrianise Sloane Square in Chelsea – a roundabout with potential to be a leafy public space, surrounded by cafes, shops, offices and residential development, as well as the great Royal Court Theatre – but it fell foul of local politics.

We developed the concept of a 'green grid', mapping London's more neglected green spaces, and visualising them as an inter-related network, for relaxation, walking, cycling, nature. We mapped high streets and town centres too, identifying more than 600 across London as hidden opportuni-ties: if infill and retrofitting could find space for 100 more units in each, we would shore up the vitality of these places, and build 60,000 more homes.

The team became increasingly involved in east London, where the London Development Agency (LDA) still had considerable land holdings. What had been London's industrial and shipping heartland had been left derelict after the shutdown of the docks in the 1960s and '70s. The brilliant planner Peter Hall had been the first to spot the area's potential, badging it the East Thames Corridor when he was advising Michael Heseltine, and it had been rebranded as Thames Gateway by the new government.

Canary Wharf, the extension of the Jubilee Line, and the Millennium Dome were some of the few notable investments in east London. Beyond these, the area offered huge capacity, but very little intelligent planning; a few developers were trickling shoddy housing out onto big riverside sites, squandering what should have been London's future with low density sub-urban cul-de-sacs.

We worked with colleagues in the LDA and the boroughs to think how much new development could be accommodated in inner east London if we worked with the grain of local communities, rather than sweeping all traces of the past away. We commissioned masterplans for Barking, Woolwich, Stratford and the eastern end of the Royal Docks. Our plans for 'City East' covered Greenwich Peninsula, the Royal Docks and the Lower Lea Valley. In these areas alone, we estimated there was capacity for 400,000 more people to live, if proper planning was put in place to make the most of empty sites and opportunities to make existing neighbourhoods denser.

In the Lower Lea Valley, I had already been talking about plans for an Olympic bid with the social entrepreneur Andrew Mawson, sports campaigner Richard Sumray and Michael Owens, who headed a local regeneration partnership. We wanted to use the network of canals and waterways in the Lea Valley as a new connective infrastructure, creating a 'Water City' based on canal-side living, with the Olympics acting as a catalyst for change right down to the Royal Docks.

By 2003 the idea of a London Olympic bid was gaining currency in City Hall. We had learned from Barcelona how the Olympics could be a catalyst for urban change. But the breakthrough came when Ken realised that the Olympics was not just a sporting event – he was not a great sports fan – but a chance to secure government investment to cut through the knot of railways, waterways, power lines, sewers, contaminated land and derelict factories that was holding the Lea Valley back.

Ricky Burdett became design adviser for the Olympic Delivery Authority, but I became less involved, not least because my practice RRP was bidding for the masterplanning contract (our Water City-based proposition lost out, I think because it looked too risky and complex for the tight Olympic timescales). However, I did sit on the jury that selected Zaha Hadid's design for the Aquatics Centre which alongside Michael Hopkins' Velodrome is a real jewel. The Olympic Park, and the plans for its future, show the value of planning such events as part of a city's strategy, not as a one-off festival.

When Boris Johnson was elected Mayor of London in 2008, he was at first very supportive of our work, declaring that he would be proud to plunder any of his predecessor's best ideas, including free bike hire and public space projects. Charming, and always ready with a classical allusion, Boris said I could be his Agrippa, referring to the architect who had designed many of the most beautiful buildings of Augustan Rome. An early round of cuts had pulled the plug on our scheme for pedestrianising Parliament Square and by the time we met him to explain that the square was already more crossed by people on foot than in cars, it was too late, though

The Shard, Renzo Piano's masterpiece at London Bridge, viewed from Greenwich Park, alongside the cluster of tall buildings in the City of London.

Boris professed that he might have decided differently if only he had had the facts. Without support from City Hall, my ability to be effective was diminished, so I resigned the following year.

Decisions should be made as close to the people as possible. I strongly believe in cities and mayors. London is immeasurably better for having a mayor. It vies only with New York today as the most dynamic and vital city in the northern hemisphere. Initiatives like congestion charging and free cycle hire, and major projects like Crossrail and the Olympics, have given the city a new vitality – and none could have happened without a mayor to support them. But the mayor's role still needs more power – to help London compete internationally, tackle its problems and lead the UK's economy. This is more important than ever following the 2016 EU referendum and the decision of a majority in the UK (but not in London) to turn its back on a community of 750 million; the mayor urgently needs the power to maintain London's international and cosmopolitan status. And while it is frustrating trying to work within the complex bureaucracies of London government, the Architecture and Urbanism Unit, and Design for London made a real difference in the city – changing the thinking of planners, developers and highway engineers, and helping them to conceive of their projects not in isolation, but as pieces of the city, elements in its ceaseless evolution.

Building New Towns in Cities

Twenty-five years after the Urban Task Force report pioneered the return to the compact sustainable city, the urban renaissance is an unfinished revolution. In many UK cities, urban planning still lags behind cities like Hamburg, Stockholm and Copenhagen. Cyclists and pedestrians continue to be subservient to car users on many city streets and security guards patrol what were once public spaces, as private ownership creeps ever further into the public realm.

Above all, 50 years after I first considered the scale of housing needed against our struggles to complete Creek Vean and Murray Mews, we are still not building enough homes. After the publication of *Towards an Urban Renaissance*, house-building rose steadily and completions peaked at just over 170,000 in 2008. Then came the financial crash, and only half of the 250,000 homes needed in the UK were built in 2014.[6] What we do build is tiny. Our space standards are some of the worst in the world; average homes are 50 per cent bigger in Japan, Belgium and the Netherlands.[7] London's shortfall is similar (50,000 homes a year needed, 20,000 built in recent years).

Zaha Hadid's outstanding Aquatics Centre in London's Olympic Park, the delicacy and fluidity of its roof reflected in the elegant diving platfoms. We began the design competition that selected Zaha's scheme before we knew London would be staging the 2012 Olympics.

A roof over one's head is one of the four basic rights, alongside health, education and food. But more and more people are being evicted by landlords, their wages stagnating while rents rise, taking 70 or 80 per cent of income, rather than the 30 per cent that is generally regarded as 'affordable'. The social consequences of homelessness are horrific: people are left on the streets, in shelters or in abandoned houses. More than 50,000 London households are in temporary accommodation,[8] and the number of people sleeping on the streets in England has risen by a third between 2015 and 2016.[9] And soaring house prices have locked a generation out of home ownership, exacerbating inequality. This is a crisis by any standards, and will get worse in cities like London if populations rise as predicted.

But we do have space to build more homes, without eating into the greenbelt that has surrounded London and other UK cities since the 1940s. The costs of greenfield development – the impact of more car-based commuting, the need for brand new social and utilities infrastructure, spread out over a wider area – are just too high. A Canadian study estimated that an average suburban household's direct costs to its municipality, for governance, police and fire services, roads, schools, parks, libraries, cultural services and waste, was $3,500 every year compared to less than $1,500 for an urban household.[10] These don't include the costs in terms of carbon dioxide emissions, congestion, health impacts from accidents and air pollution – the same Canadian study estimated these at more than $27 billion per year. And opening up greenfield sites will lead to a bonanza of speculation, diverting investment from urban sites without necessarily resulting in a single extra house being built.

Shortage of land is not the immediate problem – in London alone there is enough brownfield for the next ten years, new sites continually become free as economic change continues, and retrofitting and intensifying development around transport hubs will both strengthen neighbourhoods and accommodate growth in an environmentally responsible way. We can build new towns in our existing cities, as we have on railway land at King's Cross in London, and in disused docks at Hafencity in Hamburg.

So why aren't we building the homes we need? The most fundamental problem is the dominance of housing supply by a few large housebuilders, who have no incentive to build faster, or to adopt the new technologies that could enable that. Building slowly to keep prices high – the average house in south-east England costs ten times the average salary – works very well for the developers who have bought up land. Their shareholders want profit, not to stabilise or reduce prices.

We should be using off-site manufacture for economies of scale, and a dramatically faster build time. A number of new designs and systems are being developed, including AECOM's Rational House, and the Zed Factory's Zero Bills House. Led by Ivan Harbour and Andrew Partridge, RSHP has worked with YMCA to design the Y:Cube, which can be manufactured off-site and assembled on-site in hours for £60,000. RSHP also designed the PLACE/Ladywell scheme in Lewisham, and the modular Tree House scheme – the centrepiece of our exhibition at the 2016 Venice Biennale.

Housing is not separate from but an integral part of the urban renaissance, of planning for the development of the sustainable compact city. It should be for elected local authorities, supported by highly skilled planners, to choose the sites, the quality and quantity of buildings, the social and economic mix, the hierarchy of transport infrastructure and public space, the social infrastructure (schools, hospitals, police and fire stations, community halls) needed, the quality of the internal and external spaces. These specifications should form the basis of a clear but flexible masterplan. It is then and only then that developers should bid for projects (though they make proposals for how it could be enhanced), and commit to building it out over an agreed timescale, with a mix of houses for sale and rent to enable rapid market absorption.

We have locked ourselves into a toxic pattern of undersupply and speculation. We have sold off social housing and are pouring housing benefit subsidies into the pockets of private landlords. Something that should be treated as a basic human right – a home – becomes an asset class to be traded, and homeowners are caught up in a heady spiral of rising prices, which governments are reluctant to disrupt. But without political intervention, an ever-wider gulf is opening up between those lucky enough to be on the housing ladder (or rich enough to be able to jump on), and everybody else.

We have the wealth, we have the land, we have the materials to create vital sustainable developments, but our political and economic policies fail us. Governments should recognise housing as essential infrastructure for our economic wellbeing and as a fundamental human right, and should work with councils to build the affordable homes we need.

WHY IRAQ? WHY? NOW?

THE FACTS DO NOT JUSTIFY WAR

JOIN US IN SAYING NO

— — — — — — — — — — — — — **cut here to make your banner** — — — — — — — — — — — — —

DAVID ADJAYE, PETER AHRENDS, LIZ AHRENDS, DAMON ALBARN, TARIQ ALI, HANAN AL-SHAYKH, PROFESSOR WILL ALSOP, ADAM ALVAREZ, ALARIC BAMPING, JULIA BARFIELD, JULIAN BARNES, RONAN BENNETT, MICHAEL BERKELEY, BERNARDO BERTOLLUCI, SOPHIE BAINBRIDGE, SUE BIRTWISTLE, JANICE BLACKBURN, WILLIAM BOYD, MARTYN BRABBINS, VICTORIA BRITTAIN, BRITTEN-PEARS FOUNDATION TRUSTEES, CARMEL BROWN, JOE BRUMWELL, SANDRA BRUMWELL, RICKY BURDETT, MIKA BURDETT, LIZ CALDER, CARMEN CALLIL, JIM CAPALDI, ANINNA CAPALDI, MIKE DAVIES, DAVID CHIPPERFIELD, ELIZABETH CLOUGH, DR JOHN COAKLEY, JARVIS COCKER, IMOGEN COOPER, RAY COOPER, MICHAEL CRAIG-MARTIN, EDWARD CULLINAN, SINEAD CUSACK, JUDY DAISH, JAN DALLEY, JOHN PAUL DAVIDSON, SIR COLIN DAVIS, HOWARD DAVIES, SIR PETER MAXWELL DAVIES, DAME JUDI DENCH, SIR JEREMY DIXON, JOANNA DODSON QC, SARAH DUNANT, LINDSAY DUNCAN, MARK ELDER, DAVID ELDRIDGE, MICHAEL ELIAS, SUSAN ELIAS, TRACEY EMIN, HARRY ENFIELD, SIR RICHARD EYRE, KATE FAHY, SIR TERRY FARRELL, RALPH FIENNES, ERIC FELLNER, CLARE FRANCIS, LYNNE FRANKS, STEPHEN FREARS, MARIELLA FROSTRUP, DAVID FURNISH, ADRIAN GALE, BOB GARLAND, DAVID GILMOUR, MARCO GOLDSCHMIED, PIERS GOUGH, ROSE GRAY, SALLY GREEN, SIR NICHOLAS GRIMSHAW, ZAHA HADID, IVAN HARBOUR, DAVID HARE, ROBERT HARRIS, DEBRA HAUER, LUCY HELLER, DAMIEN HIRST, JULIA HOBSBAWM, MARLENE HOBSBAWM, ERIC HOBSBAWM, DUSTIN HOFFMAN, MICHAEL HOLROYD, EMMA HOPE, GEORGIE HOPTON, GILL HORNBY, NICK HORNBY, GARY HUME, JOHN HURT, IAIN HUTCHISON, PAUL HYETT, NICHOLAS HYTNER, JEREMY IRONS, KAZUO ISHIGURO, BIANCA JAGGER, CHARLES JENCKS, SIR ELTON JOHN, ED JONES, JAY JOPLING, ANISH KAPOOR, BARONESS HELENA KENNEDY QC, IMRAN KHAN, JEMIMA KHAN, JEREMY KING, ALAN KITCHING, VERITY LAMBERT, GRAHAM LE SAUX, MIKE LEIGH, ROWLEY LEIGH, KEN LIVINGSTON, GIORGIO LOCATELLI, CHRISTOPHER LOGUE, JOANNA LUMLEY, SIR RICHARD MACCORMAC, DAVID MACILWAINE, LINDSAY MACKIE, FOUAD MALOUF, LEONARD MANASSEH, LESLEY MCOWEN, MICHAEL MANSFIELD QC, DAVID MARKS, RICK MATHER, COLIN MATTHEWS, DAVINA MCCALL, CAROLINE MICHEL, ROGER MICHELL, JOHN MILLER, SU MILLER, SARAH MILLER, HARRIET MILLER, BILL MORRIS, SIR JOHN MORTIMER, LADY PENNY MORTIMER, MOHSEN MOSTAFAVI, LUCY MUSGRAVE, MIKE NEWELL, STUART NOLAN, MAIA NORMAN, DERMOT O'LEARY, SUSIE ORBACH, JASON OSBORN, BILL PATERSON, JOHN PAWSON, CATHERINE PAWSON, CLARE PEPLOE, CHLOE PEPLOE, PROFESSOR ANNE POWER, JONATHAN PRYCE, ALAN RICKMAN, DEBORAH ROGERS, PETER ROGERS, RICHARD ROGERS, RUTH ROGERS, JACQUELINE ROSE, HANNAH ROTHSCHILD, JOAN RUDDOCK, EDWARD SAID, MARYAM SAID, SIR COLIN ST JOHN WILSON, POLLY SAMSON, SASKIA SASSEN, PROFESSOR WENDY SAVAGE, PROFESSOR RICHARD SENNETT, BERNICE STEGERS, BARONESS VIVIEN STERN, EVELYN STERN, DAVE STEWART, STING, LOUISE STJERNSWARD, CELIA STOTHARD, TRUDIE STYLER, JON SUMMERILL, JUNE SUMMERILL, SAM TAYLOR WOOD, JEREMY THOMAS, EMMA THOMPSON, DR GABY TOBIAS, REINHARD VOIGT, PHILIPPA WALKER, HARRIET WALTER, ALEX WILLCOCK, DR ESTELA WELLDON, JOHN WILLIAMS, ANNA WING, JEANETTE WINTERSON, MATTHEW WRIGHT, NICHOLAS WRIGHT, BARONESS BARBARA YOUNG OF OLD SCONE, JOHN YOUNG.

11   The Fair Society

The biggest challenges facing us today are inequality and climate change. The first threatens the fabric of society; the second threatens our very existence. Both lead to extremism and conflict, a world of corruption, private greed and public suffering. Populist nationalists and religious fundamentalists are exploiting popular discontent, causing levels of instability that we have not seen for decades. Rather than expressing horror at the symptoms, we need to come together to tackle the root causes of the current crises.

The Brave New World of Post-War Britain

The early years of my life included both the lowest point of humanity and one of its highest, and the influence that these have had on me is deep. The horrors of fascism in the 1930s and '40s were unparalleled. After the war, I met doctors working with my father at Epsom Hospital who had been some of the first people to enter the Nazi death camps after the Allied advance; all my life I have been haunted by their stories.

  The years after the war saw a new resolve in Britain to defeat the 'five giant evils' – squalor, ignorance, want, idleness and disease – that William Beveridge identified in his 1942 report. The welfare state that resulted from this was a commitment to a fairer society, in which no one would go hungry or be homeless, or suffer from illness without support. It could not eliminate hardship completely, but it would reduce people's suffering from the lotteries of health or social class. The radicalism of this post-war government, at a time when the nation was almost bankrupted by the war, was astonishing. In addition to health and welfare reforms, in six years the Attlee government overhauled town planning, created green belts, built one million homes, and enhanced employment protection for workers.

  After I returned from national service in Italy in 1953, politics became increasingly important to me. I marched to Aldermaston against the

Ruthie and I signed up to the powerful advertisement/poster, designed by Alan Kitching, placed in *The Guardian* on 14 February 2003, protesting against the impending invasion of Iraq.

atom bomb alongside Bertrand Russell, who I greatly admired, just as in recent years I've marched for action on climate change and against military adventurism in the Middle East. But politics was about more than big demonstrations; in my profession, with my parents, with my family and friends, political debate and engagement was a constant. The majority of architects worked on housing, schools and other public projects at that time (my first job was at Middlesex County Council's Schools Department), and most of us considered ourselves socialists. Politics was always a feature of discussions around the dining table at home. Su's parents Marcus and Rene were socialists, with deep roots in the Labour movement. Ruthie's father Fred Elias allied himself to the principles of Marxism – a brave boast in Cold War America – and had served as a doctor with the anti-fascist forces in the Spanish Civil War.

For all of us 1968 was a turning point. At first it seemed like a momentous shift of power was taking place: Ruthie and I were at the Grosvenor Square demonstrations against the Vietnam War in London, we saw the *événements* in Paris, and the optimism of the Prague Spring in Czechoslovakia. Grosvenor Square ended in pitched battles with police, and the state regained control after teetering on the brink of collapse in Paris. But the world did change: civil rights, women's rights, gay rights, the withdrawal from Vietnam, the abolition of the death penalty in most civilised countries – these were all long-term victories of the popular movements of the 1960s.

The crackdown was particularly harsh in Czechoslovakia, where attempts at reform were greeted by the Soviet invasion. That was the moment when a lot of people, faced with the brutal reality of Soviet power, lost any sympathy with the USSR. It was a moment of great disillusionment. But more importantly, that was the last time that there seemed to be a clear alternative to a world ruled by money and consumerism.

Meeting Ronald Dworkin, Thinking About Fairness

My political ideas became more clearly articulated when I met Ronnie Dworkin. Ruthie and I were living in Place des Vosges in Paris when the *New York Times* journalist Anthony Lewis introduced us. I don't remember the first evening – it must have been in 1975 or 1976 – but Ronnie used to tell the story that he and his then wife Betsy were walking away from our apartment when they heard my voice calling out of the upstairs window, 'Stop, don't go, we have more to talk about!'

We never ran out of things to talk about during the next 35 years and were the closest friends until his death in 2013. We lived a few streets away from each other in London, he and Irene Brendel married in our house, and they rented a house up the hill from us in Tuscany. Our conversations were wide-ranging and endless – about ethics, music, beauty, architecture, art and politics, both of us relishing the debate and argument. I still feel they are unfinished. Ronnie was the perfect teacher, both for the originality and elegance of his thought, and the clarity of his arguments. He loved setting up the challenge, a glass of wine in his hand, then teasing out its consequences. But he was also a listener, and fascinated by Renaissance culture, art and architecture.

When we spent time together in Tuscany, walking round Florence, Pienza and Siena, our roles were reversed, and I became the teacher. Ruthie recorded one of our last discussions on her mobile phone, on the meaning of beauty and the role of absolute values. Sometimes I play it just to hear his voice and remember his words.

Ronnie also introduced me to the writing of John Rawls, who was as significant a thinker in political philosophy as Ronnie was in jurisprudence. Rawls argued for a rights-based understanding of morality. To quote an excellent article by my son Ben, 'Rawls gives priority to the "right" over the "good" – to claims based on the rights of individuals over claims based on the good that might result from violating those rights'.[11] Rawls argued that rights could be defined fairly through considering how the world looks through a 'veil of ignorance'. This famous thought experiment suggested that the only fair way to design a society would be to arrange its affairs without knowing what your own position would be – rich or poor, handsome or ugly, healthy or ill. In this way, society would choose welfare systems that maximised individual freedom, but also looked after the interests of the worst off. To quote Ben again,

> It is the duty of society, Rawls believes, to ensure that our opportunities are as little affected by our circumstances as possible. It is not that he believes that social institutions have to ensure that everyone is as happy as everyone else – that is our own responsibility. But he does insist that, as far as possible, we should all be given similar opportunities to achieve happiness – that our family upbringing, our abilities and talents, our looks and health, our whole genetic and environmental heritage, should not be allowed to give us an unfair start in life.

Ronnie, like Rawls, was passionate about these issues; *Taking Rights Seriously* was one of his most noted books. His last book, published in 2013, was called *Religion Without God,* and its title encapsulated his world view. For him, the 'religious mindset' was one that affirmed the existence of absolute and objective values – some things simply are more beautiful or better than others – however difficult it is to establish this. Ethical and aesthetic judgements could not be explained in purely scientific terms, nor could they simply be explained away as opinions, nor did they need recourse to a mystical deity. His deep conviction was that there is a right answer to moral and legal questions; it was just a matter of trying to find it. Law should be interpreted in moral terms rather than being viewed simply as a set of formal rules, which made judgement of institutions like the US Supreme Court of paramount importance.

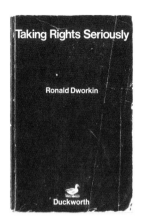

At the heart of the 'religious mindset' were two fundamental principles. One was that human lives have objective importance and dignity, and that we all have a duty to live our lives as well as we can, both in ourselves and our ethical behaviour, and in our moral responsibilities to others. The second was that the world around us has intrinsic value and beauty, and that we have a responsibility to it. These propositions seem central to me. Reading Rawls, and meeting and talking with Ronnie helped me to refine and take seriously certain principles – of humanism, of concern for fairness and justice, of environmental responsibility – that would guide my increasing involvement in politics and public life, as well as my practice of architecture.

Edward Said, whose 1978 book *Orientalism* brought to the surface the myths and prejudices that colour our depictions of foreign cultures, was another great influence on me. He was one of the most wide-ranging humanist intellectuals I have met, a professor at Columbia University and a concert pianist. He was also a passionate proponent of the Palestinian cause and opponent of the 1993 Oslo Agreement, which he described as 'an instrument of Palestinian surrender, a Palestinian Versailles'. His anger was powerful, but he also sought peace and reconciliation, for example through the West-Eastern Divan Orchestra, comprising Israeli and Palestinian musicians, which he co-founded with Daniel Barenboim. He died in 2003 from leukaemia. He was only in his sixties, and I felt robbed of a dear friend. I miss his passion.

Ronnie Dworkin gave us a copy of his book, *Taking Rights Seriously.* He wrote inside, 'This should have been called 'Taking Ruthie Seriously'. Those damned British printers!'

The Growth of Inequality

For 30 years after the Second World War, Western countries saw rises in living standards for all, and a shrinking gap between the rich and poor. From the late 1970s in the UK and USA, this trend was reversed, and inequality began to grow; it has levelled off in recent years, though not when you take the richest of the rich into account. In Britain, the top 1 per cent of earners now take fifteen per cent of national income – the same share as in 1940, and almost three times as much as in the late 1970s.[12] In terms of wealth, the richest 1 per cent in Britain have accumulated as much wealth as the poorest 55 per cent,[13] and in 2017 the eight richest people in the world have as much wealth as the poorest 50 per cent.[14] Even in a rich country like Britain, 28 per cent of children – nearly 50 per cent in some urban areas – live in poverty.[15]

French economist Thomas Piketty has argued that the situation will only get worse, as economic growth remains sluggish, and returns on capital continue to grow faster than (more widely shared) returns from labour. Unless something changes, the rich will continue getting richer, and the poor will struggle to keep up, even more so as trade union power has been eroded. However, while some measures show a dramatic reduction in extreme poverty over recent decades, nearly a billion people still live on less than $1.90 per day.[16] More and more wealth is accumulated by those at the top of the pile. The reality of modern capitalism is 'trickle up' not 'trickle down'.

Joseph Stiglitz has echoed these arguments, observing that the top 1 per cent are taking a quarter of the USA's income every year, double the amount of twenty-five years ago. He argues that there is nothing accidental about this inequality, which distorts society, chokes off investment and sows the seeds of violent protest; in his view, 'the top 1 per cent want it that way'.[17] In 2013, looking back at the aftermath of the financial crisis, President Obama described inequality as the 'defining challenge of our time':

> But when the music stopped and the crisis hit, millions of families were stripped of whatever cushion they had left. And the result is an economy that's become profoundly unequal and families that are more insecure. Just to give you a few statistics: Since 1979, when I graduated from high school, our productivity is up by more than 90 per cent, but the income of the typical family has increased by less than eight per cent. Since 1979 our economy has more than doubled in size, but most of the growth has flowed to a fortunate few. The top ten per cent no longer takes in one-third of our income; it now

takes half. Whereas in the past, the average CEO made about 20 to 30 times the income of the average worker, today's CEO now makes 273 times more. And meanwhile, a family in the top 1 per cent has a net worth 288 times higher than the typical family, which is a record for this country. So the basic bargain at the heart of our economy has frayed.[18]

We cannot sustain the inequality that consumer democracy has given us, while also claiming to believe in the dignity and value of all human beings. A system that pays bank executives tens of millions of pounds every year (FTSE 100 chief executive salaries have quadrupled in a generation), while few headteachers earn more than £100,000, has lost sight of what is truly valuable. There is no more important role in society than teaching children; for the child born with nothing, education is the best chance of escaping their circumstances. It is the most important investment we can make.

I am proud of Mossbourne Academy, the school we designed, with Ivan Harbour in the lead, in one of the poorest neighbourhoods of Hackney. But good schools need great teachers, and the amount we pay them suggests we regard their role as trivial. Instead of education we spend more and more on a penal system that is hugely wasteful of lives and money.

Such injustices are compounded by the way we tolerate tax evasion, as *The Guardian's* exposure of offshore banking demonstrated in 2015. In the words of Luke Harding, one of the journalists who worked on the story, 'Previously we thought that the offshore world was a shadowy but minor part of the economic system. What we learned from the Panama Papers is that it is the economic system.'[19]

We are told that it is the wealthy who hold society together, that the whole structure of our modern economy will be destroyed if we cause any disturbance to those at the top of the tree. People boast of how little they pay in tax, when surely one should be proud to pay taxes if one believes in a well-educated, fairer society? Others talk of their charitable giving, which privatises social responsibility, and redefines what should be seen as a fundamental civic duty as a voluntary act of generosity. When I chaired the Tate, I was envious of the ease with which US museums and galleries raised funds, but when I see their boards selected on the basis of wealth, I realise that they have lost something too.

The Myths of the 1 Per Cent

Three great myths support the status quo. The first is that the super-rich 'deserve' their wealth, as they have earned it, and that the poor are poor because they are lazy. More and more of the rich have accumulated their wealth only through what Ronnie Dworkin would call 'brute luck' (e.g. privileged birth, and the advantages it gives in education, careers and inherited wealth – Piketty estimates that more than 70 per cent of wealth in France is inherited, and that that proportion could grow to 80 or 90 per cent by the end of the century)[20] rather than 'option luck' – the opportunities created by individuals' talents.

The second falsehood, promoted by reactionary politicians intent on stripping back the state, is that it was welfare claimants and government programmes that caused the 2007–8 financial crash rather than bankers' reckless and consequence-free gambling, which is conveniently excised from debate. Millions lost their jobs and their homes after the crash, and it has proved a disaster for the taxpayers round the world, as they took on the financial consequences of the banks' recklessness, propping them up with money that could otherwise have been used to help people who had lost their homes, or to invest in health, employment, infrastructure and education.

The third myth is the assertion that the unfettered free market is a natural state of affairs rather than a political choice, that its distortions and inequalities are simply facts of life, as inevitable (if regrettable) as tooth decay or hair loss, a price worth paying for economic efficiency. The evidence suggests that this is wrong, that one can choose to make a society more or less unequal: the pre-tax income gap between the wealthiest and the rest of society has got significantly wider since 1970 in the UK and USA, but has stayed much the same in Japan and continental European countries.[21] Our society has decided, or has been led to decide, that we will tolerate this worsening level of inequality, despite the fact that it is socially corrosive and economically inefficient. Our politics cannot be made a slave to the narrow interests of the super-rich.

The Corrosive Impact of Inequality

Concentrated wealth does not enrich our society; it impoverishes, erodes and destabilises it. Far from there being an inevitable trade off between equality and economic prosperity, our unequal society is actually stifling growth. Global wealth is growing faster than the global population, but more and more of this wealth accrues to the few (in the developed world at least).[22] When companies forgo investment in equipment and people

Following page: Minami Yamashiro Primary School, completed in 2003, is not just a school but a new centre for a remote mountain community. It puts education where it should be – at the centre of civic life.

303

Share of total income going to the top 1 per cent

Anglophone counties

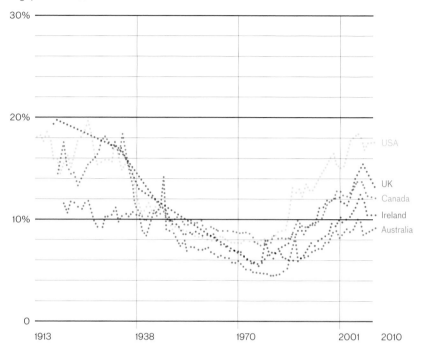

Non-anglophone countries

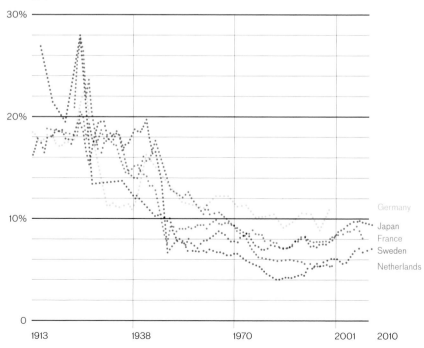

so that they can maximise dividends, they decrease productivity. When tax cuts favour the rich and welfare cuts penalise the poor, the economy is starved of consumer spending (as the poor spend more of their money than the rich do). When the public infrastructure of schools, railways and hospitals is run-down, to support bailouts and tax giveaways, we are hacking at the roots of economic growth as well as social cohesion.

This level of inequality is unhealthy for society. Richard Wilkinson and Kate Picket[23] have shown how increasing inequality undermines social cohesion and trust, and generates anxiety. Unequal societies have worse rates of mental and physical illness, violent crime and drug abuse. Material inequality brings with it social disintegration. As the 1 per cent get richer, social capital and financial capital alike diminish for the rest of society. Will Hutton has compared inequality to a slow-growing cancer; society can remain in blissful ignorance before its symptoms show themselves, by which stage it may be too late to treat.

As I write in 2017, we are starting to see the symptoms of a disease that started 35 years ago. You can see them in the rise to prominence or even power of far-right politicians across Europe and the USA, in the rise of extreme nationalism and religion across the world. You can see them in the alienation and social exclusion that led a majority of voters in the UK to choose to leave the European Union, turning their back on the most exciting experiment in international social and economic collaboration to have emerged since the Second World War. You can see them too in the US presidential election result, which has put an inexperienced demagogue in the White House, promising mass deportations, a roll-back of environmental legislation and a retreat to narrow nationalism.

We need leaders who can help us see the problems inequality is causing, who can help us work towards a more equal society. Inequality is not just unfair, socially corrosive and economically inefficient, it is also destabilising. The alienation that drives young people to fight in Syria is as much a symptom of an unequal society as is the hunger that drives people to food banks. Millions of people are suffering across the world because of war, increasingly impelled by the nationalist and religious extremism that I hoped would be banished to the past when I was young. With the possible exception of NATO's intervention in Bosnia, the West has not won a single war since the Second World War, but we have constantly jumped in – with guns and bombs, instead of economic and social aid. We have compounded, not relieved, the agony of the wounded, orphaned and displaced.

Poverty and war, combined with environmental crises, are driving hundreds of thousands of refugees to our borders. Nationalists feel threatened by what they see as an invasion, but this is a false fear. Immigrants

These two graphs, taken from Max Roser's *Our World in Data* website, show how inequality fell until the 1970s, then began to rise sharply in the UK, United States and other anglophone countries, but levelled off elsewhere. Inequality is a choice.

have always brought wealth, knowledge and abilities; we are all immigrants if we look back far enough in our history. Immigrants are often the most entrepreneurial people, who have made the decision to flee to a strange land, at huge personal risk, for the chance of a better life. They are a boon to the economy, more likely to be starting new businesses than claiming benefits. But more importantly than that, they are our fellow men, women and children. Our response should be one of humanitarian empathy for citizens of the world, not nationalistic resistance.

We should take to heart the inscription at the base of the Statue of Liberty in New York harbour: 'Give me your tired, your poor, your huddled masses yearning to breathe free!' Our social responsibility is to welcome, educate and give shelter, as we did to refugees from fascism in the 1930s. There are nearly five million displaced Syrians in the Middle East – surely careful planning would enable Europe and the USA, with a combined population of 1.2 billion, to accommodate these desperate people?

My son Roo involved me in Doctors of the World, which works in 70 countries worldwide, including emergency field clinics in refugee camps, and a clinic in east London providing longer-term care to illegal migrants and sex workers – people who have fallen through the gaps in social provision. Roo had wanted to take a year off to work on an overseas aid project during his studies at Columbia, and I knew that Robert Lion, who I had met when he was head of the design competition jury for La Défense, the first of President Mitterrand's *Grands Projets,* was on the board of Médecins du Monde (MdM). But my request for Roo to work with them was turned down. Not a chance, said Robert, we don't take people that young and inexperienced; it's a risk for us and for them.

Eventually, though, they waived the rule, and Roo went to South Sudan with MdM. The experience nearly killed him – he caught malaria several times, found snakes in his sleeping bag, and met people coming back from the war with blood on their knives – demonstrating the wisdom of the MdM policy. But when he had recovered, Roo worked with Robert to establish a UK branch of MdM (now called 'Doctors of the World'); I was one of the founding board members. Since then, Roo has co-written a book on the sharing economy, created the first eco-friendly car service in New York, and works with start-ups in Asia and Africa.

Climate Change – A Reality, Not a Theory

Long before the current climate emergency, it became clear to me that our post-war assumptions of inexhaustible natural resources were flawed. We could no longer continue to plunder the world around us, but needed to think of a more sustainable approach to the environment, the metabolism that sustains our lives. The early warning signal was sounded by Rachel Carson, whose book *Silent Spring,* published in 1962, showed the devastating impact that the use of pesticides to boost agricultural yields was having on wildlife. Since then, the threat has only grown: a 2016 report estimated that one in ten wild species in the UK are threatened with extinction. [24]

Meanwhile, Buckminster Fuller, the godfather of environmentally responsible architecture, was preaching the gospel of 'doing more with less', of minimising the energy and the materials that buildings used, of knowing – in his words – how much our buildings weigh. In 1972, the Club of Rome's report, *The Limits to Growth,* sounded the alarm, that we would soon exhaust our supply of natural resources. While their projections proved premature, the core of their message was right – there was a crisis on the way.

Now it is clear that climate change is the single most important danger facing mankind, and we have little time left to act. The concentration of carbon dioxide in the atmosphere has been accelerating over the past decade, polar ice is being rapidly eroded, and desertification is spreading. As usual, it is the poor who will feel the impact first, as crops fail and floods sweep away homes.

The shift we need to make is huge, and implies significant disruption to the status quo of late capitalism. Of course there is a level of uncertainty, much exaggerated by those paid to lobby for fossil fuel companies, but the precautionary principle should be at the front of our minds. If you see a car speeding towards you, it is best to get out of the way, rather than debating whether it may stop in time. Tackling climate change is an opportunity to rebalance our economy and our society, moving away from relentless acquisition and competition in the name of 'economic growth', and unlocking technology and creativity to find new forms of sustainable energy and agriculture that do not destroy the world.

As a first step, we can think again about how we are actively subsidising climate change. The International Monetary Fund estimates that fossil fuels will cost global taxpayers $5.3 trillion in 2015, more than all world governments spend on healthcare services. Fossil fuels receive $550 billion in production subsidies every year; renewables receive one fifth of that. [25]

As cities generate the majority of carbon emissions, building the sustainable compact city is essential to our survival, making the best use of space, and minimising private car use. Architecture needs to play its part too, building on the old adage, 'Long life, loose fit, low energy'. Adaptability ensures that buildings have a long life, and do not need to be demolished, which incurs huge costs in both financial and environmental terms. Our practice has also sought to turn away from buildings that create energy-intensive closed systems, dominated by artificial light, air conditioning, ventilation and heating systems, and entirely cut off from their environment – not just energy-guzzling, but also soul-sapping.

Schemes like the Bordeaux Law Courts and Welsh Assembly Building use thermal mass (the ability of materials like concrete and soil to hold its temperature) to mitigate the heat of midday or the cool of night, and use the natural 'stack effect' to draw cool air through the courts and assembly chamber. Earlier projects also included designs for a fully self-sufficient house in Aspen, Colorado, commissioned by Steve Martin and powered entirely by solar and wind power, and a zero-energy tower in Tokyo.

For our competition entry for the Inland Revenue's new headquarters in Nottingham we proposed slim buildings, curved to maximise airflow, and with trees planted between to cool and freshen the air that would circulate through them. In recent years, the bar of expectations has been raised ever higher, as technological advances have opened up new possibilities. One of our most recent projects, 8 Chifley in Sydney, Australia, which was led by Ivan Harbour, has been awarded the highest level of environmental certification, and is one of the greenest buildings in Australia, with 50 per cent lower carbon emissions than a standard office block. It creates public space at ground level, and has louvred blinds that track the sun to create shade through the day. It also generates heat and power on site, recycles wastewater and harvests rainwater. Its offices are grouped into two- to three-storey villages, which can be easily linked by internal staircases, rather than relying on elevators.

At times over the past 20 years, the challenges of climate change have looked almost insuperable, but there are some glimmers of light, some signs that we may be able to limit the damage that climate change is already having on our societies, and at least buy ourselves the time we need to adapt and find long-term solutions. Some of the positive signs are political: the 2015 Paris Agreement on Global Climate Change marked a new commitment to collective action, though Donald Trump's rejection of the agreement is a reckless act – privileging short-term political imperatives over the lives and livelihoods of millions across the world.

Others are technological: the price of solar technology has plummeted far faster than anyone had anticipated; by 2020 solar power will be competitive with electricity from other sources for 80 per cent of the world's population.[26] Even in the cloudy UK, there were days in early 2017 when 25 per cent of electricity was generated from solar power – more than coal or nuclear. But we need to go further: we need to cap and tax carbon emissions, and to accelerate the switch towards energy efficiency and renewables.

If we continue to exploit fossil fuels, we will accelerate our extinction, as Al Gore said in his 2006 documentary *An Inconvenient Truth*: 'what we take for granted may not be here for our children'. We need to put aside nationalism to work together for a global solution, which encompasses economic and political as well as environmental change. Redistributing energy consumption, and putting in place a global system to limit emissions, could also create a more equitable world.

Choosing a Better Society

Global instability, and the conflicts that plague the world, are fuelled by inequality, corruption, and a mounting environmental crisis. In the Middle East and North Africa, climate change is causing displacement and famine, leading to clashes between different groups – city dwellers and peasants, farmers and nomads, Arab and African. But our consumerist society continues to contribute to global warming, rather than taking the concerted action needed to tackle the problem.

The climate change agreement in Paris made me hopeful, as do the social movements that have sprung up across the world in recent years. They suggest that I am not the only one who believes that we can find a better way to live, and that our broken market system will have to be reformed, or it will come to an end. If we are to survive, we need to find a fairer and more environmentally sustainable way of running our society. We are struggling to humanise an economic system that only works for the wealthy, and to find a way of growing prosperity without wrecking our environment.

But we have to choose this new society. There is nothing inevitable about the way the world is organised at the moment. We need to clearly recognise its dysfunction and the lies we are told about what is going wrong. This is not just about redistribution and redressing the balance to help the less fortunate, but about allowing for the social structures that enable individuals and their families to flourish, and about the values that underpin them.

As I wrote earlier, there is so much more in the world than money (though I am aware how lucky I am to be relatively wealthy), and our values reflect that. Ian Hay Davison, who was brought in to clean up Lloyd's in the 1990s, was once challenged to identify where a particular sharp practice was outlawed in Lloyd's rules. 'It's not in the rules,' he said. 'It's in the Ten Commandments – Thou Shalt Not Steal.' We should not confuse legality with morality, nor ethical values with financial ones.

We need a profound social and political revolution, at the heart of which is an acknowledgement that our individual lives are wrapped up in the relationships, rights and obligations that define us as citizens. We must stop stigmatising the poorest in society and start helping them instead.

American sociologist Robert Putnam has spent many years tracking the disintegration of social ties in the USA, and the damage this does to communities and particularly to the life chances and opportunities of the poorest. In his latest book,[27] he quotes James Truslow Adams' 1931 formulation of the 'American dream': 'a dream of a social order in which each man and each woman shall be able to attain to the fullest stature of which they are innately capable, and be recognized by others for what they are, regardless of the fortuitous circumstances of birth or position'.

To achieve this dream, we need teachers, in and out of school, who will help us and our children to challenge received opinions on wealth, corruption, religious and nationalist chauvinism, politics and the good society – not telling them what to think, but showing them how to think. In a society where every other marriage ends in separation, we also need to learn how to remain civilised in our personal relationships. Essentially, our problem is one of values: if the only values that count are financial, if social and environmental considerations are excluded, we cannot be surprised that society is on such an uneven keel.

We should also rethink how we tax and spend, investing in infrastructure and creating jobs, in health services, in education, in transport, rather than obsessing about the national debt and imposing endless austerity. Government should intervene in the economy to provide financial stability and social justice, to match earnings to the real value of work, and to shut down the tax havens that enable the richest to contribute the least to society. Professor Tony Atkinson made a strong case for a range of reforms in his final book, *Inequality: What Can Be Done?*. He argued for a fairer tax system, which taxes wealth and inheritance more than earned income, together with a more progressive property tax regime. This would be complemented by higher levels of universal benefits, including child benefit and a universal minimum income, and a progressive taxation system which would enable poorer people to keep more of their money. Atkinson also argued for more active interventions to create full employment, including through active investment in technological change.

These may not be precisely the right answers – I am not an economist – but they do display the breadth of thinking that is required. The world is wealthier than ever before, and it is absurd to claim that we cannot afford to take responsibility for each other, to ensure that nobody is unfairly disadvantaged by the accidents of birth or health. We simply need to choose a better way of living, or face the consequences of a fractured society that drives its discontents to extremism.

My granddaughter Ivy at the Women's March in early 2017, almost 60 years after I first marched against nuclear weapons at Aldermaston.

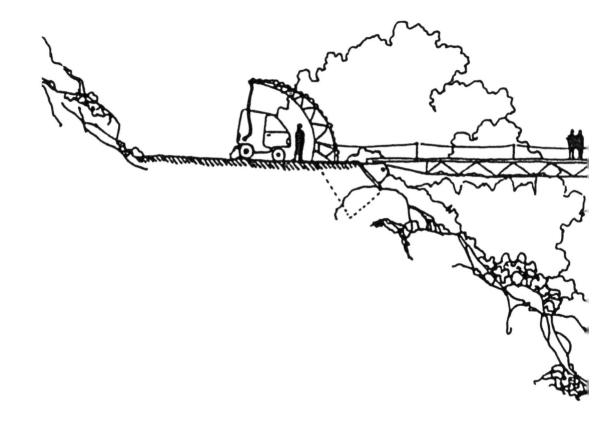

The Autonomous House that RRP designed for Steve Martin in 1978 was a prototype for a building that could be self-sufficient, in terms of power, heat and water, enabling life off-grid in the Colorado mountains.

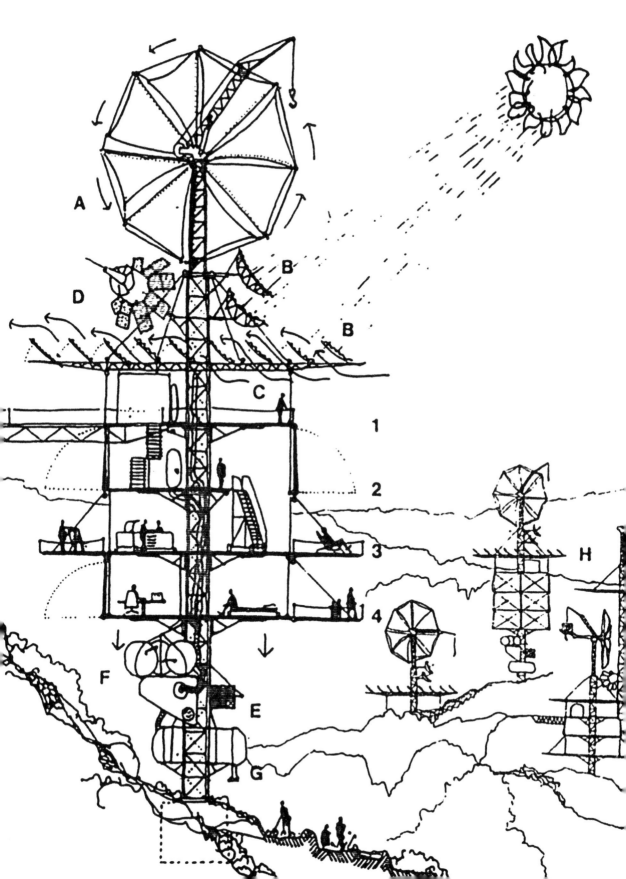

Reflections on the Future

As I have been writing this book in 2016 and early 2017, global instability has intensified. The massive swing against the traditional left and right, and towards populist and anti-establishment movements throughout the Western world is an expression of discontent at the unfairness and inequality in society, features that have been in place for a century or more, but were kept in check during the middle of the twentieth century by the moderating power of the welfare state.

There is a growing sense of anger, a feeling that the system is no longer working for the majority. Both the traditional left and right are struggling to address this, offering no solutions, no ways to address the gap between the 1 per cent and the 99 per cent. The result is that many citizens have turned to what I never expected to see again in my lifetime, extreme populist, nationalist and religious groupings. Right wing politicians like Donald Trump have taken advantage of this discontent, though there have also been voices from the left - like Bernie Sanders' and Jeremy Corbyn's - pushing the argument for a fairer society.

The need for new ideas, new politics, and new leaders is becoming urgent, especially as Brexit drives a wedge between the UK and its European neighbours, but left of centre politicians seem slow to act. I believe we should start by looking at ways of achieving a fairer distribution of wealth, starting with taxes and earnings. Tax havens must be closed; fairer taxes should be used to create a better society aimed at improving health, education, housing, as well as stimulating creativity and scientific discovery. People often challenge this and say we can't afford to tax the rich and redistribute both earnings and taxes, but it is clear that the capitalist way of the past 100 years is no longer working. It is time for change.

In classical Athens more than 2,000 years ago, when young men (ephebes) were ready to become citizens, they swore an oath, the Ephebic Oath,

Working in Tuscany, with a view that has remained unchanged for generations.

317

'not to leave my city diminished when I die, but greater, better and more beautiful'. I often conclude speeches with this quotation, which expresses a powerful democratic vision. I like its optimism, the sense that a better society is possible, and that we have it within our power to bring it about.

This book has explored the development of my architectural approach, my work with exceptional individuals and teams, and my views on social and environmental justice. It has expressed my passion for great cities, architecture and public places, a belief in education and active citizenship, my appetite for culture and food, and love for my family and friends. I want to finish on a positive note. I have always thought it a terrible mistake to think that nothing is as good as it used to be; we are endlessly recreating our culture and society, as each generation tries to leave its mark.

As I wrote in the last chapter, the two greatest challenges facing us are climate change, and economic and social inequality, but there are grounds for hope. We know what needs to be done. We must act on our knowledge. We can choose differently. The British people did so in 1945, when they chose the welfare state over their wartime leader.

We need to make an equivalent change. We should demand a new social settlement, which tackles the growing inequality and unfairness of society. We can create political and economic systems that are based not just on financial values, but on our obligations to one another, rich to poor, healthy to sick, lucky to unfortunate. This is what we owe each other as citizens, and what we need to make society work too.

A fairer society is one that would focus on education – on helping people to find a better path in life – rather than on locking people away. Creating a fair society means understanding our common humanity and acting on it, not dividing ourselves by nationality or religion, or perpetuating the patterns of discrimination – against women, disabled people, gay people, foreigners, poor people – that have disfigured society for so many centuries. In our affluent times, it is absurd to claim that we cannot afford to take responsibility for each other, to help refugees, to ensure that nobody is unfairly disadvantaged by the accidents of birth or health. We should be building bridges, not walls.

What does all this mean for architecture? At one level, that's asking the wrong question. I never planned this to be simply a book about architecture. This is really a book about creating better more beautiful places to live and a better society, about citizenship. But architecture is the profession I chose, and the culture and practice of architecture is integral to making a better society. It creates human habitat, from the individual house, to the city. As I wrote at the beginning of the book, good architecture civilises, bad architecture brutalises.

However, architecture is political – it responds to and affects how we live and work, how we share space in our cities, the stories we tell ourselves about our society. We need an architecture that responds to the challenges facing our society today, which recognises that the compact city based around public transport, walking and cycling is the only sustainable way to live. We ought to be designing for citizenship, so that buildings give as much to the passer-by and the public domain as they do to their occupants. Our built environment should also be a built society and a built culture. Our buildings should create a sense of place, reflecting topography and ecology, history and society. We must design for a fast-changing world, using contemporary technologies to create open-ended, flexible buildings, rather than retreating to the sterility of traditional techniques and built-in obsolescence. We need an aesthetic of change.

This calls for a revolution in professional training and practice. In many cities, architects seem to have been relegated to decoration and shape-making, or squeezed by project management and value engineering. Architectural training needs to become much broader, to span everything from the structures of society to the nature of materials, so that architects can help create better shelter and better cities. Architecture should be about problem-solving in the built and natural environment, and an architect should have an understanding of materials, culture, landscape and society.

Architecture should be about collective action, not individual heroics. The architect is nowhere without engineers, community workers, planners, landscape designers, surveyors. Planners and architects need to recover their confidence and re-engage in political debates, on how we can build a better society, as we chose to after the Second World War. Professional education, and professional institutions, should be about identifying common ground, rediscovering the multidisciplinary spirit of the Bauhaus, working and training together, not about defending territory or the purity of professional practice. I sometimes compare it to medicine, where the basics of physiology are understood before surgeons, anaesthetists and general practitioners refine their expertise; likewise architects, planners and engineers should understand society before they specialise.

We should not be afraid to talk about beauty, and to take it seriously. We all value beauty in our every day lives; we would all choose a beautiful place, building or painting; we all know how a piece of music can lift our hearts and humanise us. Architecture should create beauty without being marginalised as a matter of decoration and marketing. In a world of tight budgets, as John Ruskin said, 'there is hardly anything in the world that some man cannot make a little worse and sell a little cheaper'. You only need to look at the appalling architecture that lines the River Thames,

Public space is a human right, like decent healthcare, food, education and shelter.

Everyone should be able to see a tree from their window, to sit out on a stoop or a bench, or in a local square; and to stroll to a park to walk, play and enjoy the changing seasons.

A city that cannot provide these rights is simply not civilised.

London's greatest public space, to see the impact of this cheapening of the public realm, as urban development becomes a money machine, uninterested in environmental, aesthetic and social impact. The profession needs to change radically, to reassert its value, to avoid being pushed into this decorative dead end. Architects should be able to engage with cost constraints to make better buildings, not seek to mask the cheapness of their concepts.

There are reasons to be optimistic about a new generation of architects, who seem determined to dig deeper and to re-engage with the fundamentals of city life, to put people, social justice and participation at the heart of their work, but still to think radically and inventively about the possibilities of structure and materials. We have an incredible diversity of approach: from Alejandro Aravena's social engagement, Shigeru Ban's beautiful disaster zone structures made from renewable materials, Frank Gehry's, Jan Kaplický's and Zaha Hadid's radical sculptural experimentation. We need to maintain and celebrate this diversity; there is room for the big statement and the subtle adjustment.

But we, the citizens, also need a more engaged public debate, to celebrate and empower the best architects, to join the struggle for greater fairness and equality, and to demand more from the profession as a whole. As the Ephebic Oath indicates, it is not just for architects but for all of us to make our towns, cities and society better – more beautiful, more compact, more environmentally sustainable, and fairer.

Following page: RSHP's exhibition at the 2016 Venice Biennale reflected on the importance of better politics and planning, as well as better design and construction techniques, in order to create sustainable compact cities.

OUR URBAN FUTURE

BY 2050 TWO THIRDS OF THE WORLD'S POPULATION WILL LIVE IN CITIES

SUBURBAN SPRAWL FEEDS CLIMATE CHANGE, THREATENING OUR EXISTENCE

THE ONLY SUSTAINABLE FORM OF DEVELOPMENT IS THE COMPACT CITY

THE HOUSING CRISIS

ONE IN FOUR
PEOPLE ARE
HOMELESS
OR LIVING IN
SLUMS

THE HOUSING
CRISIS IS
INCREASING
INEQUALITY
AND
DESTROYING
OUR CITIES

Chronology

1933
Richard Rogers born in Florence, Italy

1939
The family moves to England

1951–3
National military service

1954–9
Studies for degree at Architectural Association School of Architecture

1960
Marries Su Brumwell

1961–3
Fulbright Scholar at Yale University, New Haven, Conneticut

1963
Returns to the UK to found Team 4 with Su Rogers (later Miller), Norman Foster and Wendy Cheesman (later Foster)

1963
Ben Rogers born

1964
Zad Rogers born

1966
Creek Vean, Team 4's first project, completed

1967
Team 4 splits following completion of Reliance Controls

1968
Ab Rogers born

1969
Richard + Su Rogers complete Parkside, Wimbledon

1971
Piano + Rogers win competition for Beaubourg Plateau Cultural Centre, Paris (later named Pompidou Centre)

1973
Marries Ruth Elias

1975
Roo Rogers born

1977
Pompidou Centre completed

1978
Richard Rogers Partnership (RRP) appointed to design Lloyd's Building, London

1981–9
Chairman of Tate Gallery

1983
Bo Rogers born

1986
Lloyd's Building completed. Made Knight of the French National Order of the Legion of Honour. *London As It Could Be* exhibition, Royal Academy, London

1987
RRP move to Thames Wharf; River Café opens

1991–2001
Chairman of the Architecture Foundation

1995
European Court of Human Rights, Strasbourg, completed. Gives Reith Lectures for BBC (later published as *Cities for a Small Planet*)

1996
Awarded life peerage

1998
Bordeaux Law Courts completed

1998–2005
Chairman of Urban Task Force for UK government

1999
Thomas Jefferson Memorial Foundation Medal in Architecture

1999
Millennium Dome completed

2000
Praemium Imperiale Architecture Laureate

2000–3
Adviser to Mayor of Barcelona

2000–9
Chief adviser on Architecture and Urbanism to Mayor of London

2005
National Assembly for Wales, Cardiff, completed

2006
Terminal 4 Barajas Airport, Madrid, completed; awarded Stirling Prize. Awarded Golden Lion for Lifetime Achievement at Venice Architecture Biennale

2007
Richard Rogers + Architects – From the House to the City exhibition at Pompidou Centre, Paris. Appointed Pritzker Prize Laureate. Richard Rogers Partnership becomes Rogers Stirk Harbour + Partners

2008
Heathrow Terminal 5 completed. Member of the Order of Companions of Honour

2011
Death of Bo Rogers

2013
Richard Rogers – Inside Out exhibition, Royal Academy, London

2014
Leadenhall Building completed

2015
RSHP moved into fourteenth floor of Leadenhall Building

1. United Nations, *World Urbanization Prospects*, 2005 and 2014 Revisions.

2. See O'Sullivan, P. and Romig, F.A. *Energy Conservation – Crisis or Conspiracy, Hospital Engineering*. Vol. 36 No. 2 (1982) pp. 9–17.

3. The guidance that the Architecture and Urbanism Unit prepared for the Mayor of London on competitions is available on the TFL website; other guidance is available from professional bodies such as RIBA.

4. Speech published on The Prince of Wales and the Duchess of Cornwall website.

5. Commission for Architecture and the Built Environment. *The Value of Public Space: How High Quality Parks and Public Spaces Create Economic Social and Environmental Value.* 2004.

6. Office for National Statistics. *Trends in the United Kingdom Housing Market 2014.* 2014.

7. KPMG and Shelter. *Building the Homes We Need.* 2014.

8. Department for Communities and Local Government data for Oct-Dec 2016.

9. Gentleman, Amelia. *Number of People Sleeping Rough in England Rises by Almost a Third in a Year, The Guardian*, 25 February 2016.

10. Sustainable Communities Analysis, based on case study in Halifax, Nova Scotia, 2013.

11. Rogers, Ben, *John Rawls*, Prospect, June 1999.

12. See Danny Dorling website.

13. Inman, Philip. *Britain's Richest 1% Own As Much As Poorest 55% of the Population, The Guardian*, 15 May 2014.

14. Oxfam, *An Economy for the 99%*, 2017.

15. See Campaign to End Child Poverty website.

16. World Bank. *Global Poverty Indicators.* 2012.

17. Stiglitz, Joseph. *Of the 1%, by the 1%, for the 1%*, Vanity Fair, May 2011.

18. Speech to Centre for American Progress, 4 December 2013.

19. Quoted in Rusbridger, Alan. *Panama: the Hidden Trillions*, New York Review of Books, October 2015.

20. Piketty, Thomas and Zucman, Gabriel *Wealth and Inheritance in the Long Run* in *Handbook of Income Distribution Volume 2B*, 2015.

21. Roser, Max. *Income Inequality.* 2015, at the *Our World in Data* website.

22. Stigltiz, Joseph. *Slow Growth and Inequality are Political Choices. We Can Choose Otherwise.* In *The Great Divide*. London: WW Norton and Co, 2015.

23. Pickett, Kate and Wilkinson, Richard. *The Spirit Level: Why Equality is Better for Everyone*. London: Penguin, 2010.

24. State of Nature Partnership, *State of Nature 2016 England Report*. London: RSPB, 2016.

25. International Energy Agency. *World Energy Outlook 2013*. Paris: OECD/IEA, 2013, at the *World energy Outlook* website.

26. Gore, Al. *The Turning Point: New Hope for the Climate*, Rolling Stone, 18 June 2014.

27. Putnam, Robert D. *Our Kids: The American Dream in Crisis*. New York: Simon & Schuster, 2015.

Bibliography

Appleyard, Bryan. *Richard Rogers: A Biography*. London: Faber and Faber, 1986.

Atkinson, Anthony. *Inequality: What Can Be Done?* Cambridge, MA: Harvard University Press, 2015.

Banham, Reyner. *Theory and Design in the First Machine Age*. Cambridge MA: MIT Press, 1980 (second edition).

Brumwell, Joe. *Bright Ties Bold Ideas: Marcus Brumwell, Pioneer of 20th Century Advertising, Champion of the Artists*. Truro: The Tie Press, 2010.

Carson, Rachel. *Silent Spring*. Boston, MA: Houghton Mifflin, 1962.

Castells, Manuel. *The Rise of the Network Society*. Oxford: Blackwell, 1996.

Chermayeff, Serge and Alexander, Christopher. *Community and Privacy: Toward a New Architecture of Humanism*. London: Penguin Books, 1963.

Cumberlidge, Clare and Musgrave, Lucy. *Design and Landscapes for People: New Approaches to Renewal*. London: Thames and Hudson, 2007.

Dworkin, Ronald. *Religion Without God*. Boston, MA: Harvard University Press, 2013.

Dworkin, Ronald. *Taking Rights Seriously*. London: Gerald Duckworth and Co. Ltd, 1977.

Evans, Huw. *Renzo Piano: Logbook*. New York: Monacelli Press, 1997.

Frampton, Kenneth. *Modern Architecture: A Critical History*. London: Thames and Hudson, 1980.

Gehl, Jan. *Cities for People*. Washington DC: Island Press, 2010.

Giedion, Sigfried. *Space, Time and Architecture: The Growth of a New Tradition*. Boston, MA: Harvard University Press, 1941.

Gray, Rose and Rogers, Ruth. *The River Café Cook Book*. London: Ebury Press, 1996.

Hacker, Jacob and Pierson, Paul. *Winner-Take-All Politics*. London: Simon and Schuster, 2010.

Hall, Peter. *Cities of Tomorrow*. Oxford: Wiley-Blackwell, 1988.

Hughes, Robert. *The Shock of the New: Art and the Century of Change*. London: Thames and Hudson, 1991 (enlarged edition).

Krugman, Paul. *End This Depression Now!* London: W.W. Norton and Co., 2012.

Le Corbusier. *Vers une architecture*. Paris: G. Cres, 1924. Published in English as Towards a New Architecture. London: Architectural Press, 1927.

Loos, Adolf. 'Ornament and Crime'. In *Ornament and Crime: Selected Essays*. Riverside, CA: Ariadne Press, 1998.

Meadows, Donella et al. *The Limits to Growth: A Report for the Club of Rome's Project on the Predicament of Mankind*. London: Macmillan, 1979.

Melvin, Jeremy and Craig-Martin, Michael. *Richard Rogers: Inside Out*. London: Royal Academy of Arts, 2013.

Piketty, Thomas. *Capital in the Twenty-First Century*. Boston, MA: Harvard University Press, 2014.

Powell, Kenneth. *Richard Rogers Complete Works, Vols 1–3*. London: Phaidon, 1999, 2001 and 2006.

Powell, Kenneth. *Richard Rogers: Architecture of the Future*. Basel: Birkhauser Architecture, 2004.

Puttnam, Robert. *Our Kids: The American Dream in Crisis*. New York: Simon and Schuster, 2015.

Rawls, John. 'Justice as Fairness: Political not Metaphysical'. *Philosophy and Public Affairs, 14* (Summer 1985), pp. 223–51.

Rogers, Richard and Architects. *From the House to the City*. London: Fiell Publishing Ltd, 2010.

Rogers, Richard and Architects (Cole, Barbie and Rogers, Ruth eds). *Richard Rogers and Architects*. London: Academy Editions, 1985.

Rogers, Richard, Burdett, Richard and Cook, Peter. *Richard Rogers Partnership: Works and Projects*. New York: Monacelli Press, 1996.

Rogers, Richard. *Architecture: A Modern View*. London: Thames and Hudson, 1990.

Rogers, Richard and Fisher, Mark. *A New London*. London: Penguin, 1992.

Rogers, Richard and Gumuchdjian, Philip. *Cities for a Small Planet*. London: Faber and Faber, 1997.

Rogers, Richard and Power, Anne. *Cities for a Small Country*. London: Faber and Faber, 2000.

Ritter, Paul. *Planning for Man and Motor*. Oxford: Pergamon Press, 1964.

Said, Edward. *Orientalism*. London: Routledge and Kegan Paul, 1978.

Scully, Vincent. *Frank Lloyd Wright (Masters of World Architecture)*. New York: George Braziller, 1960.

Silver, Nathan. *The Making of Beaubourg: A Building Biography of the Centre Pompidou, Paris*. Cambridge, MA: MIT Press, 1994.

Smith, Elizabeth. *Case Study Houses*. Cologne: Taschen, 2009.

Stiglitz, Joseph E. *The Great Divide*. London: Allen Lane, 2015.

Sudjic, Deyan. *Norman Foster, Richard Rogers, James Stirling: New Directions in British Architecture*. London: Thames and Hudson, 1986.

Sudjic, Deyan. *The Architecture of Richard Rogers*. New York: Harry N. Abrams, 1995.

Urban Task Force. *Towards a Strong Urban Renaissance: An Independent Report by Members of the Urban Task Force Chaired by Lord Rogers of Riverside*. London: Urban Task Force, 2005.

Urban Task Force. *Towards an Urban Renaissance: Final Report of the Urban Task Force Chaired by Lord Rogers of Riverside*. London: Department of the Environment, Transport and the Regions, 1999.

Wilkinson, Richard and Pickett, Kate. *The Spirit Level: Why Equality is Better for Everyone*. London: Penguin, 2010.

Yentob, Alan. *Richard Rogers Inside Out*, BBC film, 2008.

Young, Michael and Willmott, Peter. *Family and Kinship in East London*. London: Routledge and Kegan Paul, 1957.

Index

Image credits

While every effort has been made to trace the owners of copyright material reproduced herein, the publishers would like to apologise for any further omissions and will be pleased to incorporate missing acknowledgements in any further editions.

Ab Rogers p11
Alan Kitching p296
Alison and Peter Smithson/Smithson Family Collection p40 (middle)
Amandine Alessandra courtesy of Publica p267
Amparo Garrido courtesy of RSHP p218
Andrea Barletta p238
Andrew Holmes courtesy of RSHP p89
Andrew Holt/Alamy Stock Photo p278 (lower)
Andrew Wright Associates courtesy of RSHP p284
Architetti Lombardi Magazine Archive p29
Bernard Vincent/ Bernard Vincent/ Archives du Centre Pompidou courtesy of RSHP/Fondazione Renzo Piano p140-41
Bettmann/Getty Images p30 (top)
Camera Press/Steve Double, hard front cover and dust jacket
Caroline Gavazzi courtesy of The River Café p231
Central Press/Hulton Archive/Getty Images p20
Christian Richters courtesy of RSHP p202
Dan Stevens courtesy of RSHP p167 (right)
Davies/Evening Standard/Hulton Archive/Getty Images p40
Domus p27 (top)

Douglas Hess/Associated Newspapers/ REX/Shutterstock p51
Duccio Malagamba courtesy of RSHP p220
Duckworth and Co. Ltd p300
E. McCoy courtesy of RSHP/Foster +Partners p77
Eamonn O'Mahony courtesy of RSHP p86, 96 (top), 97, 102 (left)
Eddie Romanis courtesy of RSHP p285
Erich Hartmann/ Olivetti Archive, Magnum Photos p26
Ezra Stoller/Esto p46, 78 courtesy of RSHP
Finn Anson p154, 157
Foster+Partners p259
Francois Halard/ Dominique Vellay p66
Georgie Wolton p42
Grant Mudford p48 (top)
Grant Smith courtesy of RSHP p98 (top), 100-01
Hufton+Crow courtesy of Zaha Hadid Architects p292
Hugo Glendinning/ Tate p159
Hulton Archive/Getty Images p30
Ian Heide/River Café courtesy of River Café p232 (lower)
Ivan Varyukhin/ Depositphotos p192 (top)
Jacques Minassian courtesy of RSHP/ Fondazione Renzo Piano p153
Janet Gill/Nikki Trott courtesy of RSHP p186
Jean Gaumy/Magnum Photos courtesy of RSHP/Fondazione Renzo Piano p108
Jean-Marc Pascolo: Eugenio Geiringer p24 (top) licensed by Creative Commons CC0 1.0
Jeremy Selwyn/ Evening Standard ROTA/PA p286

John Donat/RIBA Collections p192
John Young courtesy of RSHP p62 (top)
Jon Miller/Hedrich Blessing/DACS 2017 p36-7
Julius Shulman/ J. Paul Getty Trust. Getty Research Institute, Los Angeles (2004.R.10) p58, 61
Katsura Imperial Villa 1953, 54 Kochi Prefecture, Ishimoto Yasuhiro Photo Center p32 (top)
Katsura Imperial Villa 1981, 82 Kochi Prefecture, Ishimoto Yasuhiro Photo Center p32
Katsuhisa Kida courtesy of RSHP p150-1 (top), p166-7, 194, 204, 206, 304-5
Ken Kirkwood courtesy of RSHP p73, 92, 94-95 (top)
Keystone-France/ Gamma-Keystone/ Getty Images p120
LafargeHolcim Foundation for Sustainable Construction p267
Laurie Abbott p160 (top)
Lionel Freedman/ Lionel Freedman Archives/Yale University Art Gallery p45
London Evening Standard p266
Louis I. Kahn Collection, University of Pennsylvania and Pennsylvania Historical and Museum Commission p48
LSE p156
LSE Cities (2014)/ LSE p287 (top)
M. Flynn/Alamy Stock Photo p28
Marion Mahony/ Dallas Museum of Art, gift of the Robert O. Lane Estate in memory of Roy E. Lane, A.I.A./ ARS, NY and DACS, London 2017 p176

Mark Gorton/RSHP courtesy of RSHP p106
Martin Argles / The Guardian courtesy of RSHP p185
Martin Charles/RIBA Collections courtesy of RSHP hard back cover p118, 144-5, 149
Matteo Piazza courtesy of RSHP p160
Max Roser/World Wealth & Income Database p306
Michael Carapetian/ Smithson Family Collection p38
Michel Denancé courtesy of RSHP p134, courtesy of Fondazione Renzo Piano p 142, 290
Mondadori Portfolio/ Electa/Marco Covi p27
Morley von Sternberg courtesy of RSHP p105, 214 (top)
Neil Harvey p158
Nick Sargeant courtesy of RSHP p95
Nigel Young/Foster+ Partners p251
Norman Foster courtesy of Foster+ Partners p78 (top), p84
Paul Kozlowski/FLC/ ADAGP, Paris and DACS, London 2017 p34
Paul Raftery courtesy of RSHP p172-3, 322-3
Paul Wakefield courtesy of RSHP p128-9
Pelican Books p270
Qui Trieste p24
Rene Burri/Magnum Photos/FLC/ ADAGP, Paris and DACS, London 2017 p34 (left)
Rene Burri / Magnum Photos/FLC /ADAGP, Paris and DACS, London 2017 p34 (right)
RIBA Collections p39
Richard Bryant/Arcaid Images courtesy of RSHP p68-9, 72, 89 (top) ,168, 170, 183, 184, 188, 216-17, 222,

223, 224, 226, 234
Richard Einzig/Arcaid Images courtesy of RSHP p62, 70-1, 72, 73, (top), 76, 79 (top left), 79, 80, 146, except p50
Richard Rogers p12, 14, 18, 25, 26, 44, 79 (top right), 124, 125, 228, 229, 233, 236, 237, 238, (top), 239, 240, 241, 276, 313, 316
R. M. Schindler papers, Architecture and Design Collection, Art, Design & Architecture Museum, UC, Santa Barbara p60
Roger Henrard/FLC/ ADAGP, Paris and DACS, London 2017 p34 (top)
Romig and O'Sullivan p83
RSHP p64, 85, 88, 90, 96, 98, 102 (right), 107, 127, 132 (top), 158, 178-9, 180, 181, 182, 208-09, 210-11, 214, 235, 246-7, 252, 253, 254, 256, 258, 260, 262-3, 264-5, 271, 273 (lower), 280-1, 314-15
RSHP/Fondazione Renzo Piano p112, 113, 114-15, 126, 136, 148
RSHP/Foster+ Partners p52
S. William Engdahl/ Chicago History Museum, Hedrich-Blessing Collection/ARS, NY and DACS, London 2017, p56-7
Sandra Lousada/ Smithson Family Collection p40 (top)
Scott Gilchrist, Archivision Inc. p151
Steve Earl-Davies/ Camercraft courtesy of RSHP p164
Su Rogers courtesy of RSHP p53
SuperStock/Getty Images p54
Terence Spencer/ The LIFE Images Collection/Getty Images p299

The Architecture Foundation p268, 272
The Inland Architect and News Record/ The Ryerson & Burnham Archives, The Art Institute of Chicago/ARS, NY and DACS, London 2017 p177
The Observer newspaper courtesy of RSHP p265
The Times newspaper p198-9
Tim Street-Porter p75
Tobi Frenzen/RSHP courtesy of RSHP p104
Tony Evans/RSHP/ Arup courtesy of RSHP p132
Urban Task Force courtesy of RSHP p287
Valerie Bennett courtesy of RSHP p215
Wang Wei courtesy of RSHP p11
Yann Arthus-Bertrand /Corbis courtesy of RSHP p130-31

I would like to thank all the partners, friends and collaborators who have made my working life as enjoyable as it has been productive. I have had the pleasure of working with great talents and exceptional designers such as Norman Foster, Renzo Piano, John Young, Laurie Abbott, Peter Rice, Graham Stirk and Ivan Harbour. Alongside these, my life has been enriched by working with Brian Anson, Michael Branch, Mike Davies, Wendy Foster, Lennart Grut, Jan Hall, Tony Hunt, Su Miller, Andrew Morris, Jo Murtagh, Anne Power, Jon Rouse, Georgie Wolton, my children and their partners. Above all, thanks go to Ruthie.

Jamie Byng has been wonderful to work with as a publisher, and Richard Brown has been an exceptional co-author. Ab Rogers has challenged our thinking, and translated the concepts of my 2013 exhibition to the printed page. Caroline Roux has done magnificent work polishing the text, and we have had a great collaboration with Andy Stevens and Daniel Shannon at Graphic Thought Facility, supported by Vicki MacGregor and Heather Puttock's work on the photographic archive. Ben Rogers has been a source of advice and challenge for my political thinking over the years, and Philip Gumuchdjian helped me bring the Reith Lectures to life. We have all benefited from the comments, skills and guidance of Josh Bryson, Ricky Burdett, Katy Follain, Jenny Lord, Lucy Musgrave, Octavia Reeve, Vicki Rutherford, Simon Thorogood, Rona Williamson and John Young.

This book was being finalised when Ed Victor, my agent and dear friend who had done so much to make it happen, died. I will miss him enormously.